EVIDENCE-BASED DECISION-MAKING

Evidence-Based Decision-Making: How to Leverage Available Data and Avoid Cognitive Biases examines how a wide range of factual evidence, primarily derived from a variety of data available to organizations, can be used to improve the quality of business decision-making, by helping decision-makers circumvent the various cognitive biases that adversely impact how we all think.

The book is built on the following premise: During the past decade, the new 'data world' emerged, in which the rush to develop competencies around business analytics and data science can be characterized as nothing less than the new commercial arms race. The ever-expanding volume and variety of data are well known, as are the great advances in data processing/analytics, data visualization, and related information production-focused capabilities. Yet, comparatively little effort has been devoted to how the informational products of business analytics and data science are 'consumed' or used in the organizational decision-making processes, as the available evidence shows that only some of that information is used to drive some business decisions some of the time.

Evidence-Based Decision-Making details an explicit process describing how the universe of available and applicable evidence, which includes organizational and other data, industry benchmarks, scientific studies, and professional experience, can be assessed, amalgamated, and funneled into an objective driver of key business decisions.

Introducing key concepts in relation to data and evidence, and the history of evidence-based management, this new and extremely topical book will be essential reading for researchers and students of data analytics as well as those working in the private and public sectors, and in the voluntary sector.

Dr. Andrew D. Banasiewicz is the director of data science and analytics programs at Merrimack College, a professor of business analytics at Cambridge College, and the founder of Erudite Analytics, a data analytical consultancy focused on risk assessment.

EVIDENCE-BASED DECISION-MAKING

How to Leverage Available Data and Avoid Cognitive Biases

Andrew D. Banasiewicz

Routledge
Taylor & Francis Group

NEW YORK AND LONDON

First published 2019
by Routledge
52 Vanderbilt Avenue, New York, NY 10017

and by Routledge
2 Park Square, Milton Park, Abingdon, Oxon, OX14 4RN

Routledge is an imprint of the Taylor & Francis Group, an informa business

© 2019 Andrew D. Banasiewicz

Library of Congress Cataloging-in-Publication Data
Names: Banasiewicz, Andrew D., author.
Title: Evidence-based decision-making: how to leverage available data &
avoid cognitive biases / Andrew D. Banasiewicz.
Description: New York, NY: Routledge, 2019.
Identifiers: LCCN 2018050172 | ISBN 9781138485198 (hardback) |
ISBN 9781138485297 (pbk.) | ISBN 9781351050074 (ebook)
Subjects: LCSH: Decision making. | Cognition. | Selectivity (Psychology)
Classification: LCC BF448 .B34 2019 | DDC 153.8/3—dc23
LC record available at https://lccn.loc.gov/2018050172

ISBN: 978-1-138-48519-8 (hbk)
ISBN: 978-1-138-48529-7 (pbk)
ISBN: 978-1-351-05007-4 (ebk)

Typeset in Bembo
by codeMantra

This book is dedicated to my daughters, Alana and Katrina, and my son, Adam, in hopes they always rely on sound evidence when making easy and difficult choices.

CONTENTS

FIGURES

PREFACE

The bulk of the two decades I spent working as a quantitative business analyst was devoted to conducting wide range of statistical analyses, and trying to persuade potential users to make use of outcomes of those analyses. Like many of my professional colleagues, I too often felt like the proverbial salmon swimming upstream, especially when my data analytic findings directly contradicted long-held, and often cherished beliefs. Although it was not always quite as clear then, I have since grown to appreciate the role intuition plays in human decision-making: It is not only an inseparable part of our conception of self but also a key survival mechanism, one that tells us to stay out of reach of predators or move out of the way of an oncoming car. Moreover, trusting our instincts is not just natural – it is continuously being reinforced by everyday experiences that strengthen our dependence on intuitive sensemaking. And yet, under some circumstances, it is exactly the wrong thing to do.

Fact-driven decision-making is a seductively compelling idea, especially in an organizational setting. After all, making sensible choices by avoiding emotionally charged or biased reactions appeals to most people's sense of reason and rationality. But according to scientific research, rational thinking occupies only about 5%–10% of our brains' capacity, with the remaining 90% being committed to intuitive decision-making. It seems that we are evolutionarily hard-wired to, first and foremost, trust our instincts. If indeed so, that could help explain why, in spite of being so compelling, fact-based decision-making is notoriously difficult to institutionalize. Even more importantly, that conclusion also carries important implications for how we approach efforts to infuse evidence-based thinking into organizational decision-making processes. Rather than being presented as a competing – with intuitive choice-making – modality, fact-based sensemaking should be framed as an educator of decision-makers' intuition.

If reliance on intuition is too ingrained in human nature, then we should focus our efforts on making sure that the informational basis of intuition is sound. That may sound a bit counterintuitive, but those instinctive feelings we all frequently experience are produced by mental heuristics that enable us to draw snap conclusions using limited information, and since we are not born knowing, intuition can be seen as a product of ongoing interpretive learning. As suggested by the notion of brain plasticity, when confronted with the same problem at two sufficiently far apart points in time, a choice-maker's intuition is likely to yield somewhat different responses because of the cumulative effect of new and the ongoing re-shaping of existing knowledge. And so while intuition is inherently subjective, it can nonetheless be shaped by objective facts.

That is precisely the inspiration behind this book, and the philosophy on which the Empirical & Experiential Evidence (3E) framework detailed here is built. By casting a wide net that brings together insights ranging from undeniably objective to inescapably subjective, the 3E framework aims to provide a balanced representation of the state of knowledge relating to a decision at hand, and the framework's mechanics offer the much needed 'how-to' dimension, so often missing from otherwise compelling conceptualizations. Although the focus of ideas described here is on individual decision-making, the ultimate benefit is described from the standpoint of organizational choice-making, which so often falls short of systematically leveraging the wealth of information that is readily available, but commonly too voluminous and too varied. And so while identification and pooling of choice-related information are both critically important and as such described in a great deal of detail, the ultimate goal of the Empirical & Experiential Evidence framework is to enable conclusive syntheses of disparate and potentially conflicting pieces of information. As noted earlier, the intent behind the information identification, amalgamation, and synthesis approach described here is not to produce a yet another external set of informational inputs, but rather to infuse decision-makers' intuition with best available knowledge.

Andrew D. Banasiewicz

PART I
Decision-Making Challenges

1

SUBJECTIVE EVALUATIONS

It is well known that the human brain has essentially the same basic structure as other mammalian brains; yet, somehow, it gives rise to capabilities that enable humans to do so much more. In addition, although manifestations of those capabilities span the spectrum ranging from tragic to triumphant, the intellectual prowess that emanates from the roughly three pounds of squidgy matter that is the human brain seem limitless. From breathtaking works of art to astounding scientific and technological achievements, the sense of purpose, the need to understand and the need to believe, the ability to admire, to marvel, to dream, to imagine, are all borne out of this seemingly unremarkable structure.

Yet, brilliance is not omnipotence. When confronted with a task of quickly making sense of a large and diverse set of situational stimuli, the brain often makes use of sensemaking heuristics, or shortcuts, producing what is commonly referred to as *intuition*. Defined as the ability to understand something immediately and without the need for conscious reasoning, those nearly instantaneous conclusions feel very natural, and typically very 'right', but can ultimately turn out to be unwarranted or outright incorrect. In the course of the past few decades, psychologists and neuroscientists documented and described numerous manifestations of *cognitive bias*, or instances of sensemaking conclusions that deviate from rational judgment. And yet in spite of voluminous and convincing evidence pointing out more and more potential reasoning pitfalls, the deference to intuition-inspired decision-making shows few signs of relenting.

The focus of this chapter is on the root causes, mechanics, and ultimately the impact of cognitive biases, in their many forms, on individual decision-making. Set in the illustrative context of machine vs. human information processing, the mechanics of human learning and remembering are examined, followed by an in-depth analysis of intuitive choice-making. The goal is to show how our – that is, human – information processing 'mechanics' can be a source of a persistent evaluative bias, ultimately leading to suboptimal choices and decisions.

Thinking and Games

Card counting is a common casino strategy used primarily in the blackjack family of games to help the player decide whether the next hand is likely to give advantage to the player or the dealer. The most basic variation of card counting in blackjack is rooted in the idea that high cards, most notably aces and 10s, benefit the player more than the dealer, whereas the low cards, particularly 5s, but also 3s, 4s, and 6s, benefit the dealer more than the player. The strategy takes advantage of basic statistics: A high concentration of aces and 10s tends to diminish the inherent house advantage by increasing the player's chances of hitting a natural blackjack, whereas a high concentration of 5s and other low cards further compounds the house advantage. Those who are able to count cards, typically characterized as skilled players, can therefore modulate their betting by altering bet sizes based on the composition of remaining cards. Thus even though, on average, a blackjack player can expect to win only about 48% of the hands dealt and lose the remaining 52% (ignoring ties which can be expected in about 9% of the hands), varying the size of bets based on card count-adjusted outcome probability – that is, placing higher bets when counts are advantageous to the player and placing lower bets otherwise – can result in a player beating the house, as measured by monetary outcomes. As famously portrayed in the 2008 movie '21',[1] card counting blackjack teams have been known to win big – millions of dollars big. Although legal in all major gaming jurisdictions, card counting with the mind[2] is, not surprisingly, frown upon by casinos, with many investing considerable resources in technological and human countermeasures.

At its core, counting cards offers blackjack players the ability to reduce decision ambiguity by relying on objective, in this case statistical, evidence. An unskilled player is likely to make betting choices based on his intuition alone – as such, that player is depending almost entirely on chance, which as noted earlier favors the house. A skilled player, on the other hand, enhances his intuition by taking into account empirical evidence which chips away at the house advantage. We certainly cannot dismiss the possibility of an unskilled player winning, and possibly even winning big – after all, virtually all lottery jackpot winners are just lucky pickers of essentially random numbers. However, there is a considerable difference between picking a favorable outcome in a single-trial event, such as a lottery drawing, and winning a game comprised of series of somewhat sequentially dependent decisions. The truly interesting point here is that decision-guiding precision of card counting-derived information is relatively low, ultimately just enabling players to develop more refined expectations regarding the likely composition of the mix of cards in the shoe[3] – in essence, it just tightens the estimated probability ranges. And yet that seemingly small amount of information is enough to deliver impressive and repeated player wins, and certainly enough to compel casinos to invest in a variety of countermeasures including decreasing deck penetration, preferential shuffling, and large wager increase-triggered shuffling, to name just a few. In short, a skilled player's mind can translate relatively small infusions of objective insights into disproportionately large benefits.

Although the exact mechanics of how that happens are still shrouded in mystery, some possible clues might be offered by considering a different game, but this time not a game of chance, but what might be considered the ultimate game of strategy – chess. This centuries-old game (it is believed to have originated in India around 6th century AD) is a true test of cerebral fitness – to prevail, a player needs to consider a wide range of available strategies and tactical moves, all while recognizing and adapting to the opponent's moves. Given its highly analytical, zero-sum (one player's gain is the other player's loss), perfect information (all positions are perfectly visible to both players), and perhaps most importantly combinatorial (each successive move generates a typically large set of possibilities) nature, chess naturally lends itself to machine learning in the form of computer-based chess-playing systems. Thus not surprisingly, the history of those systems roughly parallels the history of what is known as 'artificial intelligence' (AI).

AI is a scientific endeavor of growing interest (and controversy) that aims to answer the basic question: Can a machine be made to think like a person? Almost from the start, that question was tied to the question of whether a machine could be made to play chess, as the strategic nature of that game embodies, in many regards, what we tend to view as uniquely human combination of reason and creativity. Building on the work of Alan Turing,[4] John Von Neumann, Claude Shannon, and other early 20th-century information theory pioneers, computerized chess-playing system designers forecasted that machines would come to dominate humans as early as the 1960s,[5] but it took three more decades of algorithmic design and computing power advances for that forecast to come true (now computerized chess systems routinely beat the best human players, so much so that those systems play other such systems for the 'best of the best' bragging rights). That tipping point was reached in the famous 1997 match, which pitted the then reining chess world champion Garry Kasparov against IBM's supercomputer known as Deep Blue. That event marked the first time a computer defeated a human chess champion,[6] under regular time controls (on average 3 min per move). While the news of Deep Blue's victory stirred worldwide sensation, looking back at those events we should have been more astounded that it took that long for a computer to better the best human player. After all, the game of chess is combinatorial in nature[7]; moreover, given the ever-increasing computer processing power and advances in evaluation algorithms, the eventual dominance of computerized chess-playing systems was an inescapable consequence of technological and scientific progress – the only true question was 'when'.

Thus, the truly fascinating aspect of Kasparov's duel with Deep Blue was the astounding evidentiary asymmetry: Capable of processing more than 200 million instructions per second, in a timed match, on turn-by-turn basis, Deep Blue was able to evaluate millions of possible move sequences, whereas its human opponent was only able to carefully consider a small handful, likely fewer than ten, sequences. Further adding to that disparity was the fact that although the designers of Deep Blue had access to hundreds of Kasparov's games, Kasparov himself was denied access to recent Deep Blue's games. Thus, the contest ultimately pitted a human chess player relying primarily on *ends-and-means heuristic* to intuitively determine optimal outcomes of few move sequences, against a computer programmed with the best strategies human chess players – as a group – devised, lightning fast access to dizzying number of alternatives, and an equally lightning fast decision engine powered by the most advanced algorithms devised and programmed by leading scientists. And let's not lose sight of the fact that Deep Blue, like all machines, was not hindered by factors such as fatigue or recall decay (forgetting). In view of the enormous informational and computational disparity, it is nothing short of amazing that the human champion convincingly won the initial (1996) bout, 4-2, and was only narrowly edged out in the (1997) rematch, where in six games there were three draws, two games were won by Deep Blue and one by Kasparov. Or at least that is how it would appear to a casual observer, one curious enough to ponder those matters, but not necessarily knowledgeable enough to grasp the true essence of the answer. Let us take a closer look at the storage and processing speed aspects of human thinking, as those two considerations are at the core of perceived machine processing superiority.

Mind vs. Machine

Most of us take for granted that even the slowest electronic computers are orders of magnitude faster than our own 'mental computing'. While that is indeed the case when it comes to comparing the speed with which even a computationally gifted human can, for instance, find the product of two large numbers, the opposite is actually true when we compare the speed of our brain's computational functions with those of an electronic computer – it turns out that even today's fastest supercomputers lag far behind our brain's computational prowess.

In a physical sense, the human brain can be described as approximately three pounds of very soft and highly fatty (at least 60% – the most of any human organ) tissue, made up of some 80–100 billion nerve cells known as neurons, the totality of which comprises what scientists refer to as 'gray matter'. Individual neurons are networked together via exons, which are wire-like connectors numbering in trillions (it is believed that each neuron can form several thousand connections, which in aggregate translates into a staggering 160+ trillion synaptic connections) and jointly referred to as 'white matter'. Functionally, gray matter performs the brain's computational work, whereas white matter enables communication among different regions of the brain which are responsible for different functions (as in physical and mental processes) and where different types of information are stored; together, this exons-connected network of neurons forms a single-functioning storage, analysis, and command center, which can be thought of as our biological computer. It is also where the earlier mentioned ends-and-means heuristic, along with countless other processes, is executed, and thus to understand the efficacy of that seemingly simple process it is instructive to consider the two distinct closely intertwined aspects of human brain: storage and processing speed.

Although billions of cells linked by trillions of connections make for a very large network (160+ trillion synaptic connections, as noted earlier), if each neuron was only capable of storing a single memory, the entire human brain network would only be capable of a few gigabytes of storage space – about the size of a small capacity flash drive. However, research suggests that individual neurons 'collaborate' with each other, or combine so that each individual cell helps with many memories at a time, which exponentially increases the brain's storage capacity, bringing it to around 2.5 petabytes, or about a million gigabytes. Mechanics of that 'collaboration' are complex and not yet fully understood, but they appear to be rooted in neurons' geometrically complex structure characterized by multiple receptive mechanisms, known as dendrites, and a single, though highly branched outflow (an axon) that can extend over relatively long distances. To put all of that in less abstract terms, the effective amount of the resultant storage makes it possible for brain to pack enough footage to record roughly 300 years of nonstop TV programming, or about 3 million individual shows, which is more than enough space to retain every second of one's life (including countless chess strategies). Moreover, according to the emerging neuroscientific research consensus, the brain's storage capacity can grow, but it does not decrease. What drops off, at times precipitously, is the retrieval strength, especially when memories – including semantic and procedural knowledge critical to abstract thinking – are not reinforced (more on that later). Although electronic computers have, in principle and in practice, infinite amount of storage as more and more external storage can continue to be added, brain's storage capacity is limited, but at the same time it is sufficient.

When expressed in terms of raw computing power, as measured in terms of the number of calculations performed in a unit of time, electronic computing devices appear to be orders of magnitude faster than humans – however, that conclusion is drawn from a biased comparison of the speed of rudimentary machine operations compared to the speed of higher-order human thinking. Abstracting away from deep learning-related applications (which entail layered, multidimensional machine learning), machine-executed computational steps can be characterized as one-dimensional and explicit, which is to say they tend to follow a specific step-by-step logic built around sequential input-output processes. In contrast to that, brain's computation is dominantly non-explicit and multidimensional, which is to say that we are unaware of the bulk of computations running in our mental background, and our cognitive problem solving takes place at a higher level of abstraction. And so while it is tempting to compare the speed with which a human can consciously execute a specific computational task to the speed with which the same task can be accomplished by a machine — as was the case with the earlier Kasparov vs. Deep Blue chess move evaluation comparison — doing so effectively compares the speed of high-order human reasoning with rudimentary machine-based computation. It is a bit like comparing the amount of time required for an author to write a captivating novel to the amount of time required by a skilled typist to retype the content of that novel.

Let us then take a closer look at how the rudimentary speed of our biological computer stacks up against an electronic computer. First, some important qualitative considerations: When Deep Blue was evaluating chess move sequences, it could devote close to 100% of its computational resources to the task at hand. When Kasparov was pondering his next move, his brain had to allocate considerable resources to a myriad of physiological functions such as maintaining of appropriate body temperature and blood pressure, controlling the heart rate and breathing, controlling the entire musculoskeletal structure to allow Kasparov to remain in a particular position and engage in specific movements, and, of course, the mental activities such as thinking. And though we rarely consciously think about it, just a single one of those functions entails a staggering amount of computational work on the part of our brain. To that end, in a 2014 experiment, a group of clever Japanese and German researchers managed to simulate a single second of human brain activity using what was then the fourth fastest supercomputer in the world (the K Computer powered to nearly 83,000 processors) — it took that supercomputer 40 min to complete the requisite calculations. In other words, that which was accomplished in just a single second by the roughly three pounds of grey and white matter took the 100 or so ton device[8] made up of roughly 83,000 processors 40 min. In a more general sense, the current estimates suggest that if the human brain were a computer, it could perform about a billion billions (a quantity known as quintillion, or 10^{18}) calculations per second, which is on the next order higher than the fastest supercomputer.[9] So, in terms of the rudimentary clock speed, electronic computers are actually just trying to catch up to us though an obvious question emerges: How and why is it that our brain is so computationally efficient?

It all comes down to efficiency. The fundamental computer design separates storage and processing, which is not the case with the human brain where the same interconnected areas can simultaneously store, analyze, and redistribute information. As a result, a process that might take a computer a few million steps to complete can be achieved by a few hundred nearly instantaneous neuron transmissions in human brain. The brain's processing efficiency is perhaps best illustrated by the amount of required energy – when performed by the world's fastest supercomputer, a computational task, such as the earlier mentioned simulation of 1 second of the brain's activity, would consume an amount of energy about equal to what is required to power a sizable building, whereas the same task performed by the brain would only consume about what it would take to light a single light bulb.

Thus ultimately, neither the amount of available storage nor the rudimentary computational prowess are the reasons for the advantage that chess-playing computers enjoy over human chess players. What then gives the chess-playing computer systems an advantage? The most obvious, though somewhat obtuse, answer is that it is the ever-greater refinement of machine-based evidentiary assessment that combines crisp evaluative logic with unbiased choices.

Turning back to Kasparov's dual with Deep Blue, it is possible – indeed quite likely – that in the course of his long chess career,[10] Kasparov might have 'filed away' in his memory a deep and diverse repertoire of strategic options, but all those options were somewhat 'tainted' with his subjective and ever-changing knowledge base. As explored in more depth in the *Learning and Remembering* section, one of the amazing qualities of brain is its ability to rewire itself, a phenomenon known as *neuroplasticity* or *brain plasticity*. Though generally a desirable feature supporting ongoing learning, neuroplasticity has some distinct disadvantages, one of which is ongoing alteration of our recollection of past events, which, in the case of chess strategies, means that what were once objective will likely become somewhat subjectified by individual players. As a result, all players have a bias which can be systematically explored by computer-based systems that had the opportunity to 'study' individual player's strategies, which was precisely why Deep Blue designers studied hundreds of Kasparov's matches but did not allow him access to the computer's past matches. If programmed, and reprogrammed again and again by a team of designers, computer-based chess-playing systems are unlikely to have a bias, or at least one that would be as discernable as a human player's bias – that, coupled with ever faster processors and ever better evaluation algorithms gives rise to a superior evidence-based chess move evaluation engine. In the end, computers prevail not because they are faster or have greater memory, but because they make better use of objective evidence.

Still, considering that Deep Blue prevailed by winning just two out of the six games is a testament to the remarkable efficacy of the human player's ends-and-means heuristic, even if the underlying knowledgebase was somewhat biased. The ends-and-means heuristic is rooted in the fact that good chess players have a large array of move patterns that they know will give them an advantage – those are the 'ends'. Looking at the position at hand, they then try to determine which of those patterns is most appropriate, following which they look for moves that will push the position in that direction – those are the 'means'. In its entirety, the ends-and-means heuristic typically reduces the number of possible move patterns to a small number of alternatives, oftentimes just one. Keeping that in mind and considering that Deep Blue's play was itself entirely a product of human ingenuity – after all, the computer's decision engine was a product of strategies devised by the world's best chess players, and the choice evaluation logic developed by equally outstanding programmers and mathematicians – the ultimate supremacy of computers in chess matches can be seen as a manifestation of the power of human mind freed from obstacles impeding its potential … pure, uninhibited intelligence. (It is worth noting that to some, especially in the technology circles, this merger of human creativity with speed and efficiency of machines signals the oncoming of 'singularity', or the rise of new human-AI.) In that sense, a closer look at how our brains learn and remember is instructive to better understanding the future potential of the human mind.

Learning and Remembering

Another key to unlocking the mysteries of 'how we know what we know' lies in understanding of how we *learn*, or amass the memories that comprise our knowledge base. As noted earlier, what we remember and thus know exists in our brains as a network of linked cells, called neurons, with different clusters located in different parts of our brain being responsible for distinct types of knowledge, or memories. What we capture and, ultimately, 'file away' as knowledge is thus a product of what stimulus we consciously process and how our brain encodes the resulting imprints. The overall process is driven by our brains' biological infrastructure, the key elements (from the standpoint of learning) of which include the entorhinal cortex, which acts as a central hub for memory and navigation by relaying object-related and spatial information, the hippocampus, which is where long-term remembering begins, and the neocortex, where the results are stored.

Current neuroscientific research suggests that memories are formed by developing new neuronal connections, or synapses, through a general process that encompasses encoding, consolidation, storage, and recall or remembering, as shown in Figure 1.1.

As graphically depicted there, an observed (i.e., arousing conscious awareness) stimulus is first encoded in short-term memory, into which sensory information enters in two, somewhat fleeting forms: iconic or visual, and echoic or auditory (research suggests that short-term iconic memories have an average duration of less than 1 s, whereas echoic memories last about 4–5 s). The process of learning is then initiated, starting with the formation of new neuronal connections, or networking, in hippocampus, followed by consolidation, which is when preformed remembrances are strengthened and then stored in specific part of the brain as long-term memories. Subsequent retrieval of earlier

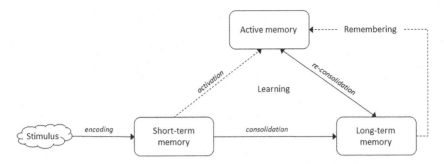

FIGURE 1.1   The Process of Learning and Remembering.

stored information from long-term to active memory results in reconsolidation, strengthening of the stored information's recall, or remembering.

In a more abstract sense, *learning* can be characterized as modifying information already stored in memory based on new input or experiences. It is an active process that involves sensory input to the brain (which occurs automatically), and an ability to extract meaning from sensory input by paying attention to it long enough (which requires conscious attention) to reach temporary, or short-term memory, where consideration for transfer into permanent or long-term memory takes place. An important aspect of human memory, however, is its fluid nature, which is very much unlike any machine-based storage and retrieval systems. Each subsequent experience, in a cyclical fashion, prompts our brain to (subconsciously) reorganize stored information, effectively reconstituting its contents through a repetitive updating procedure known as 'brain plasticity'. This process is generally viewed as advantageous because improvements are made repeatedly to existing information, but it can have adverse consequences as well, most notably when our memories of the past rather than being maintained and protected are amended or changed beyond recognition.[11] Thus, the widely used characterization of learning as the 'acquisition of knowledge' oversimplifies what actually happens when new information is added into the existing informational mix – rather than being filed away and stored in isolation, any newly acquired information is instead integrated into a complex web of existing knowledge.

Typically, long-term memories can be grouped into two broad types: declarative or explicit, and non-declarative or implicit. The former, which encompass information we are consciously aware of, can be further subdivided into semantic and episodic memories, or the knowledge of meaning and facts, and remembrances of one's personal experiences, respectively. The latter, on the other hand, encompasses an array of memories of which we may not be fully consciously aware, such as various specific skills and habits, simple classical conditioning-type responses, or nonassociative learning, which involves any change in the strength of response to a single stimulus.

A natural extension of learning and remembering considerations is the usage of one's long-term memories. Much of what and how we do to function as humans, as members of the society or as professionals, is driven by the totality of learned conscious and subconscious responses. In a more narrowly defined context of business decision-making, we rely on inferences drawn from what we know, where an 'inference' refers to a reasoning process in which we move from premises to conclusions. In that sense, inferences can be either deductive or inductive. A *deductive inference* or *reasoning* describes the use of logic to arrive at conclusions that stem from premises that are known or assumed to be true, such as natural or other laws. For example, using the law of supply and demand, an industry analyst may reach a conclusion, using deductive inference, that the glut of a certain commodity in the marketplace will lead to future price decline. An *inductive inference* or *reasoning* is the opposite of deductive reasoning – it makes broad generalizations from specific observations. Stated in more general terms, it describes learning general concepts from examples, as illustrated by the use of customer data to estimate price elasticity for a particular product.

Given that deductive reasoning works from the more general to the more specific, it is sometimes referred to as a 'top-down' approach, whereas inductive reasoning works the other way, moving from specific observations to broader generalizations and thus it is sometimes referred to a 'bottom-up' approach. These two methods of reasoning have a very different feel to them: Inductive reasoning, by its very nature, is more open-ended and exploratory, especially at the beginning, whereas deductive reasoning is narrower in nature and is concerned with testing or confirming of preexisting beliefs.

The Four Learning Paradigms

Although illustrative of the basic sensemaking modalities, continuing to only acknowledge the general inductive and deductive approaches to reasoning, and thus learning, fails to recognize the impact of advanced technologies and what has come to be known as 'big data', especially sensors-generated streaming data.[12] The burgeoning field of AI in general, and machine learning in particular, is ushering-in a new era of reasoning and learning. Taking stock of the 'old' and 'new' learning and reasoning modalities suggests four general paradigms: observational, theoretical, computational, and simulational.[13] In a very general sense, the emergence of each of the four paradigms can be seen as a product of evolution of human rationality and technological developments – if placed on a timeline, the observational learning paradigm could be considered the oldest, followed by theoretical, computational, and exploratory.

Observational learning paradigm is built around systematic examination of sensory experiences, particularly those obtained by means of observation or experimentation (in fact, the terms 'experience', 'experiment', and 'empirical' are derived from the ancient Greek word 'empeiria' and a more familiar sounding

Latin translation 'experientia'). In many regards, empirically minded learning can be seen as a natural consequence of a curious mind driven to understand the world through careful observation and subsequent generalization. It connotes a view of mind as an originally blank or empty recorder on which experience leaves marks – as such, observational learning effectively rejects the existence of innate ideas. Chronologically, it represents the oldest approach to reasoning and learning; although it is difficult to pinpoint its exact origin, many historians point to Aristotle and his theory of potentiality and actuality.[14] Known today as *empiricism,* this philosophy has many adherents who believe knowledge comes only or primarily from sensory experiences.

Tycho Brahe, a 16th-century Danish astronomer, is best known for having taken and recorded the most detailed and accurate celestial observations of his time, but it was his assistant, Johannes Kepler, who used Brahe's data to discover the laws of planetary motion. In doing so, Kepler became one of the first theoretical scientists – as a group, they blazed the trail for what eventually became the *theoretical learning paradigm.* A product of maturing human critical and intellectual thinking, that learning modality is reflected in abstract formulations such as those exemplified by Kepler's laws of planetary motion, Newton's laws of motion, and Maxwell's equations describing the behavior of electromagnetic field. An important aspect of the theoretical learning modality is its principally infinite causal chain, which contrasts sharply with the comparatively dimensionally flat empiricism. Within the confines of theoretical learning, the initial conjectural insight, such as Galileo's assertion that, in the absence of a force, a moving object will continue moving, subsequently gives rise to Newton's first law of motion,[15] which, in turn, elicits more refined derivative explanations, such as the principles of aerodynamics. Although continued empirical learning demands ever more observational or experimental data, theoretical learning can continue by means of deriving deeper and deeper insights from a single underlying theory, as is the case with the earlier mentioned Kepler's, Newton's, and Maxwell's abstractions.

Although the Age of Reason and the Age of Enlightenment produced the theoretical learning paradigm, the earlier discussed 'mechanized thought' ideas of Babbage and Turing gave rise to a new era of machine-based information processing, which, in turn, gave rise to the third learning paradigm – *computational.* The mid-20th century emergence and rapid growth of computer science and computer systems ushered-in the simulation-based knowledge era, which can be seen as the coming together of empirical and theoretical paradigms. Not all physical phenomena are directly observable, especially at the extremes. Direct observations of subatomic particles are hindered not only by the extremely small scale of those particles but also by fundamental limits to the precision with which such observations can be taken[16] while direct observations of distant galaxies are hindered by a combination of their scale and distance. Yet, combining the available measurements with the current theoretical understanding enables computer-equipped scientists to study those systems by creating their representations using advanced computing applications. Thus, we continue to learn more about the behavior of the super small and the super large phenomena, and countless other physical, social, and other systems by computationally estimating their behavior.

Although the computational learning modality can be characterized by 'batch periodicity', or interval data capture and analyses, countless sensors now generate nonstop data streams that record ever more phenomena in ever more detail, and are processed by sophisticated systems capable of automated, even autonomous data capture, curation, and analyses. And so the never-ceasing march of technological innovation, now particularly pronounced in the area of automation, is propelling the computational learning modality to the next evolutionary stage, which can be characterized as *simulational* learning. Seen by many as pervasive, the steadily encroaching digitization of countless aspects of private, social, and commercial life is supplying the 'raw materials' while the already formidable and still rapidly growing data processing capabilities are supplying means of extracting knowledge out of those raw inputs. The coming together of immense volumes, diversity and granularity of data, and the already lightning-fast and still rapidly improving data processing capabilities are making it possible to create knowledge through 'constructed reality' – artificial representations of reality, broadly referred to as 'virtual reality' (VR), that become progressively less and less distinguishable from physical reality. VR not only enables generation of previously inaccessible insights – such as conditions that existed shortly after the Big Bang[17] – but it also changes the very manner in which learning takes place, and even 'who' is learning. Within the confines of observational, theoretical, and computational learning paradigms it was always the human investigator who was the learner – as the term 'machine learning' implies, now man-made devices are also beginning to learn.

Sensemaking

What is the essence of learning? Years of formal education endowed most of us with an almost-intuitive understanding of the notion of 'learning', so much so that we are rarely inclined to ponder that term's epistemology. It is when confronted with the task of teaching computers how to learn from data that the complexity of the underlying processes becomes more evident, particularly in the context of text mining. Consider the generalized natural language processing, which encompasses the broadly defined ability of computer systems to decode and make sense of written or spoken human language, summarized in Figure 1.2.

Described in very broad terms, natural language processing subjects a corpora of text to a series of sensemaking steps comprised of lexical, syntactic, and semantic analyses. However, the lexical-syntactic-semantic progression conveys an unwarranted sense of simplicity as it does not expressly address a number of distinct sensemaking steps. When considered from the more in-depth analytical

FIGURE 1.2 Generalized Text Mining Process.

perspective, the lexical-syntactic-semantic part of the natural language process-ing requires more rudimentary word-structuring inputs; similarly, the 'output transformation' of the outcomes of that three-step process into 'data outputs' necessitates discerning of the more general – that is, cross-sentence – meaning. All considered, a more complete accounting of the natural language processing elements suggests the following computational steps:

• Phonology, or interpretation of sounds within and across words;
• Morphology, or breaking down of words into 'morphemes', which the smallest grammatical units;
• Lexicology, or assigning of meaning to words;
• Syntax, or discerning of grammatical structure to make connection be-tween words within a sentence;
• Semantics, or disambiguation of individual words;
• Discourse, or making connection between sentences;
• Pragmatics, or derivation of contextual or situational meaning.

Human brain handles the above tasks largely subconsciously, and so it is typ-ically not until an attempt is made to replicate the totality of human learning processes that the complexity and the intricacy of how we learn comes to light.

Knowing

From the perspective of machine-like information processing, a motion picture (e.g., a movie) is essentially a series of still frames shown in fast succession, but to a human spectator it is a story with a distinct, though implied theme. Our senses capture the ultimately discrete audio-visual stimuli and our brain effort-lessly (assuming a well-made production) infers the multitudes of causally and otherwise interconnected meanings necessary to understand and appreciate the underlying plot. At the end of a show, we can then say we know what the show was all about, and we are so accustomed to claim that we 'know', whatever it might be, that we rarely ask the age-old epistemological[18] question: How do we know that we know? Consider Figure 1.3.

As summarized there, our conception of what constitutes 'knowledge' can be understood in terms of two separate sets of considerations: *sources,* which captures the 'how' aspect of what we know or believe to be true, and *dimensions,* which represents the 'what' facet of what we know, in the sense of

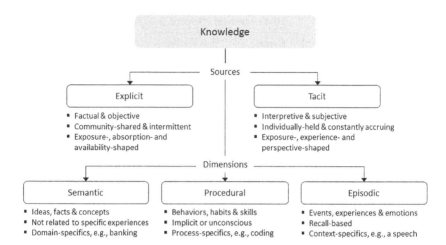

FIGURE 1.3 Dimensions of Knowledge.

the type of knowledge. The source of knowledge can take the form of formal learning, commonly labeled *explicit* knowledge, or informal learning, also known as *tacit* knowledge, best exemplified by skills, familiarity with, or understanding of topics or endeavors encountered while working or pursuing a hobby. The second and somewhat distinct set of considerations instrumental to dissecting the essence of how we know what we know characterizes the typologically distinct dimensions of knowledge. Here, our individually held knowledge can be grouped into three broad, general kinds of knowledge: (1) *semantic*, which encapsulates abstract ideas and facts, (2) *procedural*, which captures behavioral abilities to perform specific tasks, and (3) *episodic*, which encompasses an array of hedonic or emotive memories.

Insofar as decision-making is concerned, the differently acquired and differently oriented aspects of knowledge impact each other so that, for instance, one's explicit knowledge of how to fit regression models will often be somewhat altered by one's practical experience (tacit knowledge) acquired in the course of fitting regression models. We could even go as far as suggesting that the ongoing interplay between explicit and tacit knowledge, in relation to a relatively specific area of human endeavor, can produce distinct *effective topical* knowledge. Quite often, individuals might start with the same knowledge of a particular topic – as would tend to be the case with those who took the same course, taught by the same instructor – only to end up at some point in the future with materially different effective knowledge of that topic because of divergent tacit influences. Perhaps the most compelling example of that phenomenon is offered by advanced degree, most notably Ph.D., students. Let us say that two individuals of similar age and comparable abilities enrolled at the same time in the same statistics doctoral program. Those two individuals ended up taking the same set of courses, and upon completing their degree requirements graduated at the same time. At the point of receiving their doctoral degrees, both individuals could be assumed to have comparable levels of knowledge of the topic mentioned earlier – regression analysis. Their degrees in hand, two, however, chose to pursue different career paths, with one taking a position as an assistant professor at another academic institution, whereas the other instead opting to join a consulting organization as a statistical analysis expert. Over the course of the next decade or so, the academic engaged in theoretical research focused on the use of matrices in linear least square estimation (a subset of mathematical considerations addressing an aspect of regression analysis), whereas the consultant focused his work efforts on developing applied solutions for his corporate clients, such as predictive models to forecast future cost of insurance claims. If we were to reassess their knowledge of regression analysis, lets' say a decade or so later, we should expect their respective effective knowledge of regression to be materially different. Why? Primarily because of the confluence of several factors, including the obvious dissimilarity of their respective newly acquired tacit knowledge, coupled with the manner in which the new knowledge interacts (i.e., reinforces vs. replaces) the existing knowledge. Moreover, the earlier discussed non-reinforced information retrieval decay would also likely have profound impact on reshaping the composition of one's effective knowledge, especially over a longer period of time.

It thus follows that from the decision-making standpoint what matters most is the decision-maker's effective topical knowledge, hence to be complete, the conceptualization of knowledge depicted in Figure 1.3 needs to incorporate that key element, as shown in Figure 1.4.

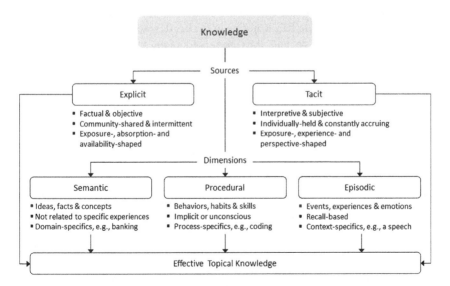

FIGURE 1.4 Effective Topical Knowledge.

Effective topical knowledge is what we draw on when presented with a task or confronted with a choice. At what could be characterized as a 'decision point', effective knowledge represents the totality of what we are able to do and what we believe to be true, within the confines of the problem at hand. The otherwise conceptually distinct sources and dimensions of our knowledge all converge into our ability – or lack thereof – to perform the task in question or make a rational choice, under conditions of uncertainty. Recalling the earlier mentioned task of fitting a regression model, when presented with a task of building a regression model to estimate, for instance, customer-specific product repurchase probability, an analyst will need to draw on his semantic knowledge of different types of regression techniques (e.g., linear, nonlinear, logistic, etc.), his familiarity with the appropriate data modeling tools and procedures (e.g., R, SAS, or other language/application), and, quite possibly, past episodes of performing similar type of work (to pinpoint specific anticipated challenges, etc.). Stated differently, that analyst will draw on what appears to be a singular reservoir of expertise within a particular task, which at that time represents the net sum of the combination of explicit and tacit sources of knowledge, as well as the semantic, procedural, and episodic dimensions of knowledge.

There is a yet another aspect to knowledge that is important to address, one that captures far more broadly scoped learning, in the sense of knowledge creation traditions. Much of Western intellectual tradition finds its roots in the Big Three of ancient Greek philosophers: Socrates, Plato, and Aristotle. The starting figure, Socrates, did not write any books but instead channeled his efforts into publicly asking probing and at times humiliating questions, which gave rise to the now-famous Socratic Teaching Method.[19] Given the fact that he did not write any books, Socrates' wisdom might have slowly dissipated with the passage of time had it not been for his devoted and talented student, Plato, who wrote down and thus preserved many of his teacher's dialogs. Building on Socrates' teachings, Plato subsequently contributed more formally described abstract, almost other-worldly notions of Forms, Ideals, and Ideas (such as Equality or Justice), which were then adapted and further refined by his most outstanding student, Aristotle, by many considered the first empirical scientist. Less other-worldly than Plato in his philosophical approach, Aristotle injected a substantial dose of realism into his teacher's abstract conceptions, laying the foundations for logical theory, or the use of reason in theoretical activity. The many thinkers who followed and carried forward Socrates, Plato, and Aristotle's ideas ultimately gave rise to Western intellectual tradition, characterized by the use of reason in knowledge creation, built around of what is now known as the *scientific method*, or a set of procedures consisting of systematic observation, measurement, and experimentation, and the formulation, testing, and modification of hypothesis.

But what if Socrates did not have Plato as a student? Would the Socratic Teaching Method exist? Would we even know his name, or would his ideas and his memory be long forgotten? It seems reasonable to speculate that there were a number of other insightful thinkers who had much to offer intellectually, but were not fortunate enough to have talented and dedicated students, willing and able to capture, enshrine in written word, and further refine their teachers' ideas. In a very practical sense, we could say that those unknown to us today thinkers had no first followers,[20] no one to, in a manner of speaking, pick up their torch of wisdom, and carry it forward. In that sense, it might be quite possible that the reason we celebrate and embrace Socrates' ideas is as much due to their universal, timeless wisdom, as it is due to a pure stroke of luck that resulted in Plato, a brilliant and committed student, picking up Socrates' wisdom and carrying it forward.

A Curious Aspect: The First Follower

It is hard to imagine a student or a practitioner in the area of computer science unfamiliar with Alan Turing's notion of 'mechanized thought', which is one of the conceptual pillars of that field. Embodied in the so-called 'Turing machine', which was first proposed by Turing in 1936 and eventually operationalized in the form of the first fully functioning mechanical computer built during the Second World War to help the Allies break the German Enigma code (used by the Nazi forces to communicate movements and locations of their military assets, such as U-boats and troops). Today, the Turing machine is best known as a mathematical model of computation that can simulate any computer algorithm, no matter how complicated it is (as originally conceived by Turing, it was a device which could manipulates symbols on a strip of tape according to a table of rules). Unquestionably, it was a brilliant invention, both as a concept and a functioning device, but Turing should be given credit as a re-inventor, not the original inventor of the concept of mechanized thought. It was Charles Babbage, an English mathematician and computer pioneer, who developed the first design for a general-purpose computer (which he called the 'analytical engine') a century earlier, in 1837. However, due to technical and funding difficulties, Babbage never completed construction of this device – also, following Babbage's death, his ideas, and his unfinished prototype were largely forgotten. Why?

One plausible explanation points to Babbage's design being simply too far ahead of its time. This conclusion appears to be supported by the fact that while during the century that separated Babbage's and Turing's designs numerous mechanical calculating machines, such as adders and multipliers, were built and improved, none of those devices could perform conditional branching, which was one of the key design elements of Babbage's (as well as Turing's) computing devices. In that sense, it might be reasonable to further speculate that Babbage's device offered a brilliant solution to a problem before it was recognized as a problem (which would help to explain his inability to raise the capital needed to construct his device). This explanation appears to be further corroborated by Turing's experience, whose proposal promised to solve a then-intractable problem of deciphering a very sophisticated – in fact, believed to be unbreakable – military communication code at the time when England (where Turing lived and worked) was facing a truly existential threat in the form of Nazi forces. And though in the midst of England's struggles with the German onslaught resources were scarce, the computational problem, and thus the need, was paramount. And so, without the first follower, the true pioneer of mechanized thought – Babbage – got lost in the annals of history while the re-inventor – Turing – helped to reshape the history, in large part because his work was done at the right time (Second World War) and at the right place (England under German naval and aerial attack) to entice the first, and subsequent followers.

Babbage's story, however, is only one of many – consider the legendary inventor Thomas Edison, widely credited with the invention of the incandescent light bulb (among other things). According to a recent book by Friedel, Israel and Finn titled *Edison's Electric Light: Biography of an Invention*, there were no less than 23 different inventors of the incandescent light bulb before Edison, but since none garnered sufficient following, as in other individuals adapting or otherwise embracing their breakthroughs, they are only known to a small handful of biographers. In terms of more recent inventions, the origin of the now-ubiquitous computer icons is often erroneously attributed to Apple, but it was actually another US firm, Xerox, that first developed graphical function representations. Those are just a few of many such examples that underscore the fallibility of what we hold to be true.

Thus, it is not just our information recall related limitations but also the validity and reliability of what we know – or at least what we believe we know – that can undermine the efficacy of our decision-making. *Validity* of knowledge can be broadly characterized as truthfulness, which encompasses factual accuracy as well as logical correctness – incorrectly crediting Turing with the idea and the design of the first mechanical computer is an example of invalid knowledge. On the other hand, *reliability* is an expression of dependability, or stability of what we know, in the sense that reliance of an element of knowledge will lead to stable and consistent outcomes. Regardless of who is the original designer of 'mechanized thought', the device based on that design produces stable and reliable results. Although the two concepts jointly attest to what can be considered *informational legitimacy* of an element of knowledge, the interplay between these two notions is a bit tricky. Within the realm of psychological testing, for instance, a test has to be reliable to be valid, but at the same time can be reliable without being valid. Thus, a particular test of intelligence, such as the Wechsler Intelligence Test, can produce consistent results across repeated applications, but may ultimately not be a sound (i.e., valid) assessment of one's true intelligence. Similarly, a statistical model aiming to predict the probability of a shopper choosing a particular brand must be reliable to be valid, but does not have to be valid to be reliable, as captured in a common statistical aphorism stating that 'all models are wrong but some are useful'.[21]

The Decision-Making Brain

In a very general sense and as detailed earlier, knowledge can be thought of as a library – a collection of systematic, procedural, and episodic remembrances acquired via explicit and tacit learning (see Figure 1.4). However, unlike physical libraries, neural networks-stored 'collections' are subject to ongoing change because while trying to assimilate new memories into the network of already-in-place ones, the brain continuously rewires itself (a property known as 'brain plasticity'). Consequently, one's *effective* topical knowledge is ever-changing as a function of the combination of cumulative past learnings and current additions. The ongoing interpretation and re-interpretation of the totality of one's knowledge has direct, and at times profound impact on one's perception, judgment and the broadly defined decision-making processes.

However, before delving into finer details of decision-making, it is important to expressly define the core notion of *decision*. From the perspective of cognitive human functioning, decision can be characterized as a commitment to course of action, intended to serve a specific purpose or accomplish a specific objective. That commitment can be seen as a product of implicit, or subconscious, and explicit, or conscious, cognitive processes, commonly characterized as *boundedly rational*,[22] or simply put, imperfect. It is also worth noting that the mental heuristic processes or proximal mechanisms that produce judgments and choices are not well understood not only because of the nearly paradoxical complexity of human sensemaking (how does one make sense of one's sense-making?) but also because decisions are ultimately shaped not only by cognitive but also by emotional, cultural, and social factors.

And yet, making decisions is an inescapable aspect of human functioning – in fact, it has been estimated that a person makes, on average, about 35,000 decisions a day. If that estimate seems exceedingly large that is probably because many choices are so routine or unordinary that they don't seem like 'real' decisions, as illustrated by numerous 'mundane' decisions required to cross a street. Thus, in a more general sense, decisions can vary significantly in terms of frequency, importance, and difficulty. Many everyday choices, such as street crossing, are routine (i.e., frequent) and important (given the potentially dire consequences), but typically fairly easy because, under most circumstances, the available information is nearly perfect, the time to make a decision is typically adequate, and requisite cognitive processing is straightforward. In a way of a contrast, other decisions, such as choosing a college, can be characterized as nonroutine, important, and complex.

Moreover, when considering basic cognitive functions, it is also important to, well, keep in mind (no pun intended) the enormous number of background, or subconscious computational brain tasks, such as regulation of heartbeat and blood pressure, maintenance of physical balance, and so on. As astounding as human brain's computational capabilities are, they are ultimately finite, which at times necessitates information processing trade-offs. As a result, when presented with a large amount of inputs, our brains will often make use of decision heuristics, or shortcuts. Recalling the 'ends-and-means' heuristic used by top chess players, such decision shortcuts can work amazingly well, especially when one considers the sheer number of alternatives.[23] But then again, there are situations when taking shortcuts can lead a decision-maker astray.

Decades of research in cognitive psychology point to numerous *cognitive biases* that permeate individual level decision-making. Altogether, researchers pinpointed significantly more than a hundred distinct manifestations of cognitive bias, which jointly attest to the many ways brain heuristics, typically engaged subconsciously, can derail the validity of interpretive conclusions. To make matters worse, individuals are generally unaware of the perception-warping impact of those complex, mental processes, which makes rectifying their effects all that much more difficult. That is not all, however. Unlike computers that 'remember' all information stored in them equally well at all times, the brain's plasticity or its persistent self-rewiring renders older, not sufficiently reinforced memories progressively fuzzier and more difficult to retrieve. One of the direct consequences of that is that memory tends to be incomplete and selective – for instance, we almost habitually retain more complete recollections of positive than of negative events, and those events that occurred more recently appear to be more significant and thus likely to recur. Moreover, details of individual events are often filled after the fact, leading to self-deception, a situation which is further exacerbated by the almost instinctual inclination toward generalizing from (often) nonrepresentative anecdotal evidence.

Further chipping away at the representativeness of one's self-captured evidence is that, even under the best of circumstances, the totality of one's individual, subjective experiences typically constitutes only a small and likely nonrepresentative sample of such experiences. In other words, one person's slice of reality is just that – a set of experiences encountered and encoded (into memory) by a particular person, which may differ substantially from experiences of others. And if all of those information processing hindrances were not enough – cognitive psychologists have still more bad news to deliver: Numerous clinical research studies suggest that the amount of information human brain can cognitively process at any given time is limited, a phenomenon known as *channel capacity*.[24] The human information processing offshoot of this idea, known as *human channel capacity* was originally proposed in 1956 by G. A. Miller, a Princeton University psychologist who placed a numeric limit of 7 ± 2 of discrete pieces of information an average human can hold in his/her working memory. According to the proponents of that notion, the reason the number of informational 'chunks' a person can simultaneously process in attention is finite, and fairly small, is due to limitations of short-term and working memory, which can be likened to physical storage restrictions of a computer system, or a physical container for that matter.

Clearly, in an attempt to perform all necessary (i.e., life functioning related) computations in an environment permeated by overwhelming volume and diversity of stimuli, the human brain can at times engage suboptimal heuristics. Considering the subliminal nature of those information processing shortcuts, the first and the necessary step in mitigating their potentially conclusion-warping effects is to develop a sound understanding of their origins and the manner in which they influence one's decision-making processes, a discussion of which follows.

Cognitive Bias

Defined as a systematic pattern of deviations from norm or rationality in judgment, *cognitive bias* leads to logically or factually faulty inferences, ultimately resulting in irrational choices. It commonly manifests itself in otherwise competent individuals reaching factually unfounded or logically irrational conclusions because of factors such as peer influence, the desirability of options under consideration, or illusory associations. It is important to note that to be considered biased, one's conclusion has to be a product of a persistent departure from what an informed and objective observer would deem to be rational or factually sound. There are numerous situations in which a person may draw an irrational or otherwise unfounded conclusion because of nonsystematic situational factors, such as time pressure, but given another chance (or more time, as in the case of time-constricted decision-making) would likely reach a different conclusion – in other words, care must be taken to not confuse an error in judgment with biased judgment. Perhaps because of that somewhat fuzzy distinction between errors in judgment and biased judgment, the idea of persistent cognitive bias was met with some skepticism when it was first suggested in the early 1970s. However, hundreds of cognitive experiments carried out over the past four or so decades by dozens of independent researchers not only lead to widespread acceptance of the existence of subconscious reasoning related predispositions, but it also produced a deluge of scientifically valid and documented manifestations of those proclivities.[25]

Still, there is no agreement on the source of cognitive bias. Numerous origin explanations have been suggested over the years, which can be grouped into two broad categories: (1) reasoning and (2) emotions. The former attributes cognitive bias to brain's cognitive limits, or more specifically the need to counteract brain's finite information processing capabilities, especially when presented with an overwhelming volume of stimuli or alternatives (recall the earlier discussed 'ends-and-means' heuristic utilized by expert chess players). According to that school of thought, bias-causing heuristics are permanently ingrained into our cognitive processes through evolution or learning and can be seen as natural countermeasures to the brain's finite information processing capabilities.

A noticeably different explanation is offered by the latter of the two cognitive bias origin explanations, which attributes those predispositions to the impact of emotions on cognitive processes. On the one hand, that explanation appears to be supported by research suggesting that reasoning and the emotions are indeed closely interconnected,[26] but on the other hand, it is widely held that brain processes underlying emotions are distinct and separate from those responsible for cognitive functions, which is the main counterpoint made by the critics of the 'emotional' explanation. All considered, while it is tempting to conclude that cognitive processes that are responsible for rational reasoning give rise to cognitive bias, and emotional processes give rise to emotional bias, it would be a mistake to ignore the well-established connection between reason and emotions and thus unwise to entirely dismiss the role of emotions in the formation of cognitive bias. More on that shortly.

Interestingly, the origins of cognitive bias are of secondary importance to the recognition of the potentially profound impact those predispositions can exert on an individual's decision-making. But to truly understand and, more importantly, to remedy the potentially disadvantageous consequences of those mental processes, it is essential to develop a more substantive understanding of the manner in which the otherwise dependable reasoning processes can lead us astray. It is not an easy task – the earlier mentioned 40 or so years of cognitive sensemaking research produced quite an array of cognitive bias manifestations, with some of the better known including the availability heuristic, base rate fallacy, confirmation bias, omission bias, or gambler's fallacy. The bias-enumerating research output has been so rich that it is difficult to discern the exact count of distinct expressions of those mental predispositions – in fact, Wikipedia-hosted page dedicated to this topic lists nearly 200 distinct types of cognitive bias.

Are there indeed that many distinct manifestations of cognitive bias? To answer that question, one must first address the notion of 'distinctiveness' in the context of latent, or not directly observable concepts. Known as *construct validity*,[27] it aims to answer a basic question: Does the notion of interest communicate insights not already communicated by other concepts? In other words, are there reasons to believe that it is not just a different name for an already described phenomenon?

It is difficult to offer a definitive answer to such an existential question though the widely used double-blind (identities of researchers are hidden from reviewers and vice versa) scientific research review process can be assumed to have affirmed the individual bias manifestations' independence, or construct validity. Given that, a more meaningful question might be: Are there distinct, broader truths that similar-sounding biases have in common? Synthesizing evidence produced by individual research studies using *systematic reviews*, the aim of which is to provide as complete as possible summary of published research relevant to a question at hand, individual studies-reported cognitive bias variants can be combined into larger, more general categories. Starting with approximately 100 of the more commonly cited bias manifestations (see Appendix A for the full list), a two-tier bias categorization schema was derived, suggesting three broad types of cognitive bias, each comprised of several more narrowly scoped subtypes. Recalling the earlier discussion of sources of cognitive bias, the resulting bias categorization representation is predominantly information processing focused but it also hints of the role of emotions in the formation of cognitive bias. This is an important consideration insofar as it suggests material amounts of cross-person and cross-situation variability in the extent to which irrational or evidence-refuting reasoning may arise.

Figure 1.5 offers the graphical depiction of the meta-structure of cognitive bias.

The structure shown in the aforementioned summarization is meant to illustrate the dominant cognitive bias contributors, which are *influences*, or external reference elements, such as peers, *effects*, or internal states-of-mind, and

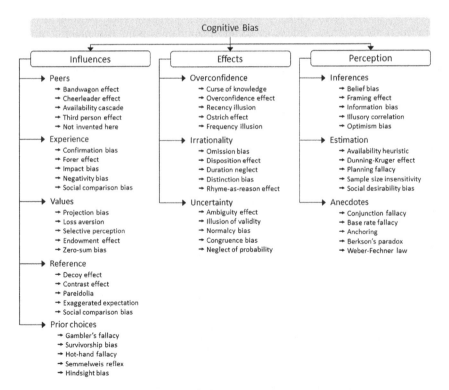

FIGURE 1.5   The Structure of Cognitive Bias: A Meta-Model.

perception, or observation and processing of external stimuli. A decision-maker's judgment can be adversely impacted by several types of influences, including opinions of peers, accumulated past experience and prior choices, as well as latent values and applicable aspects of his or her frame of reference. In addition, one's ability to arrive at a rational conclusion can be further impeded by internal-to-self effects, which include overconfidence, general irrationality, and the more situationally emergent feeling of uncertainty. Lastly, the efficacy of one's decision-making can be even more degraded by perception-based influences such as skewed inferences, flawed estimations, and overvaluing of anecdotal evidence. In a sense, human decision-making can be likened to an athlete trying to complete an obstacle course – while the challenge associated with surmounting individual obstacles cannot ever be completely eliminated, knowledge of, and experience in dealing with each obstruction will greatly enhance the athlete's overall performance.

Perhaps the greatest challenge emanating from the various forms of cognitive bias summarized in the meta-model depicted in Figure 1.5 is that those are consequences of what could be described as natural brain functioning. A decision-maker does not willfully make a choice to, for instance, ignore base rate information (base rate fallacy) or inaccurately perceive a relationship between two unrelated events (illusory correlation) – those, and dozens of other fact and logic-warping 'mental instincts' are automatic, subconscious information processing, sensemaking mechanisms that feel as natural as those that produce rational and fact-conforming conclusions. It takes a great deal of mental discipline, focus and awareness (of the many forms of bias) to shield one's reasoning from cognitive bias, and even the partial list of its many manifestations shown in Figure 1.5 suggests an overwhelming task, given the sheer number of ways the brain can trick itself. What steps can be taken, especially in the context of organizational decision-making, to at least noticeably reduce the potentially adverse consequences of cognitive bias? The answer is both simple and complex: Make better, more systematic use of the available data – that is the simple part. The 'how' to do that, on ongoing, systemic basis, is the complex part of the answer, and it is the focus of the Empirical & Experiential Evidence (3E) framework detailed in this book.

Notes

1 Loosely based on a somewhat fictional (according to the Boston Globe) 2003 book by B. Merrich titled *Bringing Down the House: The Inside Story of Six MIT Students Who Took Vegas for Millions*, featuring a group of MIT card counters commonly known as the MIT Blackjack Team.
2 As opposed to using external applications or systems, which are generally not legal.
3 A gaming device, used mainly by casinos, for holding multiple decks of playing cards.
4 The famed Turing's Machine, originally built to break the Nazi's Enigma code and designed around the concept of 'mechanized thought', now forms one of the core theoretical constructs in computer science.

5 For instance, following their 1957 discovery of 'refutation screening', which is a method for optimizing move evaluation, a team at Carnegie Mellon University predicted that a computer would defeat the world human champion by 1967.

6 It should be noted that the 1997 event was a re-match between Kasparov and Deep Blue; Kasparov won the initial match held a year earlier, 4–2.

7 It is commonly held that to play well, a competitive player has to look at least five moves ahead; given the average of about 30 legal moves per chess position, there can be as many as 10^{15} (quadrillion) possibilities.

8 An estimate based on the fact that the fastest (and thus larger) supercomputer weighs over 150 tons.

9 At the time of writing of this book, the Chinese Tianhe-2, aka Milky Way 2, holds the record as the fastest supercomputer in the world, able to perform 54.902 quadrillion calculations per second, using over 3 million Intel processors.

10 Kasparov was 34 years old at the time of his loss to Deep Blue; he became a chess master at the age of 15 years, and the youngest ever undisputed world chess champion at 22 years.

11 This is one of the reasons eyewitness accounts become less and less reliable with the passage of time.

12 Refers to uninterrupted flow of long sequences of data, such as audio or video captured by security devices; it presents distinctly different management and analysis challenges that batch data, which tend to be captured intermittently.

13 Loosely based on Jim Gray's four scientific paradigms as elucidated in Hey, Tansley & Tolle's *The Fourth Paradigm: Data-Intensive Scientific Discovery*, published by Microsoft Research.

14 *Potentiality* refers to any 'possibility' that an entity can be said to have, whereas *actuality* is the motion, change, or activity that represents an exercise or fulfillment of a possibility.

15 An object will remain at rest or in uniform motion in a straight line unless compelled to change its state by the action of an external force.

16 The Heisenberg's indeterminacy principle postulates that the position and the velocity of subatomic particles cannot be measured exactly.

17 The leading explanation about how the universe began postulates that the universe as we know it started with a small singularity, then inflated over the next 13.8 billion years to the cosmos that we know today.

18 Epistemology is a branch of philosophy concerned with understanding the nature of knowledge and belief.

19 It is worth noting that many of his contemporaries, especially those in Athens' ruling elite, were significantly less enamored with his approach, as evidenced by the fact that Socrates was brought to trial (before a jury of 500 of his fellow Athenians) on charges of failing to recognize gods recognized by Athens and corrupting the youth; he was sentenced to death.

20 Credit for this idea should be given to Derek Sivers and his 2010 TED (technology, entertainment, design) talk.

21 Most often attributed to a noted statistician George Box.

22 Bounded rationality is a notion suggesting that rational decision-making is constrained by the tractability of decision problems, cognitive limitations, and time constraints.

23 As earlier noted, a skilled competitive chess player tends look at least five moves ahead, and given the average of about 30 legal moves per chess position, there can be as many as 10^{15} (quadrillion) possibilities.

24 As used in computer science and information theory, it refers to the upper limit of the rate at which discreet amount of information can be reliably transmitted over a noisy communication channel. Originally proposed by C. Shannon in 1948, as a part of his information theory.

25 For instance, a Wikipedia page devoted to that topic lists nearly 200 different cognitive biases, and the list keeps growing.
26 For more details, see a recent research study by N. Jung, C. Wranke, K. Hamburger, and M. Knauff titled 'How emotions affect logical reasoning: evidence from experiments with mood-manipulated participants, spider phobics, and people with exam anxiety'.
27 One of the three types of *evidence validity*, with the other two being content (also known as logical) and criterion validity.

2

NON-GENERALIZABLE OBJECTIVITY

Anecdotal evidence can be irresistibly compelling. After all, there are entire product categories, even industries that owe their existence to consumers relying on nonfactual data. Antiaging or skin care products are commonly bought on recommendations of friends, diet plans and miracle pills that promise to deliver a lot (of weight loss) and fast are typically sold by passionate spokespersons – in fact, one of the pillars of advertising, a compensated endorser, is rooted in the persuasive power of anecdotal evidence. Consumers tend to conclude that a product or a brand is 'the best' or 'the worst' not based on any kind of scientific evidence, but on word-of-mouth, television, and other similar forms of influence.

A more recent phenomenon of online product reviews seemingly fixed the problem associated with relying on a single, or a very small number of influencers by bringing to bear an often large pools of ad hoc reviewers (which created a cottage industry of professional product reviewers). The idea of 'verified' product purchasers offering their independent evaluations is now one of the mainstays of online commerce, and countless consumers base their brand choices on the resultant buyer satisfaction comparisons. After all, how can one not trust hundreds of independent impressions?

And while relying on a compensated opinion of a star professional athlete when buying, let's say, a car or car insurance is very visibly questionable, relying on (sometimes compensated and sometimes not) opinions of hundreds of anonymous buyers may seem reasonable, or at least until the representativeness of a particular opinion pool is called into question. Would brand reviews sourced mostly from younger, let's say under 30 years of age, drivers offer meaningful decision-related insights to a retired baby boomer looking for a new automobile? Perhaps, but probably not likely. Although the difference may seem obvious to a statistician, many decision-makers tend not to be adequately cognizant of the difference between the number of product reviewers and the degree to which opinions of those reviewers may or may not be representative of a larger universe of all product users.

The focus of this chapter is on the widespread practice of treating as generalizable insights extracted out of samples and analyses that do not meet the basic generalizability criteria. The goal of the ideas discussed in this segment is to clearly lay out the reasons for why overreliance on conclusions drawn from anecdotal evidence or nonrepresentative samples can lead to unwarranted conclusions, further compounding the adverse impact of biased perception.

Familiar Clues

Two business consultants, Mary and John, have been retained to evaluate the root causes of a business organization's growing customer attrition problem. After a few weeks spent independently analyzing the company's sale and related data, conducting customer interviews, reviewing peer practices, and cataloguing and analyzing the currently in place customer relationship management practices, the consultants presented their findings to their client. Interestingly, though both were manifestly analyzing the same underlying problem and, to a large extent, used the same or similar data, the results of their analyses were quite different: Mary's findings largely paralleled what the organization already believed to be the leading causes of growing customer attrition, whereas John's findings effectively disputed the current organizational beliefs, pointing instead to different culprits. Which of the two competing sets of conclusions is the organization more likely to embrace?

According to a psychological *theory of self-affirmation*, information that is congruent with one's preexisting beliefs is more likely to be accepted than information than contradicts those beliefs. The theory postulates several reasons for that, most notably:

- Protection of self-integrity. There are numerous dimensions to one's self-integrity relating to values, roles, and belief systems – within the confines of the above consultant reports, believing oneself to be an intelligent and knowledgeable professional is likely to compel one to defend the beliefs one held, and possibly communicated with others.
- Defensive instinct. When information that contradicts previously held beliefs is presented, it often triggers defensive reactions in the form of denial or disbelief. In the context of the consulting example, it may mean questioning the validity of the underlying data, the efficacy and/or accuracy of the analysis of data, etc.
- Self-serving evidence. Anecdotal or one-sided evidence is often offered in support of self-affirming beliefs, as illustrated by detractors of predictive

modeling. One of the common strategies used by those resisting the use of predictive modeling to support, for instance, identification of at-risk (of attrition) customers is to point to instances of incorrect model prediction. It matters little that, in aggregate, the accuracy of a particular model may be three or four times greater than when no predictive models are used – a model-based approach is deemed flawed merely because some of the model-based predictions are inaccurate.

Turning back to the competing explanations of customer attrition offered by the two consultants, the one that affirms the already held beliefs is more likely to be positively received and, ultimately, believed. The explanation that contradicts the currently-in-place view will likely face more disbelief, leading to heightened scrutiny of the underlying data and data analytic methods, because it contradicts currently held beliefs. The informational content of the current-beliefs-bucking explanation is of secondary importance insofar as the resultant dissonance is concerned – it is the disconfirmation of existing beliefs that triggers an almost automatic defense of the current knowledge response.

This tendency, often characterized as *confirmation bias*, compels individuals to search for and favor information in a way that confirms one's preexisting beliefs, effectively infusing systematic error into inductive reasoning. It is why more than 90% of college professors believe themselves to be better at their jobs than their colleagues, why 70% of college students believe themselves to be above average leaders, and why 25% of students believe themselves to be in the top 1% in terms of their ability to get along with others[1]; gamblers swear by their 'hot' and 'cold' streaks and alter their bets accordingly; sky gazers see faces of God in cloud formations, etc. When coupled with the manner in which human brain processes information (detailed in the previous chapter), self-affirmational tendencies compel individuals to look for familiar clues, which, in turn, predisposes decision-makers to affirm the familiar, rather than to embrace the new. Thus, the tendency to impose order, to find coherence among diverse, often random events or characteristics can ultimately lead to self-deception, if and when relying on anecdotal or otherwise non-generalizable evidence, which explains the pervasiveness of numerous organizational management-related fashions, fads, and lores.

Management Lore

Learning organization's, 'knowledge management', 'emotional intelligence', 'total quality management', 'employee engagement' are all examples of quick fix, templated management frameworks. Easy to communicate and comprehend, seemingly applicable to everyone's problems everywhere, and in-tune with the zeitgeist, or perceived problems of the day, those and numerous other management fashions offer novel, though rarely radical solutions to even intractable problems. Filled with fun anecdotes and buzzwords, supported by stories of excellent companies, and communicated by eloquent, confident sounding gurus, those universal management recipes usually offer to deliver a lot and fast, and help their adaptors feel effective and cutting edge.

Broadly characterized, the above exemplified *management fashions* encompass a wide range of transitory collective beliefs that certain management techniques are at the forefront of management progress, and as such represent proven solutions to nagging management problems. And in fact, bits of ideas imbedded in, for instance, total quality management or emotional intelligence frameworks might indeed work in some contexts, which is often used as 'evidence' of those techniques' overall efficacy. Though clearly analytically flawed leaps of faith (akin to believing in generalizability of inferences drawn from statistically nonrepresentative samples), when coupled with the status of gurus promoting those ideas, along with memorable, upbeat and entertaining stories, quick fix management solutions can sound quite compelling.

Moreover, decision-makers' desire to impose order by finding coherence in barrages of distinct characteristics or events can manifest itself in a yet another form of self-deception known as *management lore*. Defined as flawed management beliefs, axioms or anecdotes that are so pervasive that they erroneously achieve the status of immutable facts, management lore tends to be a product of faulty logic, overreliance on common sense, or unfamiliarity with applicable and factually robust evidence. Exemplified by Walt Disney's famous axiom 'if you can dream it, you can do it', or the widely repeated expression 'sky is the limit', the idea that thinking big leads to big outcomes is one of the fundamental, nearly axiomatic beliefs underpinning Western society and culture. And yet, empirical evidence from social psychology shows that dreaming big can actually be detrimental to individuals' performance, even to their career success. Research-derived explanation suggests that adopting unrealistic fantasies of success can lead to becoming accustomed to the fantasy as it is was already a reality, which, in turn, can lead to overconfidence and failure to commit the effort required to actually achieve the big goals. Along similar lines, another commonly encountered management lore suggests that, in a group setting, creativity always benefits from diversity. Although diversity is indeed desirable for a wide range of social justice and equality-related reasons, there is no empirical evidence supporting the widely believed creativity-diversity link. In fact, group dynamics-related research suggests that even if diverse individuals privately generate substantially different ideas, teams do not often discuss all ideas thought of by individual members, and thus distally related concepts do not necessarily produce coherent wholes. Similar belief vs. reality incongruence also characterizes the idea of emotional intelligence, or the ability to identify, assess, and control the emotions of oneself as well as those of the group.

Popularly advertised, often by self-proclaimed gurus as one of the best predictors of organizational employees' performance, that seemingly compelling notion actually lacks sound theoretical basis or meaningful practical measurement approaches, thus cannot be backed either by scientific research or verifiable and directly applicable practical outcomes.

Validity and Reliability

The concepts of validity and reliability, first addressed in Chapter 1, are often used somewhat interchangeably, mostly because both are tools that are useful in ascertaining the efficacy of measurement qualities of indicators of abstract, latent constructs. Consider the following informational challenge: A group of political scientists is trying to estimate the possibility of a politically destabilizing event taking place at a particular part of the world in the next 12 months. What are their respective definitions of a 'politically destabilizing event'? Restated in more operational terms, the problem at hand can be phrased as follows: What tangible benchmarks or indicators could signal an onset of a larger, politically destabilizing event? In essence, the challenge of quantifying the likelihood or the severity of somewhat abstractly expressed events is twofold: First, it is of identifying the right indicators, which are any directly observable proxies for the event in question. Second, it is that of ascertaining the accuracy of those indicators – in other words, how good an indicator of the latent construct of interest (the said politically destabilizing event) is particular observable events, such as anti-government demonstrations?

Implied in the above considerations are two distinct dimensions of validity and reliability of observable events as proxies for the underlying latent construct of interest. An important consideration in assessing the degree to which particular observable proxies can be indeed taken as valid and reliable indicators of an underlying unobservable idea lies in understanding the core tenets of *latent*[2] *construct measurement*, which is a set of procedures used by social scientists to formulate and test hypotheses that further our understanding of group (social) and individual (psychological) phenomena. Broadly speaking, those procedures are comprised of two conceptually distinct components: (1) examination of the 'truthfulness' of individual latent and observable constructs and (2) assessment of the degree to which observable characteristics and events are indeed indicative of the broader latent ideas. Hence, the notions of validity and reliability encompass aspects of cogency of individual concepts, as well as the efficacy of the observable indicator – latent construct specification.

Keeping the above considerations in mind, *validity* is the degree of truthfulness of a particular concept, often expressed as the degree to which the construct's conceptualization and operationalization are in agreement. Recalling the distinction between the assessment of 'construct truthfulness' and the 'observable-latent specification', the different manifestations of validity can be grouped as follows:

1　Construct truthfulness assessment

　a　Face validity: A fairly superficial and subjective assessment of whether or not a particular idea captures what it is supposed to capture;

　b　Content validity: The degree of logical completeness of a particular concept;

　c　Discriminant validity: The degree to which two notionally distinct concepts are actually unrelated;

2　Observable-latent specification assessment

　a　Convergent validity: the degree to which two measures of constructs that theoretically should be related, are in fact related;

　b　Predictive validity: The degree to which an observable indicator correctly signals change in the latent construct of interest;

　c　Concurrent validity: The stability of the observable indicator – latent construct association.

Reliability captures the repeatability or consistency of a particular operationalization. A measure (i.e., an observable indicator) is considered reliable if it gives us the same result over and over again, of course assuming that what we are measuring (latent construct) is not changing. Conceptually, reliability can be thought of as a ratio of the true level of the measure to the entire measure. In practice, however, the 'true' measure is rarely known hence in an applied sense the best way of estimating reliability is to express it as a correlation among multiple observations of the same measure. There are several different types of reliability, which can be grouped into internal, which assesses the extent to which a latent construct – observable indicator specification is consistent within itself, and external, which captures the extent to which the same specification produces materially different cross-usage results.

1　Internal reliability

　a　Split-half method: Assesses the extent to which individual observable indicators contribute equally, or comparably, to the assessment of the latent construct;

2　External reliability

　a　Test-re-test: The cross-usage stability of the latent construct – observable indicator specification;

　b　Inter-rater: The cross-user stability of the latent construct – observable indicator specification.

The preceding brief overview of the key validity- and reliability-related considerations is meant to heighten awareness and help formulate more operationally granular understanding of those important aspects of evidence assessment. In most situations, it is simply not feasible to engage in an extensive mental validity and reliability assessment calculus – that said, being more keenly aware of the operational meaning of those two notions should nonetheless lead to more cautious and thoughtful consideration of new evidence.

Anecdotal Evidence

Whether it is in professional, business, or personal life, a good story is a verbal equivalent of a picture that is worth the proverbial thousand words. Anecdotes, which are brief, often amusing or humorous revealing accounts of a person or an event, have the power to capture attention and deliver a clear message. Widely used to convey abstract ideas underpinning many core human values such as morality or justice, anecdotes have been used by teachers and preachers to deliver important messages, as it has been long known that people are more likely to remember notable rather than typical examples. But that, however, can also be a problem.

Any informal account or a testimonial can become *anecdotal evidence*. In most situations, anecdotal evidence is limited to either a single case (an event or an individual) or a very small set of cases, and it is intended to communicate a specific story, often in the form of a personal account or testimony. For instance, a person may argue against compulsory use of seatbelts by citing an example of an acquaintance who was not wearing a seatbelt while driving, got in a head-on collision as a result of which was ejected from the car, which shortly thereafter burst into flames. Using that example as anecdotal evidence, the individual then may claim had his friends been wearing the seatbelt he would have likely died in the ensuing fire; thus, seatbelt laws should be abolished. This hypothetical case illustrates the key characteristics of anecdotal evidence which are face value truthfulness (the event either actually occurred or its occurrence is plausible) and non-typicality (the event represents a rare, isolated example). Although in that particular case not wearing a seatbelt might have indeed resulted in a better outcome, that is a very atypical, rare case and there are many more instances where wearing a seatbelt prevented, or at least materially diminished accident-related injuries.

Implicit in the notion of an anecdote is that such evidence does not need to meet any specific standards of appropriateness, or to use more scientifically clear language, it does not need to exhibit satisfactory degree of validity and reliability. In most instances, to be appealing, anecdotal evidence is expected to be on-point, which is to say it needs to depict a topically related person or situation, in addition to also being interesting. However, as noted earlier, it is usually the atypical cases or situations that are interesting and memorable however, being atypical renders such examples nonrepresentative, which can be problematic from a decision-making perspective. Unorthodox business schemes that led to successful outcomes are described in case studies and many business schools devote substantial parts of their teaching to dissecting those preternatural cases, ultimately further conditioning future business managers to trust anecdotal evidence. Unique events, maverick leaders, and norm-bucking choices are all so much more colorful and thus captivating than systematic and persistent review and synthesis of a broad spectrum of representative evidence, in the same sense that overnight sensation, rags-to-riches success stories are so much more captivating than a slow and predictable building of a successful career. Years of formal and informal education instill in all of us fascination with the rare and the atypical, leading to an almost natural acceptance of anecdotal evidence as sufficient proof.

And to be fair, there are notable instances where atypical offers the best guidance – after all, just replicating the ways of the past is unlikely to produce new, in the sense of different, future. In fact, now dominant companies such as Google, Amazon, or Walmart all started by breaking with established norms. However, from an organizational decision-making standpoint, the vast majority of decisions made by the vast majority of decision-makers are of operational nature – as such, those decisions entail predominantly tactical resource allocation and related choices, where preponderance of evidence likely offers better decision-guiding insights than out-of-the-ordinary cases.

Best Practices & Benchmarks

Regardless of what facet of organizational functioning and performance one considers, it is difficult to assess it without an appropriate frame of reference. Is 6% ROI good? Is 5% chance risk of incurring an adverse event high? Is 50% probability of repurchase high? The short answer is – it depends. If the industry average ROI is 4%, 6% is comparatively speaking quite strong, but if the industry average ROI is 10%, 6% would likely be seen as poor performance. The same applies to the said 5% chance of incurring a damaging event, and 50% repurchase probability: The qualitative 'high-' vs. 'low'-risk exposure and repurchase probability conclusion would typically be a function of the company or customer, respectively, specific estimate compared to a pertinent benchmark, such as the industry average or the average across all customers. This illustration underscores the importance of benchmarks as the key component in arriving at decision-guiding conclusions.

This is an important point. Let us consider again the sample 5% chance of incurring an adverse event, and let us further assume that the average across all comparable companies (a peer group) is 7% for that particular exposure. From the risk management-related decision-making point of view, granular numeric estimates are ultimately interpreted in a more general context of conclusive categories such as 'low', 'average', or 'high' because risk response choices distinguish among categorically, not merely mathematically different values. In other words, the conclusion of high-risk exposure would likely compel materially different risk responses (in terms of specific risk mitigation, risk financing, and related decisions) than the conclusion of low-risk exposure while the estimate of 3% vs. 9% risk probability would not, by itself, trigger differentiated responses due to lack of proper contextualization (i.e., numeric estimates such as those don't convey universally recognizable meaning in the way that 'high' vs. 'low' categories do). Hence, the importance of benchmark validity and reliability: To yield robust conclusive, decision-guiding categories, the underlying benchmark has to be sound (i.e., valid and reliable); only then will the mathematical estimates produce robust conclusions.

One of the key considerations entailed in defining an appropriate benchmark is the composition of the peer group. For some organizations, such as public utilities or insurance companies, it may be a relatively straightforward and objective task, given the well-defined industry boundaries and easily enumerable like organizations. For other organizations, however, such as diversified conglomerates, the peer selection process tends to be more subjective, and the resultant peer group noticeably more heterogeneous, in terms of composite companies' profiles. Under most circumstances, the more heterogeneous the peer group composition the greater the within-peer-group variability of focal characteristics, such as exposure to specific risks, and outcomes, such as operational and other performance, which reduces the efficacy of benchmarking. A yet another frequently encountered challenge is that of limited sample size, as even well-defined industry segments, such as leisure and hospitality, are comprised of very small numbers of dominant firms,[3] which effectively severely limits the number of true peers. Here, the same is true as in the case of high within-group variability mentioned earlier: The small sample size leads to greater benchmarking metrics' variability, which, in turn, diminishes the efficacy of benchmarking.

The challenge associated with delineation and use of the so-called 'best practices' is considerably more vexing, primarily because of the far greater degree of subjectivity associated with the identification and interpretation meaningful and applicable praxis. Popularly characterized as professional or commercial procedures or courses of action prescribed as offering the most effective means of producing desired outcomes, *best practices* can be a product of experience or research, though in business management it tends to be overwhelmingly the former. The implied intent behind the pursuit and embrace of best practices is the desire to achieve superior results by replicating, or mimicking, processes or methods developed and used elsewhere.

Conceptually, it is a compelling idea, but practically it is fraught with problems as its premise is rooted in a number of questionable assumptions, the most fundamental of which is 'that which worked there will also work here'. Even organizations that compete in the same industry producing functionally substitutable products and/or services are likely to exhibit material cultural, organizational, and structural differences that make some methods or practices more applicable in one organizational setting than in another. The obvious differences might include leadership style, which can be centralized in one organization and decentralized in another, risk appetite, with some companies being risk-averse, whereas others aggressive risk takers, or insourcing vs. outsourcing posture, with some organizations committed to reliance on their in-house operational infrastructure (insourcing) while others equally committed to using outside suppliers (outsourcing). A practice that has been shown to work well in an organization characterized by centralized leadership style, risk-averse decision-making and insourcing focused operations may be ill-fitted to a decentralized, aggressive risk taking, and outsourcing-minded organization.

The notion of best practices implies the degree of universality that may be found only in selected few areas of organizational management such as data management or business continuity planning. Those organizational domains are characterized by a considerable degree of cross-firm similarities due to a combination of structural- and oversight-related factors. Regarding the former, virtually all business enterprises use commercially procured (vs. in-house developed) data capture and management hardware/software systems which naturally lends itself to cross-organization standardization. In terms of the latter, laws and regulations addressing certain sensitive aspects of data capture and storage, such as privacy and security, apply uniformly to all companies that capture and maintain in storage certain types of data, such as financial or health care details. Consequently, identifying and adhering to industry best practices in the areas such as data security is highly desirable.

There is yet another reason why best practices could be less-than-ideal standards to emulate: At least some are rooted in tradition rather than good economic sense. For example, the widely accepted publishing industry's best practice is that a bookseller can return any unsold books to a publisher, at that publisher's expense, which is a practice that dates back to the time of the Great Depression. Not only did the demand for books declined precipitously during that time, but the vast majority of booksellers were small, independent shops that could not assume the financial risk of buying books that might not be able to sell to the public. One of the major publishers at that time, Simon & Schuster, came up with ingenious solution by offering to assume the financial risk of unsold inventory by allowing book retailers to return, expense-free, unsold books. The solution worked well for Simon & Schuster as it allowed the publisher to continue to sell books, so not surprisingly it was quickly copied by other publishers and it remains the industry best practice, in spite of fundamentally different demand characteristics and industry structure. One would be hard-pressed to defend the wisdom of embracing that particular practice today, or even to characterize it as 'best practice' as it is nothing more than an outdated norm that continues because of tradition, and in spite of lack of sound economic reasoning.

Still, perhaps the most significant downside to overreliance on industry best practices is that it can stifle innovation or strategic creativity. How many of today's most admired companies – Amazon, Google, Apple, or Toyota – rose to prominence by emulating their industry peers? Setting aside a handful of structural and oversight areas briefly discussed earlier, industry benchmarking and best practices are rarely, if ever, thresholds of excellence – typically, they demark baselines of acceptable, that is, average, performance. It is more rational, in fact more statistically sound to think of industry benchmarks and best practices as guidelines to not being left behind (competitors), rather than a roadmap to attaining leading results. An investor with a highly diversified portfolio will most likely earn average returns, just as a business organization with peer benchmarking and industry best practices focused managerial mindset will also likely realize average results. For those who want to 'play it safe', that might indeed be an appropriate and a rational mindset – for those, however, who aspire to above average results, sound but independent decision-making might be a better bet.

Even worse, adoption of the industry best practices can ultimately (meaning, in the long run) adversely impact organizational performance. Business process reengineering, agile management, and lean/six sigma are among the many consultant-popularized frameworks that promised to streamline operations, increase productivity, enhance efficiency, or increase profitability. And to be sure, some of those frameworks deployed in some organizations indeed delivered short-term benefits, but there are few documented and empirically validated examples of those 'best in class' practices delivering sustained long-term benefits. Managers continue to embrace those ideas not only because of the almost universal desire to be on the cutting edge (which those approaches presumably represent), but also due to their auras of simplicity, making them easy to communicate, comprehend, and, when needed, defend.

Nonrepresentative Samples

Industry benchmarks and best practices discussed in the previous section are largely products of qualitative and observational research – for example, retailers and other direct-to-consumer business organizations often utilize the Pareto principle[4] based '80/20 rule', according to which 80% of revenue can be attributed to approximately 20% of customers. That generalized insight is a 'rule of thumb', meaning it is based on practical experience rather than specific empirical insights (it should be noted that the original research published by V. Pareto was based on empirical evidence showing that roughly 80% of land in Italy, at that time, was owned by 20% of the population). Rules of thumb, such as the 80/20 rule, serve as general guides, and are accepted to be true from the onset. In contrast to those and other external-to-the-organization standards, businesses can also develop their own, internal-to-the-organization rules by exploring the available data.

Data as Asset

An *asset* is defined as something of economic value that the organization owns and controls and that is expected to provide future benefits; in an investment sense, an asset increases the value of a firm or benefits the firm's operations. Under most circumstances, the asset-worthiness of data stems from the potential to improve the firm's operations through the generation of unique knowledge, which, in turn, can give rise to competitively advantageous decisions. Stated differently, it is more appropriate to think of data as a *potential asset*: It contains the 'raw material' which can be transformed into an *actual* asset in the form of competitively advantageous managerial decisions.

Thinking of data as a potential asset also has a secondary benefit of redirecting the emphasis away from storage and maintenance and toward the usage of data. Since the 1980s, organizations across industries have been investing heavily into data capture and maintenance-related infrastructure while dedicating disproportionately little effort and resources to data exploration. Although the relatively recent emergence of 'data science' and 'business analytics' as recognized business disciplines is beginning to change that trend, historically approximately 85%–90% of total data-related expenditures were directed at the hardware and software infrastructures, with only the remainder going toward extracting insights out of data. Thus, only about 10¢ out of every $1 of data-related spending went toward actually making data into a true organizational asset.

But even the 10% or so of the total information technology expenditures that in one way or another was dedicated to data exploration has not always been utilized as much as possible. Oftentimes, a good part of that spending went toward production of generic information (e.g., the standard, summary focused reporting) that could bring the organization up to the level of competitive parity, but not endow it with competitive advantage. Some of that is due to proliferation of commercial (i.e., generic) data capture, storage, and management platforms, coupled with the ever more standardized approach to data analysis, together leading to within-industry, and at times even cross-industry *informational convergence*. Further fueling that trend is the proliferation of third-party analytics, or data analysis vendors offering fundamentally the same type of information to organizations across industries – that said, unlike the technological standardization, the degree of analytical convergence varies across industries. Nonetheless, there is a distinct trend of relatively few, large data providers and aggregators providing informationally non-distinct analytical products and services to a wide cross-section of the marketplace.

The slow but persistent process of technological and informational convergence underscores the importance of developing forward-looking informational vision built around analytically innovative approaches to data analysis. Raw data have the potential of becoming an asset, but its asset-worthiness hinges on the organization's analytical skills. Some organizations are able to systematically extract competitive edge producing insights out of data, but others struggle to move beyond generic reporting that lacks the informational power to push those organizations ahead of their competitors.

Data Selection

There are three key, sequentially dependent steps to use data as a source of decision-guiding insights: *data selection → data analyses → result interpretation.* All three are equally important, but being the starting point, data selection sets the tone, as captured by the long-standing computer science GIGO (garbage-in, garbage-out) concept. Given that, for reasons ranging from statistical appropriateness to practical accessibility, the vast majority of data analyses use subsets or samples of all available data, one of the core aspects of data selection is embodied in the notion of *sampling.* Defined in simple terms, it is the process of selecting units (e.g., some people, organizations, product purchases, insurance claims) from a population of interest (e.g., all people, organizations, product purchases, insurance claims) in a manner such that sample-based results can be generalized onto the population from which that sample was chosen. This often a multi-step process is graphically depicted in Figure 2.1.

The universe → population → initial sample → final sample progression shown in Figure 2.1 is quite common and it reflects a combination of theoretical and practical considerations. The starting point in the sampling process is to clearly define an all-encompassing *universe* – for instance, in marketing analyses it could mean conceptually delimiting the totality of all purchasers of a particular brand, whereas in insurance claim analyses it could point toward all personal automotive claims filed during a particular period. The next step is to specify the reachable *population*, or a subset of the earlier defined theoretical universe. In the case of marketing analyses that could be all

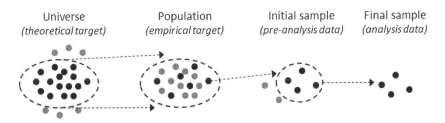

Universe	Population	Initial sample	Final sample
(theoretical target)	*(empirical target)*	*(pre-analysis data)*	*(analysis data)*

FIGURE 2.1 The Generalized Sampling Process.

identifiable brand purchasers, such as those registered in the brand's loyalty program, whereas in the case of insurance claim analyses, reachable population could be defined as claims filed against a particular insurance company. Quite often, a population can be quite large and diverse which typically necessitates selecting a more narrowly defined *sample*, which in the case of marketing analyses could be limited to brand purchases made, or insurance claims filed within a particular region or during a particular timeframe. Almost always the initial sample needs to be further engineered to make sure it exhibits statistically desirable properties, the result of which is analyses-ready final sample – in marketing- and insurance-related analyses alike the creation of the final sample typically entails eliminating or otherwise correcting for outlying/atypical (e.g., exceedingly large) values, along with other data molding steps.

All analyses of data comprising the final sample are subject to the composition of that sample. Within the confines of the sample selection logic outlined above, projectability of sample-derived insights is of primary concern. *Projectability* addresses the fundamental question of usability – do sample-based estimates represent sufficiently accurate approximations of the population-wide values? Regardless of what sampling technique[5] is used, a sample encompasses a typically small subset of all cases, which means that a sample is just about guaranteed to be a somewhat imperfect representation of the population (and the universe) it is meant to depict. The question is how imperfect – setting aside technical details surrounding sampling error and related statistical considerations, let it suffice to say that the efficacy of sample-derived estimates notwithstanding, the degree to which those estimates can be generalized onto the population of interest is a direct function of the degree of similarity between the sample and the population it is meant to represent.

Another important sampling related consideration is that of *recency*, which reflects the newness of data. It is well known that more recent the data tend to be more indicative of the future – what is somewhat less obvious is that the most recent set of behaviors represent but a snapshot of reality, which may not necessarily be most indicative of more persistent, cross-time propensities. In more general sense, just focusing on the most recent outcomes of interest may lead to loss of *longitudinal dimensionality*, which may ultimately hamper any forward-looking forecasts. There is an element of randomness or chanciness that is confounded with recency – minimizing its impact typically requires going further back in time to discern more general trends or propensities. The difficult part is knowing how far back, for which there is not universally applicable threshold or choice calculus.

Overall, data selection is prone to two types of errors: sample composition outlined earlier, and sample sizing. One of the core statistical ideas taught in introductory courses is that too small a sample will lead to unreliable parameter estimates; however, excessively large sample may lead to even inordinately trivial differences becoming statistically significant, while not being statistically significant at a smaller sample size,[6] everything else being the same (the notion of 'statistical significance' is discussed in more detail later). Thus, extremely small effects can be deemed statistically important, even if their magnitude renders them practically inconsequential.

Data Usage

Recall the earlier introduced data selection → data analyses → result interpretation progression. Having addressed the 'data selection' part of the generalized data usage process, let us now take a closer look at the remaining two parts of the process: 'data analyses' and 'result interpretation'.

First, a brief disclosure: As it is intuitively obvious, the topic of data analyses is incredibly broad, given the dizzying array of data available to organizations, an equally rich array of data analytical tools, techniques, and approaches, and the seemingly endless list of business questions. It is not the purpose of the ensuing discussion to offer even a rudimentary overview of those considerations[7] – our focus is limited to delineating and addressing potential informational challenges emanating from analyses of nonrepresentative samples. That may seem like a very narrow, exception-rather-than-the-norm-oriented aspect of data usage but in fact it is not, as a surprising number of applied business data analytical initiatives is based on nonrepresentative samples. It is the proverbial elephant in the room – though hardly a secret, little is done to acknowledge and remedy this rather pervasive problem.

When considering data usage from insight generation point of view, a commonly encountered problem stems from the use of *statistical significance tests* (SSTs), as a way of validating the truthfulness – in the sense of correctness and generalizability – of sample-based conclusions. SSTs are a hypothesis testing tool, the purpose of which is to identify universally true effects. SSTs' secondary and closely related objective is that of generalizing sample-based insights onto a larger population. Although principally a theory development method, significance testing is also widely used in applied analyses, but the manner in which it is used often outstretches its intended usability limits.

Operationally, statistical significance testing utilizes any of the known distribution statistical difference tests, such as F, t, or χ^2, to compare means (F-test and t-test) or frequency counts (χ^2 test) with the purpose of distinguishing between spurious and persistent relationships. Although the statistics utilized in significance testing are themselves methodologically sound, the manner in which they are used can lead to troublesome misapplications. Setting aside random user error (such as using F-test to compare differences among sets of counts), applied business analyses are permeated by systematic SST misuse stemming from the fundamental lack of fit between theory development and applied insight extraction. The former aims to uncover universally true knowledge claims, whereas latter aims to contribute to sustainable competitive advantage, from which it follows that significance testing is used as a mean of ascertaining sample-to-population generalizability when used for scientific theory building purposes, and a mean of quantifying the magnitude of impact when used in applied business analytics. Sidestepping a technical discussion of confidence intervals,[8] *generalizable relationships* (theory development) are estimated using 'value ± error' ranges, whereas estimation of *incremental benefits* (applied business analytics) demands exact magnitudes – SSTs were designed, and should be used, in the former, but not the latter setting. In more operationally clear terms, it is methodologically invalid (and thus practically incorrect) to use SST to characterize any sample-derived magnitudes, such as incremental sales of, let's say, 3.6%, as being 'statistically significant' (at any of the commonly used levels of significance, with $\alpha = 0.05$ being the most widely employed threshold) – to ascribe statistical significance to any such effect, it would need to be recast in terms of an appropriately estimated confidence interval (e.g., 2.1%–5.1%).

Notes

1 Gilovich, T. (1991), *How We Know What Isn't So: The Fallibility of Human Reason in Everyday Life*, The Free Press, New York, NY.
2 From Latin *lateo*, meaning 'lie hidden'; those are abstract, no directly observable ideas such as 'honor', 'compassion' or 'loyalty' – to assess the extent to which, for instance, a customer is loyal to a particular brand we typically look for observable behaviors, such as brand repurchase.
3 For instance, the largest hotel groups: Marriott International/Starwood Hotels & Resorts (a recent merger-created single company), InterContinental Hotels Group, Hilton Worldwide Holds, Wyndham Hotel Group and Choice Hotels own, on average, more than 16 hotel brands each (Marriott/Starwood owns over 30), making them significantly more diverse (both offering types- and geography-wise) than their smaller peers.
4 Based on the distribution of income and wealth in population (derived in 1906 by Italian economist V. Pareto), it states that, for many events, roughly 80% of effects stem from about 20% of causes.
5 Broadly speaking, sampling approaches can be grouped into *probability* and *non-probability* methods – the former are all built around random selection and include simple, stratified, systematic, and cluster methods; the latter do not make use of random selection and can be further subdivided into 'accidental', best exemplified by convenience sampling, and 'purposeful', which includes quota, expert, and modal instance sampling.
6 A minimum acceptable (i.e., exhibiting sufficient statistical power) sample size can be determined with the help of widely used sample size determination formulas, but no analogs exist for approximating maximum acceptable sample size.
7 Which are covered by already extensive and growing library of sources explicitly focused on business analytics, data science, statistics, data mining, and machine learning and related.
8 A measure of the probability that a population parameter will fall between two set values computed using sample statistics to estimate an unknown population parameter with a given (i.e., user selected) confidence level.

3

MASS ANALYTICS

The technological singularity, or simply the singularity hypothesis, argues that humanity is headed toward the creation of artificial superintelligence in the form of accelerating self-improvement-capable computers running software-based general artificial intelligence, destined to ultimately far surpass human intelligence. Although the idea may seem far-fetched at first, it is actually quite rational: Since one of the ultimate manifestations of human intelligence is the creation of artificial intelligence, an ultra-intelligent system initially designed by mankind will subsequently continue to improve upon its initial design, leading to what is often referred to as 'intelligence explosion', and ultimately leaving its creator – the mankind – far behind. Just an idea for now, though one that encapsulates a seemingly inescapable conclusion to the clearly evident accelerating technological progress, especially in the area of information technology. In that context, some futurists are promoting the view that within the next couple of decades, humans will connect our neocortex, or the part of brain responsible for thinking, to the cloud, which is effectively a metaphor for the Internet. That may seem far-fetched as well, but wouldn't the now ubiquitous addiction to the Internet as a source of information and the primary mean of communication seem far-fetched a couple of decades ago?

Scary or exciting, future turning points, as exemplified by the speculation surrounding the idea of technological singularity, can rarely be predicted simply be extrapolating observable trends. At the same time, emerging trends can offer credible cues in relation to important although perhaps not quite as existentially themed developments. One of those near-term, fairly practical considerations is extracting value out of the explosive torrents of data. More and more of business and other organizations see their future tied to productive consumption and monetization of data, yet relatively few have clear and operationally sound vision that spell out not only the desired end states but also the means of getting there. The rapidly developing domain of *data science* is emerging as a new field of study and a new domain of practice, and it is bringing the much needed conceptual and methodological discipline to the broadly defined pursuit of extracting valid and reliable insights out of data. The term 'insight extraction' itself is taking on a broader meaning, as its meaning is no longer synonymous with generation of decision-guiding inputs into human decision-making, but now also includes curation of multi-sourced data used to power automated (e.g., online recommendation engines), and even autonomous (e.g., self-driving cars) systems.

The explosion in the variety of data and the growing interest in analytics have fueled 'mass production' of a wide array of data analytic outcomes, ranging from simple summative reports to sophisticated predictive models. Yet, in spite of the growing torrents of those informational products, many key organizational decisions are still driven by subjective factors, rather than objective evidence. It is the goal of this chapter to address the often seen scenario of organizations being not only data but also information-rich while remaining comparatively (decision-guiding) knowledge-poor.

Digitization of Life

Why is *big data* 'big' and why are business and other organizations in a frantic race to leverage big data's informational content? The obvious answer is self-evident – namely, because of potential value of insights hidden therein. That, of course, does not address the true spirit of the question contained in the first part (why is big data 'big'?) – here, the answer is equally obvious to even a casual observer: More and more aspects and details of individual and organizational behaviors are recorded, encoded, captured, and stored in the form of digits, words, and symbols that jointly comprise big data. (We are not going to address the implications of that on the idea and the reality of privacy, not because those considerations are not important, as they clearly are, but simply because they fall outside of the scope of our analysis.) Ironically, much of that stems from what could be described as 'voluntary disclosures', where entities, be it individuals or organizations, willfully share their opinions, positions, and even actions via a plethora of outwardly directed means, including websites, blogs, online reviews, discussion forums, etc. Some other data-encoded disclosures are made in a manner that is not overtly willful, though in effect produces personal data recorded by commercial entities. Consider various wearable devices, such as the now ubiquitous Fitbit, Apple Watch, and similar tracking devices worn by millions of consumers to track and record plethora of biometric and behavioral factors. Do those wearing the said devices actively consider what happens to all that physical lifestyle (e.g., daily physical activity) and general well-being (e.g., sleep patterns) data? Do they know who captures and stores that data? Do they know how are those data – if at all – used? And from a more general legal perspective, who owns the resultant data and what rights and responsibilities come with that ownership?

Patterns of change are generally easy to discern looking back in time, but considerably harder to note at the time when change is taking place, especially when the process of change is evolutionary and constantly ongoing. Not too long ago, the bulk of individual- and organizational-level communications were evanescent due to the dissipative nature of sound or radio waves carrying the content of those communications – now, many of the same types of communications are captured and encoded as bits of data that are stored, exchanged, and analyzed. It is in this sense that lives of organizations and individuals are being 'digitized', as readily evidenced by the rise of big data. The seemingly never-ending flow of new devices and applications results in the ever-expanding flow of data, as data capture is now almost an inseparable part of functioning of the modern communication infrastructure. And governments, business and other organizations continue to amass more and more data in hopes of using those reservoirs of potential knowledge for anything ranging from better informed public policies to design of more compelling products, all the while also grappling with potentially economically and reputationally costly consequences of failing to properly secure and protect data entrusted, or not, to them.

Data Breaches

Experts in the field of electronic data security generally agree that data breaches are, in principle, unavoidable. They advise data managers to, of course, focus on securing their data as much as possible, but at the same time to also accept the inevitability of some sort of a breach, and thus to be equally vigilant about putting in place means and mechanisms aimed at minimizing the potential damage, and assuring speedy recovery.

The statistics of data breaches are quite staggering: In the first half of 2015 alone, 245,919,393 records have been breached, representing 888 individual incidents; of those, the top 10 individual breaches accounted for about 82% of the total records breached (it is worth noting that in roughly 50% of individual data breach cases, the exact number of compromised records is unknown). On a more microscale, every day an estimated 1,358,671 records are lost or stolen; about 62% of breaches are attributed to malicious outsiders, followed by accidental loss (22%), malicious insiders (12%), hacktivists (2%), and state sponsored (2%). The bottom line: More and more of life is going online, so more crime is going online as well. In a physical world it is relatively easy to know when one is, or is passing through, a high crime neighborhood, but it is not so online. As business organizations continue to amass more and more data, and as their data become more distributed throughout their organizational ecosystems, their exposure to malicious or unintended data breaches continues to increase.

Legal Standard of Care

One of the most cherished values held by many individuals is the right to privacy, simply defined as the right to be let alone. Widespread, ongoing data capture can, at least in some situations, run afoul of privacy considerations, given that substantial share of data captured and/or acquired by business organizations contains customer/client/patient details, inclusive of *personally identifiable information* (PII), which is defined as any information that can be used on its own or with other information to identify, contact, or locate a single person, or to identify an individual in context. That said, just as the individual's right to privacy is not absolute,[1] not all PII poses threat, if publicly exposed, to individuals' privacy. More specifically, all PII can be categorized as nonsensitive or sensitive. Nonsensitive PII is exemplified by information gathered from public records, phone books, corporate directories, and websites; as that information is already public, its loss (via data breach discussed earlier) does not pose the risk of causing harm to the individual. On the other hand, sensitive PII is information which, when disclosed, could result in harm to the individual whose privacy has been breached; examples include biometric information, medical information, personally identifiable financial information (PIFI), as well as unique identifiers such as passport or Social Security numbers. Hence, it follows that business organizations, and others, that capture, store, and/or maintain sensitive PII are obligated to safeguard that information.

However, the ever-rising cyber threats coupled with the volume and variety of (potentially) sensitive personal data held by business organizations are compelling regulatory bodies to go beyond the already-in-place legal framework, in an effort to bring about greater data protection vigilance on the part of data amassing organizations. For instance, the US Federal Trade Commission (FTC) has been using its authority to take legal action against business organizations that, in view of the Commission, failed to maintain reasonable cybersecurity measures. To that end, since 2002, the FTC has brought and settled more than 50 enforcement actions against companies for alleged failure to adequately safeguard their customers' sensitive personal information.

Not surprisingly, regulatory compliance, or conformity to applicable laws and rules, is paramount. To date, 90 or so individual countries adopted data protection laws which prohibit the disclosure or misuse of information about private individuals (Sweden is believed to have been the first country to adopt a comprehensive national data protection law, with its Data Act of 1973). Although country-specific laws vary in terms of their breadth of coverage, they nonetheless spell out what amounts to minimum acceptable data protection standards. Still, to be deemed socially responsible, it would be unwise on the part of business organizations to just focus on legal dos and don'ts, as those formal rules tend to lag the emerging social consciousness. Stated differently, the pursuit of corporate social responsibility dictates that data capturing, storing, and using organizations pay attention not only to legally binding rules, which fall under the general umbrella of compliance, but also those deemed to be morally important, which fall under a related but distinct category of ethics.

Ethical Considerations

If you were an employee of a local bank and knew that some of your friends had accounts at your bank, would you be tempted to look up their account balances? Considering that any organization is at its core a collection of individuals working together, there is a seemingly infinite number of situations in which data, especially sensitive PII discussed earlier, can be accessed and used in an unwarranted, or even harmful manner. Consider the following scenario: As insurance claim handler reads the description of an accident, which (the accident) the policyholder finds embarrassing and would like to keep confidential. The claim handler finds the details of the accident amusing enough to post them on a blog – although he did not include the name of the policyholder, the readers of the blog are nonetheless able to piece together the posted details, and ultimately identify the person involved in the accident. Finally, given the locally high profile of the individual involved, the story makes it into the local newspaper, much to the embarrassment of the policyholder who was promised his claim would be handled confidentially.

Broadly defined as a set of fundamental principles describing decent human conduct, *ethics* encompasses the essential fairness and equality of all men and women, respect for laws, as well as concern for general well-being of others. In the above example, the claim handler behaved unethically because he acted with disregard for the emotional and social well-being of a policyholder, as he should have kept all claimant information confidential, and used it only for the purposes directly related to processing of the claim. Thus, while the claim handler was in compliance with applicable data protection and privacy laws (since he did not disclose any personally identifiable information, as defined by the law), he nonetheless did not do the right thing in the ethical sense (which ultimately adversely impacted his employer's reputation and the claim handler's career).

Data as the New Normal

The risks associated with data ownership notwithstanding, organizational data holdings are not only a potential asset – they are a centerpiece of a thriving industry encompassing capture and storage hardware, manipulation and reporting software, and exploration-focused consulting. Business organizations tend to view database infrastructure as a competitive necessity, investing heavily in ever larger and more complex data capture, storage, curation, management, and analysis systems. However, the results of billions of dollars of aggregate database infrastructure spending, coupled with large-scale capture and cata-loguing of data are all too often disappointing, as the hoped-for informational enlightenment is reduced to just a barrage of inconclusive reports, contributing more to clutter than to the quality of decision-making.

Nowadays, virtually all mid-size and larger business organizations either al-ready have in their possession or have a ready access to a variety of transaction-recording and/or descriptive data. In fact, the vast majority of these organizations own multiple databases, maintained and used by a variety of functional areas, such as sales, claims management, human resources, industry analysis, market-ing, and so on. And, as pointed out in the opening chapter, most organizations subscribe to the flawed belief that data is an asset, which is to say that the often considerable expense required to capture, store, and maintain the ever-growing volumes of diverse data is absolutely justifiable. Underscoring that unwavering conviction is the fact that, in total, over the past 25 years or so, businesses in the US alone invested in excess of $1 trillion in data-related infrastructure, with mixed results. Some, including Walmart, Google, Capital One, Harrah's, or Marriott, to name just a few, clearly benefited from their data-related invest-ments; many others put a lot more into the database endeavor than they ever were able to get out of it. In fact, it could be argued that, overall, the database revolution did more for the fortunes of data service suppliers than it did for the competitiveness of an average database using organization.

Getting more out of data is a function of two, somewhat related consider-ations. First, it requires what could be called an intimate knowledge of data sources. Let us not forget that the vast majority of data capture is a by-product of business process digitization, particularly what is broadly termed electronic transaction processing. It means business databases tend to be large in terms of size and esoteric in terms of content. Typically, they encompass millions of re-cords and hundreds or even thousands of individual metrics, many of which are far from being intuitively obvious. The bottom line: The attainment of robust knowledge of a particular database requires dedicated effort, which is perhaps why an average user will just scratch the surface.

The second prerequisite to getting more out of data is the amalgamation of dissimilar data into a singular analytical source. Now, if getting to know a sin-gle database seems like a lot of work, getting to know several and finding a way of combining their contents could well be considered a Herculean undertaking. And frankly, it can indeed be a hard and an arduous process. Is it worth it? Any organization that is not convinced should probably reconsider stockpiling data in expensive databases.

As illustrated throughout this and the remaining chapters, the most signif-icant difference between information-savvy organizations and their data-rich but information-poor counterparts is the data analytical know-how. In other words, while virtually the same hardware and software technologies are avail-able to all organizations, it is the power of the subsequent data exploration and utilization that determines the ultimate return on the overall data infrastructure investments. And it all starts with a solid grasp of the available data.

Fundamental Data Challenges

Broadly defined, *data* are facts. There are multiple ways of categorizing data: by source, type, usage situation, etc. From the standpoint of informational content, data can be broadly divided into *events* and/or *behaviors*, and *attributes* that describe or otherwise augment individual events and/or behaviors. Within the realm of business analytics, the former are exemplified by product purchases (behaviors) or automotive accidents (events), whereas the latter can be exemplified by purchase describing details, such as selling price and location, or accident describing details such as cause and nature; moreover, both can be further contextualized by a broad spectrum of potentially explanatory factors, such as purchaser or claimant demographics. From the informational point of view, those rudimentary differences between events/behaviors and attributes are indicative of the informational value of the two data types: The former offer the basis for summarizing, trending, and reporting on 'what' happened, whereas the latter enable more granular contextualization of the observed outcome by way of contributing to better understanding of 'why' it happened, and in the case of more advanced data analytical capabilities, to making forward-looking predictions regarding 'what is likely to happen next'. A closer look at the difference between events/behaviors and attributes, also addressing some of the unique challenges associated with both, might make the distinction more meaningful.

Events   Nowadays, in virtually all aspects of business – and life in general – events and behaviors leave an electronic imprint – a data record. Consider an example of an on-the-job employee accident and the subsequent processing of the resultant worker's compensation claim: The initial accident is entered into an appropriate electronic repository, along with numerous evidentiary details, such as time and place, cause and nature of an injury, initial treatment and diagnosis, etc. The claim is assigned to a handler (a claim adjuster) who manages the record communicating with the injured worker, reviewing requests for medical treatments, salary continuation payments, injury-related expense payments, etc.; all handler actions and activities are also recorded electronically (as adjuster notes in a diary system). Any other activity by other parties, such as medical examinations and the subsequent treatment, return to work activities or any legal actions are also captured electronically, all of which result in a web of ultimately interconnected (via a widespread use of a common record identification, such as Claim ID) but otherwise dispersed (because of being located in different files and, possibly, different databases) details of the aforementioned on-the-job accident.

Attributes   Every event and every behavior can be contextualized using a plethora
               of descriptive characteristics. As noted earlier, a product purchase
               can be described in terms of purchaser demographics, location,
               price, time, presence of promotional incentives, etc. Although
               not always obvious, some of those characteristics are captured
               concurrently with the event/behavior (as is the case with price,
               location, and time), whereas others have to be 'attributed', or
               ascribed to the event/behavior of interest, due to being captured
               independently of the event/behavior of interest (as is typically the
               case with metrics recording presence of promotional incentives,
               such as temporary price reduction). Although it may seem
               straightforward, ascribing attributes to events and behaviors they
               contextualize is prone to error. While the reason for that is fairly
               technical and beyond the scope of this text, the consequences of
               incorrect attribute-to-event/behavior assignment can materially
               alter conclusions of follow-on analyses, so much so that a closer
               look seems warranted.

Ascertaining Event-Attribute Ascription

Considering the challenge of correctly assigning descriptive attributes to appropriate events and/or behaviors, it could be argued that the proper context
for such analysis is that of ascertaining causation. This is not to say that ascribing a separately captured Attribute A to Event X is tantamount to saying that A
caused X, but rather it is to say that the general logic that is used to weigh the
possible cause-effect linkage between two metrics could be applied to evaluate
the appropriateness of the aforementioned A-to-X attribution.

Given its central role in knowledge creation, the notion of *causality* or
causation has been a subject of centuries-long debate among scientists and philosophers alike. At the core of the debate has been the line of demarcation
separating cause-and-effect from just simple concurrence-based relationships.
Is factor A causing B, or do the two merely coincide? From the standpoint of
philosophy of science, to be deemed causal an association has to exhibit temporal sequentiality (A has to precede B), associative variation (changes in A
must be systematically associated with changes in B), the association between
A and B has to be non-spurious (it should not disappear upon introduction of
a third moderating factor), and lastly, it also has to have sound theoretical rationale (it has to 'make sense' or exhibit basic face validity). Temporal sequentiality and associative variation have a very simple meaning and application
(in spite of their somewhat foreboding names), as the conditions of occurring
in sequence and doing so persistently are both intuitively obvious and relatively easy to demonstrate. For instance, one has to receive purchase incentive, such as a discount coupon, prior to making a purchase during which that
coupon is redeemed (temporal sequentiality), and that sequence can easily be

observed on recurring basis (associative variation). However, the rationale and the proof are often more elusive with the remaining two causality thresholds (non-spurious association and theoretical support). For instance, given the observational, in the manner of speaking, nature of transactional data, it is usually quite difficult to arrive at a conclusive evidence of non-spuriousness[2]; the main challenge with showing evidence of sound theoretical rationale is that, absent a well-established scientific theory, any such rationale tends to be subjective.

Insights: Theory of Data Driven?

How do we know that we know? Ascertaining the validity and reliability of what is considered 'knowledge' is probably one of the oldest controversies in science. The issues here are not only the availability of objective evidence – that is, knowledge, but also its believability. In other words, how do we separate facts from fiction? Consider the Galileo Affair to appreciate the potential difficulty of distinguishing between objectively verifiable facts and subjective beliefs. The story is anchored in the idea of empirically testing the key postulates of the heliocentric system originally proposed by Copernicus. As the inventor of telescope, Galileo was the first to be able to gather closer celestial observations and more precise measurements that allowed him to empirically verify the soundness of Copernican thesis. Yet lacking an appreciable understanding of optics, many of Galileo's contemporaries were skeptical of his findings, suspecting the apparent celestial phenomenon to be tricks of the lenses. And so in their eyes, the great scientist was a heretic.

Obviously, our understanding of the world has increased immensely over the near four centuries that elapsed since Galileo's struggles, but as we continue to push beyond the familiar, we continue to wrestle with some of the same types of challenges. Some of our greatest scientific theories, with quantum theory being the prime example, are based on what are, to many, nonsensical assumptions,[3] and as outlined in earlier chapters, our minds continue to trick us into believing what may ultimately not be true. Is one better off grounding one's explanation in theory or in observation?

From the standpoint of philosophy of science, the creation of objective knowledge can be either theory-or data-laden. The former is carried out by means of hypothesis testing, which is a method of empirically assessing specific theory-derived suppositions. It means that theory-laden knowledge creation springs from the foundation provided by a particular conceptual and rational paradigm – and it is limited to test specific predictions derived from that framework. It also means that results of empirical analyses are interpreted within the confines of the guiding theory. There is a certain amount of intuitive appeal associated with that stance, but more importantly, it is supported by neuroscience studies detailing the mechanics of functioning of the brain (discussed in Chapter 1). Those studies suggest that cognitive processing of information requires the brain to hold some beliefs about reality, as absent those we would be unable to learn from the available information. In that sense, at least some aspects of the human knowledge creation process appear to be confirmatory, that is, theory-laden. It is important to keep in mind, however, that a handful of loosely stated suppositions or insights generated by past analyses do not necessarily constitute a theory, at least not one that can offer an adequate explanation and/or prediction of the phenomenon of interest. On the other hand, there can be multiple competing theoretical frameworks available, which can be confusing, but nonetheless tends to be the case in social sciences.

In the way of contrast, the data-laden approach assumes no existence of an underlying theory and instead approaches the pursuit of decision-guiding insights as a purely exploratory endeavor. The resultant knowledge is built from scratch, cobbled together from individual insights extracted from the available data. The data-laden approach certainly has merit, but at the same time it is more likely (than the theory-laden approach) to be blotted by data imperfections, which is a significant drawback, both in science and in business. In particular, it poses greater result validity and reliability challenges, which stem from the combination of heightened dependence on the accuracy of data, and the inherent imperfections of data. Ultimately, the question asked earlier – how do we know that we know? – becomes more difficult to answer; overall, being guided by pure data exploration tends to heighten the likelihood of arriving at erroneous conclusions. This limitation is illustrated by the drawbacks of automated data mining applications frequently used in conjunction with large event-tracking databases – those systems tend to spawn large numbers of statistically significant but practically trivial 'insights', which does more to distract than to inform.[4]

Theory-laden knowledge creation is certainly not immune to the dangers presented by poor data quality, but it is significantly less impacted by it, for a number of reasons. First, virtually no theory is ever validated or refuted on the basis of a single test, or even a handful of tests, which obviously reduces the danger stemming from a chance encounter with an aberrant dataset. Second, a single study typically tests multiple hypotheses derived from the theory of interest, and under most circumstances, not all of those hypotheses would be impacted in the same fashion by data imperfections. And perhaps most importantly, theory-laden approach takes fuller advantage of the cumulative nature of knowledge creation, by offering a way of leveraging previously uncovered insights and building on that base with the help of additional analyses. In short, though there are undeniable benefits to exploring pertinent and available data, one should not lose sight of the fact that essentially all data used in business analyses are imperfect and noisy, which means that relying on pure exploratory analyses extracted insights is fraught with validity-related challenges.

Data in Organizations

Why so many business organizations continue to lament that they are data-rich, but information-poor? Such a broad and deep question does not necessarily lend itself to a simple, direct answer, but it nonetheless draws attention to the manner in which organizations tend to consume data. So perhaps that question could be rephrased to instead ask: How are the available data consumed by the organization, and how beneficial is that consumption?

The Curse of Reporting

Starting with the premise that all business organizations exist for the sole purpose of creating and serving customers,[5] the most obvious, almost natural first step in data utilization journey is to develop an organized, ongoing way of tracking customer-related outcomes, such as sales. The advent of electronic transaction processing, coupled with computerized data storage and automated data processing and management capabilities, gave rise to now-ubiquitous standardized, periodic summary reports. There are clear benefits to organizational managers to being able to keep track of key business outcomes; thus, reports that deliver that information are undeniably valuable. The problem many organizations continue to struggle with is that what could be called 'reporting culture' became the primary mode of organizational data consumption, which continues to contribute to the data-rich, but information-poor feeling for two basic reasons: First, outcome-based reporting is focused, by definition, on enumerating 'what' happened without addressing managerially critical question of 'why' it happened. Second, reporting culture is incestuous in nature as reports beget more reports, ultimately leading to proliferation of unnecessary and at times even conflicting accounts that contribute negligible-to-no value to the organizational decision-making. In large business organizations in particular, countless reports are produced because they can be produced, not because they should be produced. In such situation, it is easy to see how an organization can be data-rich, but information-poor.

Moreover, production of those superfluous summaries uses organizational resources, which means that an organization can expand at times significant resources to produce outcomes that do not materially add to the organizational value creation process. In a sense, it is not that different from expanding resources to create products or services without the intent of selling them or otherwise using them for productive purposes. But that is not all: Industry estimates suggest that more than 80% of business analysts' time is spent on managing, joining, and preparing data, with bulk of that effort supporting reporting related requirements. Looking beyond the obvious direct costs involved, a perhaps even more significant (though far harder to quantify) is the opportunity cost – analysts readying data for superfluous reports do so at the expense of sifting through data in search for decision-guiding insights. Again, it is easy to see why in such a scenario a business organization would deem itself to be information-poor.

Too Much of a Good Thing

Much has been written about the already overwhelming and continually grow-ing torrents of data available to organizations. According to recent (early 2018) statistics, more than 5 billion people worldwide are calling, texting, tweeting, and browsing on mobile devices, all of which is captured and stored; Walmart, the world's largest retailer, handles more than a million customer transactions per hour and its private cloud processes more than 2.5 petabytes[6] every hour – in fact, according to International Data Corporation (IDC), a research firm, by 2020 the overall volume of business-to-business and business-to-consumer transactions will surpass 450 billion per day. It should be noted that the lion's share of those relentless torrents of data is captured not because of a specific need, but largely because the electronic transaction processing and communications infrastructure records all aspects of its functioning. Consequently, captured data are a mix of potentially useful, informative 'signal', and informationless 'noise'. A direct con-sequence of that is that making the available data 'fit' a particular question often requires significant amounts of data manipulation and reengineering, which can be difficult and taxing, and gives rise to a yet another obstacle to a wider data usage.

Looking beyond the hotly debated risks and benefits of the rapidly emerging digital reality, the volumes of data generated by the totality of commercial and noncommercial transactions and other interactions, with much of it available to business organizations, are nothing short of staggering.[7] And while in principle lots of diverse data can be beneficial from the decision-making point of view, lots of diverse data can also present a formidable utilization challenge, as evi-denced by Forrester Research's estimates suggesting that 60%–73% of data be-ing collected is never successfully used by organizations. Those conclusions are echoed by New Venture Partners' 5th annual survey of corporate executives, which found that although more than 85% of the surveyed firms were aiming to establish a data-driven culture, only 37% felt they were successful in doing so. It is clear that although the idea of data-driven decision-making is compel-ling, turning that idea into operational reality is quite challenging. Why?

Although it is tempting to dismissively conclude that each situation is differ-ent and look past the underlying causes, there are indeed some communalities that recur with startling regularity. First, setting aside small, specialized ana-lytical consulting firms staffed primarily with highly skilled data science and business analytics professionals, the majority of prospective data users in the majority of business organizations lack the requisite analytical literacy. This is a macro, or system-level impediment which exists at the intersection of two commonly seen trends: On one hand, to make more data more readily available to more users, business organizations are rapidly embracing self-service business intelligence (BI) solutions, but the bulk of prospective data users do not have the necessary data manipulation, assessment, and analysis skills. Just providing tools for those who do not know how to use those tools, and are often apprehensive about 'jumping into data', is simply unlikely to bring about the desired cultural transformation.

The second of the core reasons companies struggle with instituting data-driven culture is that it requires some degree of silencing of one's subjective intuition, which is difficult, even unnatural. Recall the discussion of cognitive bias in Chapter 2 – every one of the many distinct perception- and decision-warping biases is a natural consequence of brain's wiring. As clearly evidenced by numerous psychological and neuroscientific studies,[8] it takes a considerable effort and focus to overcome those natural mental impulses. In short, there is nothing natural about being data-driven. Making the already difficult task even more daunting, the granularity of the available data effectively pushes decision-making down to ever more micro considerations, often below the comfort zone of decision-makers. All considered, these can be considered micro- or individual-level impediments that ultimately manifest themselves in the lack of workflow integration of data analyses and the lack of adoption of analyses-generated insights.

The third key reason behind the difficulty of establishing data-driven organizational culture is that it requires structural re-wiring of organizations, especially those that reached operational maturity in the pre-'data everywhere' period. Given that the main objective of organizational structure is to ensure that the chosen strategy is effectively executed, it requires the right mix of people, in terms of skills and capabilities, being in the right place, doing the right thing; it also needs data analytics-aligned decision triggers. Just adding a team of data scientists and business analysts to an authoritative organization where decisions are made hierarchically and driven by the often-biased (see Chapter 2) subjective evaluations is unlikely to produce data-driven culture, because in such an organization data-derived insights tend to be (informally) validated against prior beliefs and other, often subjective, considerations. Plato wrote in his great work, *The Republic*:

> Until philosophers are kings, or the kings and princes of this world have the spirit and power of philosophy, and political greatness and wisdom meet in one, and those commoner natures who pursue either to the exclusion of the other are compelled to stand aside, cities will never have rest from their evils...

In order for an organization to become truly data-driven, its decisions need to be rooted in sound, empirically derived evidence, and the key decision-makers need to themselves be analytically competent. Thus as so eloquently stated by one of the 'big three' of ancient Greek philosophers, either analysts should become the key decision-makers or the key decision-makers should become analytically competent. So long as the broadly defined organizational data analyses endeavor exists as an appendage to the preexisting organizational structure, the organization will struggle with becoming data-driven.

The Analytics Industry

Commercial business analytics is a thriving industry – it surpassed $130 billion in 2016 and is expected to top $200 billion by 2020, according to IDC, a research firm. Overall scope-wise, business analytics encompasses the broad domain of *data exploration*, which is focused on uncovering new knowledge by means of open-ended mining of the available data, *prescriptive* and *predictive analyses*, which encompass activities aimed at estimation of predetermined outcomes to produce decision-guiding knowledge, and *optimization* and *impact measurement*, which aim to identify the best, in probabilistic sense, courses of action, and estimate the effect of those actions on someone or something. Looked at as an industry, business analytics can be thought of as being comprised of three distinct segments: (1) BI, seen here as practice-oriented and tool-enabled embodiment of data exploration, (2) prescriptive & predictive analytics, seen here as applications of data modeling techniques to clearly delineated business problems, and (3) measurement & optimization. That perspective of business analytics implicitly assumes focused on self-generated or otherwise already available data (e.g., ongoing data feeds from outside suppliers), which typically reside in the organization-owned operational platforms such as production, logistics and inventory management, or in-house marketing activities. However, many, if not most business organizations also source data from outside of the organization; thus, it is appropriate to take a more expansive view of the broader data and analyses ecosystem. Consequently, in addition to the three analysis-focused clusters, two more distinct groups of contributors can be singled out: (1) data generation and (2) data aggregation entities.

Business Intelligence

BI encompasses technologies, applications, and practices for the collection, integration, analysis, and presentation of business information derived from the available data, with the purpose of supporting better business decision-making. Although it encompasses more than tools, BI is nonetheless acutely focused on tools – primarily in the form of software applications – that support data curation, summarization, visualization, and reporting. Broadly characterized, BI tools streamline the effort needed to search for, merge, and query data to obtain information needed to make good business decisions. For example, using a

BI system, a company that wants to better manage its supply chain will be able to determine where delays are happening and where variabilities exist within the shipping process; that company could also use its BI capabilities to discover which products are most commonly delayed or which modes of transportation are most often involved in delays.

Given BI systems' wide scope, there are some prerequisites a data processing application needs to meet to be considered a BI tool – to qualify for inclusion in that category, a product must:

- Consume data from any source through file uploads, database querying, and application connectors
- Provide an architecture to transform data into a useful and relatable model
- Support data modeling, blending, and discovery processes
- Create reports and visualizations with business utility
- Create and deploy internal analytics applications.

According to Gartner, a consultancy, there are two somewhat distinct types of BI: (1) traditional BI, where IT professionals use in-house transactional data to generate reports and (2) modern BI, where business users interact with agile, intuitive systems to analyze data more quickly. Organizations tend to favor traditional BI for certain types of reporting, such as regulatory or financial reports, where accuracy is paramount and the questions and datasets used are standard and predicable; modern BI systems are preferred for extraction of ad hoc insight in changing circumstances, as is the case with marketing or risk management.

Offering-wise, there is a rich assortment of BI tools available in the marketplace – as of the time of the writing of this book (late 2017/2018), some of the better-known systems include MicroStrategy, Tableau, Sisense, QlikView, Dundas BI, Business Objects, Oracle BI, SAS BI, IBM Cognos, and Easy Insight. Although in an abstract sense all of those tools offer similar capabilities, the competitive landscape varies considerably in terms of the sophistication, learning curve requirements, and, of course, price.

Prescriptive & Predictive Analyses

This is not as much a defined industry, as a fairly amorphous collection of service providers offering services focused on exploratory, prescriptive, and predictive analyses of data. The term 'service', however, is beginning to take on an extended meaning in this context, as it can be seen as a continuum ranging from the traditional conception of a service where an entity endowed with specialized knowledge performs activities requiring such specialized knowledge, as exemplified by statistical modeling services offered by a statistician, to complex technology (software + hardware + know-how) solutions, as exemplified by IBM Watson.[9] Thus, loosely defined, the data analysis industry encompasses three somewhat distinct sets of providers: (1) specialized service suppliers, (2) technology-based analytic platforms, and (3) all-in-one integrated solutions.

Specialized service suppliers can be thought of as the legacy segment of the analytics industry. Historically employing classical statistical data analytic tools and approaches where statistical experts and other skilled professionals conduct (typically) need-tailored analyses using open-source (e.g., R, Python) or proprietary (e.g., SAS, SPSS) tools. More recently, responding to needs emanating from the emergence of very large, often unstructured data sources (e.g., the much talked about big data), coupled with the rapid growth of streaming data,[10] those traditionally intellectual skills (e.g., statistical modeling know-how) focused suppliers have been aggressively adding more technology-intensive capabilities, particularly for automated data, including text, mining and insight discovery, machine learning, and more recently, even more technology-intensive deep learning.

Technology-based analytic platform providers offer unified technology-based tools designed to address the needs of its users. Manifestly, those solutions aim to simplify the task of extracting insights out of data by automating common data manipulation and analysis steps, ultimately allowing relatively technically unsophisticated users to conduct at least rudimentary analyses of data. Design-wise, technology-based analytic platforms join different tools to create analytics systems together with an engine to execute, a database to store and manage the data, data mining processes, and techniques and mechanisms for obtaining and preparing data that is to be used. Thus, in contrast to the capability-delivering and made-to-order solutions offered by specialized service suppliers, providers of technology-based analytic platforms offer do-it-yourself solutions engineered to allow wider swaths of organizational data users to become de facto analysts. Depending on the level of sophistication and software-hardware integration, those solutions are usually generically characterized as software-as-service (SaaS) or platform-as-service (PaaS) offerings. More and more, those platforms are focused on the emerging need of processing explosively growing data streams coming from device interconnectedness, commonly referred to as the Internet of Things (IoT), which by 2020 is expected to link together more than 20 billion devices.[11]

The last of the three broad categories of data analytic service suppliers, the all-in-one integrated solution providers, offer even more technologically evolved solutions, promising to altogether obfuscate the need for technical data analysis related knowledge. Arguably, the best known of those offerings is IBM Watson – an artificial intelligence, machine learning system that gained mainstream notoriety for its 2011 victory on a TV quiz show *Jeopardy!*

Artificial intelligence systems like Watson learn without being explicitly programmed by leveraging complex mathematical algorithms, many of which were built to emulate the functioning of human brain, as exemplified by artificial neural networks. Broadly characterized, the goal of those algorithms is to develop the ability to use large pools of heterogeneous data to *classify*, or assign records to groups (e.g., high-value vs. low-value customers), and to *regress*, or predict the future value or state (e.g., expected future spending). The so-framed 'learning' takes place by continually rejiggering the selected algorithm's internal processing routines to produce the highest possible percentage of correct answers on some set of problems, such as which customers pose the highest threat of attrition. The correct answers have to be already known[12] so that the system can be told when it gets something right and when it gets something wrong. The accuracy of predictions or classifications produced by such a system is, to a large degree, dependent on two key factors: First, it is the volume of appropriately labeled (i.e., containing correct answers) training data, as quite in line with human learning ('practice makes perfect'), the more such training data is available, the better the algorithm's classification or regression focused predictions. Second, it is the training-to-application data resemblance, or the degree of similarity between the problems that were used to learn and problems that the system is to analyze. A system trained on robust sample of automotive accidents would, under most circumstances, perform far better flagging high-risk automotive insurance applicants than flagging high-risk health insurance applicants.

Though in the context of the above example the training-to-application data resemblance might seem reasonable, there is a yet another, less obvious implication which is significantly less reasonable, especially given the hype[13] surrounding those technologies: Machine learning based systems are trained to detect that which happened in the past, and typically with some degree of repetition – stated differently, those systems cannot foresee that which they have not encountered in the training data. To be able to sift through vast pools of data and pull out the few pieces of information important to a single case – be it a customer, an insurance claim, or a patient – someone has to do it by hand first, for thousands and thousands of cases. To recognize the signs of customer dissatisfaction, an impending illness or an insurance claim that is likely to become very costly, a machine learning system needs thousands of records of customers/patients/claims, respectively, that have specific combinations of attributes and outcomes. But those unique, risk-predicting combinations can be hard to come by; in many cases, the requisite data may not exist in the appropriate format or not exist at all, or data may be scattered throughout multitudes of different systems and may be difficult to work with. Those are tremendous limitations, especially given the lofty expectations (which, to a large degree, are a direct consequence of system providers overhyping their wares). Consider a simple insurance claim management example: To many claim managers being able to pinpoint claims that exhibit a combination of characteristics that have been known to inflate cost is of little benefit because those capabilities have long been in place. Those managers are interested in pinpointing claims that, for reasons previously unknown, are likely to become very costly, but that is where the machine learning systems, for reasons noted earlier, tend to underperform. Those limitations are further compounded by the black box nature of those systems – the 'how' of a system-generated answer tends to be completely hidden from view, and even it was somehow made visible, it would likely be too complex to make human sense. In other words, just as that feeling of something being right or wrong one may experience in a particular situation is difficult to describe in terms of specific reasons,[14] machine learning applications, many of which overtly aim to emulate the processes involved in the human brain's sensemaking, make predictions that cannot be validated in terms of how they were produced.

Measurement & Optimization

The bulk of business decisions come down to choosing to engage, or not, in specific activities, and selecting the most appropriate course(s) of action. Thus, it is natural to want to assess the efficacy of those choices, typically in terms of *impact*, or the effect on someone or something. Doing so also fits perfectly with data-driven culture, as data offer both the opportunity to conduct more thorough impact assessment, along with an imperative to do so.

Scope-wise, impact assessment can be macro- or micro-focused. Valuing aggregate social, environmental, and economic benefits of strategic or tactical choices are all examples of the former, whereas estimating the incrementality of a predictive model-driven customer retention efforts and customer segmentation-inspired brand repositioning are examples of the latter. Measurement of very broad and, frankly, ill-defined social, environmental, or even economic macro benefits is fraught with difficulties, with perhaps the most visible ranging from those that could be categorized as theory-laden, such as political or social views and agendas, or data-laden, often taking the form of what evidence is used and how it is evaluated. Moreover, not all macro factors can be, or for that matter should be, measured directly. For instance, although the immediate (and most easily shown) benefit of reduced dependence on fossil fuels, such as coal, is the reduction in airborne pollutants, the ultimate benefit is the anticipated slowing of global warming which poses a more existential threat to humanity. However, doing so requires a level of research expertise, commitment to longitudinal study, and allocation of resources that are typically beyond the capabilities of individual organizations. Thus, from a more pragmatic point of view, organizations may want to think in terms of when it makes sense to invest time and resources in measuring impact, and when it might make more sense to simply stick with tracking of key outcomes – especially when an organization's control over results is limited, and causality remains poorly understood.

A very different reasoning applies when considering the measurement of micro effects, such as the earlier mentioned value of using predictive models to guide, for instance, customer retention efforts. Unlike the fairly vague definition of what constitutes impact in values- and perception-permeated social or environmental initiatives, the value of investing organizational resources in developing informational assets, such as predictive models, is quite unambiguous – a dollar spent should produce more than a dollar worth of *incremental* benefits measured in terms of key business outcomes, such as revenue or profitability. That means that, for example, the impact of a marketing campaign geared toward new customer acquisition should be expressed in terms of the number of additional customers, or those that would not have been acquired had it not been for the campaign in question. This is critically different from attributing all newly acquired customers to the said campaign, as some of those customers would likely have been acquired without its help.

One of the core benefits of systematic and sound impact measurement is that it enables decision-makers to make better choices in the future, particularly when choosing among competing alternatives. In that context, impact assessment generated insights support what could be considered *post hoc choice optimization*, or identification of the most advantageous (given the problem at hand) courses of action. In situations where sufficiently valid and reliable impact assessment results are not available, *predictive choice optimization*, typically utilizing machine learning choice algorithms or classical predictive modeling approaches,[15] can offer objective, albeit more speculative decision-guiding insights.

There are situations where choice optimization may require more data than an organization may actually capture – in fact, building robust choice models almost always benefits from use of the widest range of data possible. In addition, optimization – in the sense of fine-tuning – of common organizational endeavors, such as customer relationship marketing (CRM), hinges of maximally informative inputs, which in the case of CRM entails the development of the so-called '360° view of customer'. All told, there are numerous reasons a business organization may consider adding to its, often already quite rich, data universe.

Data Generation

It is hard to think of a business organization that does not generate data, given the ubiquity of electronic transaction and communication enabling systems, virtually all of which capture detailed operational information. Yet, most of the data generated by most business organizations are, ultimately, only of use to those organizations; a notable exception to that rule are organizations that can be described as operational or communication intermediaries. Operational intermediaries encompass three somewhat distinct subgroups: transactional, which support sales and marketing functions or link manufacturers and retailers; logistical, which enable physical distribution of goods; and facilitating, which supplements product distribution by offering storage and supply services.

Communication intermediaries, on the other hand, are those that enable inter-actions among varieties of entities (individuals, organizations) using variety of modes (voice, email, social media).

In addition to what could be characterized as incidental data capture, there are organizations that exist for the sole purpose of generating very specific, or special purpose types of information. Capture of specialty data takes place through online and offline tracking, as exemplified by tracking of Internet browsing behaviors or in-store promotions, direct research, as exemplified by consumer opinion panels or secondary-data-derived overlays, as illustrated by lifestyle segmentation or geodemographics. While typically not operationally or otherwise 'connected' to the organization, the specialty data can potentially enhance the value of the organization's total informational reservoir; thus, those sources may warrant consideration.

To identify and ultimately secure the widest range of organizational decision-making-pertinent data, a business organization can delimit its unique *informational ecosystem,* a loosely defined network of entities that contribute to the overall data pool. Doing so can deliver multiple benefits, not the least of which is a more thoughtful and systematic outside data procurement strategy.

Data Aggregation

Imagine the task of shopping for a particular product in a world in which there are no business intermediaries, such as retailers. Imagine how taxing it would be to choose a product as basic as bread, milk, breakfast cereal, a shirt, or a pair of shoes. Although perhaps not to the same extent, nonetheless the same reasoning applies to outside data procurement, given the rich array of data that exist outside of business and other organizations – not surprisingly, there are organizations that specialize in compiling large pools of data that combine nu-merous source- and type-distinct data inflows.

Beyond offering one-stop – or at least simplified – data procurement ser-vices, data aggregators also typically offer extensive data curation services, in-cluding aggregation, de-duplication, missing value imputation, distributional corrections (e.g., outlier rectification), file amalgamation, and other important data usability enhancing improvements. Although generally desirable, primar-ily for technical reasons, data usability enhancements do not come without a cost. Recalling the earlier discussed challenges encountered by machine learn-ing based systems, most notably the general inability of those systems to reliably pinpoint as aberrant outcomes or scenarios that were not present (or labeled as such) in the training data, the technically justifiable attempts at making data more usable can culminate in making data more generic, as illustrated by the case of geodemographics.

As clearly suggested by their name, geodemographic data are a product of merging of two otherwise distinct dimensions of social descriptors: geography, or location based, and demography, or human attribute based. In short, geodemographics are vital, social statistics ultimately derived from individual-or household level descriptors but ultimately attributed to geography-defined groups of persons or households. It is an imperfect but best available solution to the problem of being able to access social statistical information for any segment of the population, anywhere in the country. It is imperfect because the individual variables such as age, income, or education level are derived by means of averaging of individual values comprising a particular group (typically comprised of 20–30 households living in close physical proximity[16]), which results in a phenomenon known as the *regression to the mean*, or a tendency for observed values to cluster near the average. A direct consequence of that tendency is that the resultant geodemographic data tend to exhibit artificially small degrees of variability, which means that geodemographics described differences tend to understate true differences. Still, for those looking for comprehensive demographic data in the US and other developed countries, national census bureaus are usually the only source of country-wide demographic information, and are also usually prohibited from selling individual or household-level data, but not group based averages which mask individual differences. So though imperfect, the resultant geodemographic data can be the only commercially available glimpse of population level social statistics.

Notes

1 For instance, in the US, where individual freedoms, including the right to privacy, are particularly cherished, personal matters or activities which may reasonably be of public interest, like those of celebrities or participants in newsworthy events, are usually excluded from privacy protection.

2 Without delving into technical details, making that determination typically requires setting up of a (at least somewhat) controlled experiment, which is often not feasible.

3 The phenomenon known as 'superposition' offers perhaps the best illustration. In the realm of quantum mechanics (behavior of subatomic particles), rather than being in one state or changing between a variety of states, particles are thought of as existing across all the possible states at the same time. Likening that phenomenon to human existence realm, superposition would stipulate that we all are simultaneously alive and dead.

4 One of the main culprits is the use of the earlier discussed statistical significance tests with large sample sizes, which is nearly inescapable in transactional data reservoirs. As is well known, sample size alone systematically inflates the probability of concluding that a relationship is statistically significant because of the central role played by standard error, the magnitude of which decreases as the sample size increases.

5 A view first put forth by Peter Drucker, a renowned author, educator, and management consultant.

6 1 petabyte equals 1 million gigabytes, or 2^{50} bytes (same amount of storage is about 1.5 million CD-ROM discs); incidentally, it is estimated that the human brain can store about 2.5 petabytes of memory data.

7 According to International Data Corporation, about 2.5 exabytes of data, roughly the equivalent of 250,000 Libraries of Congress, is created every day.

8 A convenient and compelling summary of pertinent research is offered by D. Kahneman in his 2011 *Thinking Fast and Slow* book.

9 Named after IBM's first CEO, industrialist Thomas J. Watson, Watson is a computer system capable of answering questions posed in natural language, developed in IBM's DeepQA project.

10 Traditionally, data generation and capture could be characterized as 'batch' in the sense that data were captured, processed, and analyzed periodically; the proliferation of always-on sensor-based (e.g., surveillance, product movement tracking, weather recording) data capture mechanisms gave rise to a new, uninterrupted flow data sources.

11 Anticipating that the cloud/data center based processing power might become insufficient in the near future, a new approach to handle vast quantities of data generated by smart sensors is currently emerging – known as 'edge computing', it is based on a design where sensors and connected devices communicate with a gateway device, instead of the cloud or server, which provides initial processing of sensor data.

12 This is known as *supervised* machine learning, to be contrasted with *unsupervised* machine learning which is where correct or otherwise desirable states or outcomes are inferred by the analytic algorithm used (there are numerous types of algorithms that are used in both supervised and unsupervised learning).

13 For instance, as far back as 2013, in a Forbes write-up, IBM claimed that 'a new era of computing has emerged', even going as far as suggesting that Watson '...tackles clinical trials'. A couple years later, a 2015 Washington Post article quoted an IBM Watson manager saying that the system was establishing a 'collective intelligence model between machine and man'. Based on published evidence (e.g., the ill-fated collaboration between IBM Watson and the University of Texas MD Anderson Cancer Center) that followed, those appear to have been exuberant claims.

14 Primarily because those brain-generated impulses are products of a complex interactions among large numbers of neurons, invoking situational (i.e., sensory input) as well as stored-in-memory information, and representing different facets of sensemaking.

15 Before the advent of widespread machine learning capabilities (which itself is a product of rapid growth of computing speed and capabilities, coupled with decreasing cost), the most common approach to build predictive models was to use established statistical techniques (e.g., logistic regression, multinomial logit, discriminant analysis for choice modeling) to 'hand-fit' those models, typically with the help of either open-source languages, such as R or Python, or proprietary applications, such as SAS or SPSS.

16 It is known as a *census block*, which is the smallest geographic unit used by the US Census Bureau for tabulation of 100% data (data collected from all houses, rather than a sample of houses); the US (including Puerto Rico) was divided into 11,155,486 blocks during the most recent (2010) census.

PART II
Evidence-Based Practice

4

EVIDENCE-BASED MOVEMENT

Although intuitive decision-making feels extraordinarily natural, using objective evidence as basis for decision-making can also feel as natural, which begs an obvious question, why? A part of the reason could be that, unconsciously, those two very different choice-making modalities appeal to very different types of decisions. When choosing friends, for instance, intuition tends to play the dominant role because for reasons that are often difficult to put into words, we all feel natural closeness or even attraction to some individuals, but not to others. But when making other choices, such as car purchases, rational evaluation of objective criteria tends to be the most commonly used decision-making mode because in that context relying on objective evidence feels more natural than trusting that elusive 'warm and fuzzy' feeling. What in some regards is considerably less clear, however, is the extent to which objective evidence is utilized, or even what exactly constitutes 'evidence'.

In many professional practice areas such as medicine, law or social work, practitioner skill sets can be seen as combinations of tacit and experiential knowledge. The former is typically acquired through appropriate formal education and as such tends to be relatively uniform (setting aside any differences in teaching and learning efficacies), whereas the latter is a product of practical experience; thus, it tends to be prone to considerably more variability across practitioners. A yet another potential source of cross-practitioner competency variability is ongoing professional learning, or the degree to which new approaches, techniques, strategies, and other practice-enhancing changes and innovations are learned and utilized. Ideally, newly produced practice-related knowledge enabling practitioners to deliver better quality outcomes should be incorporated by individual practitioners, but that does not always happen due to a couple of basic reasons. The first of those is the sheer volume of new knowledge, which even in relatively narrow domains of practice can be overwhelming. The second reason can be characterized as professional habituation, typically taking the form of an enduring belief that solution X offers the best remedy to problem A. Working together, the vast quantities of new information and innate tendencies to develop enduring beliefs can erect powerful barriers to advancing individual practitioners' competencies, ultimately resulting in unnecessarily variable outcomes. Evidence-based practice (EBP) movement represents an attempt aimed at remedying such undesirable situations.

The goal of this chapter is to offer a high-level overview of the genesis and growth of what has come to be known as EBP. Starting with its roots in the practice of medicine and subsequently spreading onto other domains of practice including management, the philosophy behind EBP is outlined, in the context of the basic considerations of 'why' and 'how'.

The Practice and Science of Management

The notion of *management*, defined as a general process of controlling things or people, is as old as human civilization. The very functioning of civilizations, the emergence of cities and states, and the great artefacts of past civilizations, such as the Egyptian and Mayan pyramids or Greek, Roman and medieval temples, churches and palaces required that special 'tool'. Timeline-wise, the earliest evidence of somewhat formalized management dates back more than six millennia, to around 4,500 BC, and the organized record keeping developed by Sumerians[1]; the development of more systemic management practice can be attributed to Hammurabi's formal organizational controls codified in written documents. The emergence of management as a separate domain of study and practice can be attributed to a Greek philosopher Xenophon (a student of Socrates), who in his work titled *The Oeconomicus* discusses the tasks and challenges of estate management. The rise of modern management science is widely attributed to Frederick W. Taylor, an American mechanical engineer who, in the late 19th and early 20th centuries, developed scientific foundations for effective job and incentive compensation design, focused on achieving higher productivity.

Despite its long history and important organizational function, management is not a profession, but merely an occupation. Although many managers tend to have received some form of business education, unlike professionals such as physicians, engineers, or attorneys, organizational managers do not receive standardized education based on an agreed upon body of knowledge. Moreover, managers do not need to be accredited to practice management and are not required to engage in continuing professional education – lastly, the fact that managers cannot be sued for professional malpractice[2] is perhaps the clearest indication of the 'unprofessional status' of the occupation of organizational management.

The practice of management is also noticeably different from professional practices, as exemplified by medicine or law. A physician, for instance, tends to deal with largely fixed sets of problems and constraints: A manifestly un-well patient exhibits certain symptoms based upon which the physician is tasked with, first correctly diagnosing the underlying disease, then with iden-tifying the best treatment means and protocols, all while taking into account patient-specific factors such as the patient's age, general health, medical history, etc. Assuming patient cooperation, the physician has a high degree of control over the outcome of the treatment because the problem he or she is trying to solve is contained, and if properly diagnosed and treated, the effectiveness of that physician's decision-making can be objectively assessed (which forms the basis for the professional malpractice mentioned earlier). It is also important to note that physician-patient dyads are united by commonality of goals, most no-tably the well-being of the patient. The reality of managerial decision-making, however, is considerably different.

First, although definitionally an organization can be described as a group of individuals joined together in pursuit of share goals, the notion of 'shared goals' obscures numerous not-so-shared individual factors and considerations. Most notably, the behavior of individuals is influenced by a combination of genetic or inherited traits such as gender, temperament, race, or religion; learned characteristics such as values, attitudes, or emotions; and general as well as situational goals such as career objectives. Although group function-ing demands at times considerable degrees of interdependence and sharing in the common purpose, the individual group members' own needs and goals may not be in alignment with shared goals, which poses considerable, but difficult to identify (and remedy) obstacles to effective management. Second, in contrast to the relatively stable and controlled diagnosis-treatment context that characterizes common, that is, non-emergency medical practices, orga-nizational decision-making commonly takes place in a largely uncontrollable environment. Final outcomes of managers' decisions are almost always shaped not only by the efficacy of their choices but also by managerially uncontrol-lable factors such as actions of competitors, aggregate demand characteris-tics, technological and business process innovation, regulatory developments, and other external forces. Third, the practice of management is permeated by far greater (than the practice of medicine or law) degree of uncertainty, or what could be more precisely characterized as 'diagnostic imprecision'. Stated differently, organizational ailments can be hard to precisely diag-nose, especially in large, complex organizations, and are perception- and interpretation-prone. For instance, conclusions such as 'low performing' or 'high customer attrition' do not have universal meaning, but instead tend to reflect peer- or expectation-based evaluations. Moreover, there is often an informational gap in terms of that which needs to be known and that which is knowable to organizational managers – interestingly, and perhaps even coun-terintuitively, it is as much a function of not enough as it is a function of too much information.

Too Much and Not Enough Information

In their 2006 Harvard Business Review article, Pfeffer and Sutton argued that 'executives routinely dose their organizations with strategic snake oil: discredited nostrums, partial remedies, or untested management miracle cures'.[3] And indeed, what may seem like an enlighten solution to a vexing problem may in retrospect turn out to be nothing more than a passing fad. Now largely forgotten, business process re-engineering, total quality management, knowledge management, or learning organizations management frameworks once enjoyed widely shared, albeit short-lived enthusiasm, in spite of the lack of objectively verifiable benefits. Still alive and well are talent management, emotional intelligence, employee engagement, or agile management, offering solutions for everyone and everywhere. Promising to solve even the intractable problems in a manner that is easy to understand and fast, those management miracle cures are full of buzzwords, acronyms, and fun anecdotes, supported by stories of excellent companies and recognizable gurus and, perhaps most importantly, resonate with trends and problems of the day. Although less obvious, the continuing reliance on management fads is usually also fueled by informational overload – the earlier mentioned human channel capacity places a numeric limit on the number of distinct pieces of information (7 ± 2) a human decision-maker can consciously consider at a given time. Overwhelmed by dozens and dozens of different and possibly conflicting informational inputs, organizational managers are more likely to fall victim of the simple, straightforward, universal, tried-and-true decision-guiding frameworks, even if there is little-to-no evidence attesting to their efficacy.

A notionally opposite problem is brought about by the 'it is all about the data' mindset. Many organizations are indeed awash in data, but data are incomplete and messy, in the sense of combining insightful facts and distracting noise, thus not intrinsically informative. Moreover, it is reasonable to now assume that most competitors have access to essentially the same data and the same data management and processing technologies, which means that being all about data is akin to being like everyone else … most of whom are quipping about being data-rich but knowledge-poor. An organization with lots and lots of data is a bit like a farmer with lots of usable land – it is certainly a good start, but not a guarantee of a good harvest.

As clearly illustrated by successful organizations, the biggest single source of informational advantage is the superior knowledge creation know-how. Overall, the most significant factor that consistently explains why some data-rich organizations are also knowledge-rich, whereas other, equally data-rich and technologically enabled firms are comparatively knowledge-poorer is the advanced data analytical skill set of the former. At the time when data are ubiquitous and standard data processing tools yield informationally generic outcomes, it is the ability to go beyond the basic data crunching functionality that is the key determinant of the ultimate value of data.

And that, for many organizations, is a problem. Though manifestly important, the knowledge creation know-how is arguably the least developed and certainly the least formalized aspect of the new, digital world. That may be surprising as, after all, the domain of quantitative analysis is a well-established, long-standing field of study. And indeed it is, but mostly in the academic, rather than applied sense. Similar to a number of other fields of study, quantitative methods tend to be inwardly oriented and primarily focused on methods rather than outcomes. Those trained in that domain tend to acquire substantial amounts of abstract knowledge, but comparatively little understanding of application-related considerations. The emergence and rapid proliferation of business analytics and data science curricula, coupled with growing emphasis on hands-on experiential learning, is beginning to change that, but the process is slow while needs are urgent. And even if and when more and better trained analysts are mining the vast quantities of organizational data, the problem of informational overload will not disappear – in fact, it may grow as more analysts doing more analyses will translate into higher volumes of information. At the same time, as more and more data are transformed into usable insights, the opportunity to thoughtfully amalgamate those insights into more conclusive, ambiguity-reducing decision inputs will grow. In short, a solid foundation for evidence-based decision-making will have been laid.

Evidence-Based Practice

The emergence of the idea of EBP cannot be traced back or attributed to a singular event, but rather a gradual organizational embrace of more manifestly rational and fact-supported mode of decision-making. Starting in the 1980s, the British government began to emphasize the need for public policy and practices to be informed by accurate and diverse body of objective evidence. In the US, the notion of EBP first took roots in medicine, most notably as an outcome of the Evidence-Based Medicine Working Group's 1992 release of *Evidence-Based Medicine: A New Approach to Teaching the Practice of Medicine.* Framed as a new paradigm which 'deemphasizes intuition, unsystematic clinical experience and pathophysiological rationale as sufficient grounds for clinical decision making and [instead] stresses the examination of evidence from clinical research', it advocated integration of individual clinical expertise with the best available external research evidence. Shortly, the originally medicine focused EBP spread into other domains of practice including management and psychology, as demonstrated by the 2005 Academy of Management presidential address and the formation of the American Psychological Association's Presidential Task Force on Evidence-Based Practice in 2006.[4]

As captured in the original evidence-based medicine characterization, the intended main source of evidence is scientific research, which is to be critically reviewed and synthesized as a mean of generating external and unbiased source of knowledge. The means of accomplishing that task are provided by two somewhat related but nonetheless distinct research review and synthesis tools: *systematic reviews* (SR) and *meta-analyses* (MA). The former are focused on collecting and summarizing research evidence that addresses a pre-specified research question, whereas the latter makes use of statistical methods to summarize the empirical results of those studies. It follows that SR in particular are time-consuming and so while summative research offers promising benefits, time and resource requirements can be overwhelming, even with narrowly scoped research questions. Large, resource-pooling collaboratives, best illustrated by the Cochrane Collection, a large database of SR generated by tens of thousands of volunteers from more than 100 different countries, can and do offer a compelling solution to that problem. Still, more endemic problems associated with large-scale summarization of research outcomes remain, with subjectivity and selection being of primary concern. The first of the two challenges is most evident in SR, which even with steps that can be taken to reduce reviewer bias[5] are shaped by perspectives of individual researchers. The very essence of those efforts, as embodied in the five main SR stages – research question definition, search for relevant data, extraction of relevant data, assessment of data quality, data analyses, and amalgamation – is geared toward researcher judgment, which is particularly pronounced when searching for, extracting, and assessing the quality of data. The problem of selection, which is the second of the two problems endemic to the task of research summarization, is particularly pronounced in the context of MA (often considered a subset, or a special case of SR). Although manifestly more quantitatively minded than the somewhat more narrative SR, that approach has been criticized as giving insufficient attention to heterogeneity of research in its search for congruence.

Although SR and MA related methodological concerns are certainly not trivial, it is difficult to question the soundness of the broader evidence-based approach in natural science fields, such as medicine, where the bulk of new knowledge is generated by scientific, largely academic research. Often characterized, or mischaracterized in view of some, as self-referential, jargon laden, obsessed with theory while at the same time unconcerned, if not outright dismissive of practical considerations, organizational-management-related academic research does not offer quite as firm and compelling evidentiary foundation as the one offered by medical and other natural scientific research. In fact, there is a substantial volume of writings, by both academics and practitioners, that detail the academic-practice gap, in particular as it regards the general trend of academics lagging in studying topics of interest to practitioners, and rarely being able to compel practitioners to pay attention to what academic research deems important. Whatever the specific spoken or unspoken reasons, the disconnect between the theoretical management research and the practice of management is so fundamental that limiting the scope of evidence-based practice to primarily academic research just about guarantees greatly reduced informational value.

A yet another stumbling block to mimicking evidence-based medical practice in organizational management is illustrated by the Cochrane Collection mentioned earlier. Different physicians treating their respective patients suffering from the same or similar ailments are ultimately united in the common goal of helping their patients, which means that a common body of knowledge is very beneficial to all. That, however, is often not the case with managers of organizations that compete with one another. Here, not only do those managers have no incentive to contribute to a common-to-all database of knowledge – the perceived benefit of using common-to-all informational reservoir flies in the face of the basic tenets of competitive advantage. Of course, that is not the case for academic management researchers, but as noted earlier, relatively few of their ideas and recommendations are attended to by practitioners. And lastly, the timing of so-derived knowledge is also a concern, as unlike ailments that may remain relatively unchanged in terms of their key characteristics (i.e., knowledge that may take months or even years to be produced will likely still be of considerable value), organizational managers' decision time horizons are often prohibitive of lengthy fact-finding missions.

Moreover, looking beyond practical applications, the very scientific vitality of academic management research has been a subject of vigorous critique from academicians themselves. For instance, some management researchers lament the lack of intellectual coherence of the overall research output, pointing to contradicting outcomes of research focusing on some of the field's most studied conceptual frameworks, such as goal theory, where some published studies conclude that setting challenging goals enhances performance, whereas others find that doing so reduces productivity. Others bemoan the highly disjointed nature of research efforts, asserting that management research base is less than the research base in natural sciences, such as medicine, concerned with cumulating reliable and replicable knowledge. Still others point out what they view as the lack of objectivity in management research efforts, and the focus on search for universal generalizations, which effectively ignores the highly context- and situation-dependent character of management problems. The search for conclusively true patterns and relationships contrasts visibly with tentative and situationally specific nature of organizational decision-making.

Challenges and limitations impeding wider utilization of academic research outcomes' notwithstanding, there are kernels of important knowledge that can be found in those volumes. The potential value of those insights becomes even clearer when the capacity of human cognitive reasoning (recall the human channel capacity concept discussed earlier) is brought into picture, underscoring the need to simplify organizational decision problems. To be more specific, those research-derived kernels of knowledge can aid in the rudimentary sensemaking or reasoning processes. Broadly defined, human *rationality* is bounded by mental skills, habits, and reflexes, all of which play a role in solving a problem at hand. It thus follows that the efficacy of managerial decision-making can be improved by learning-based enhancements of a decision-maker's mental skills, and providing informationally compelling evidence that can overcome a potentially biased habits and reflexes. Scientific research plays a particularly important role in shaping decision-makers' mental skills, and while medicine-originated 'flavor' of EBP may not be especially well suited to the realities of organizational-management-related research, the idea of EBP is very well suited to the needs of managers, especially when one considers the alternative – management by intuition, which is hard to defend outside of a small number of hand-picked examples of truly exceptional leaders who were able to see further than others, and might have also benefited from an ounce or two of good luck.

Evidence-Based Management Practice

Within the domain of organizational management, the Center for Evidence-Based Management (CEBMa) is emerging as the leading proponent of EBP. An independent nonprofit foundation, CEBMa serves as the hub of EBP-related learning, teaching, and research; its founding members which include professors Denise Rousseau, Rob Briner, Eric Barends, and Jeffrey Pfeffer are among the most prolific and widely cited management EBP researchers.

The Center officially defines EBP as 'making decisions through conscientious, explicit and judicious of the best available evidence from multiple sources by

1   Asking: translating a practical issue or problem into an answerable question
2   Acquiring: systematically search for and retrieving the evidence
3   Appraising: critically judging the trustworthiness and relevance of the evidence
4   Aggregating: weighing and pulling together the evidence
5   Applying: incorporating the evidence into the decision-making process
6   Assessing: evaluating the outcome of the decision taken to increase the likelihood of a favorable outcome'.[6]

Defining evidence as 'information, facts or data supporting (or contradicting) a claim, assumption or hypothesis', CEBMa further asserts that evidence may come from four distinct sources:

1   The scientific literature, which embodies findings from empirical studies published in academic journals,
2   The organization, or more specifically data, facts, and figures gathered from the organization,
3   Practitioners, in the form of professional experience and judgment, and
4   Stakeholders, in particular the values and concerns of people who might be affected by the decision.

Guided by the idea that 'good-quality decisions should be based on a combination of critical thinking and the best available evidence', the information gathered from each of the above four sources should then be subjected to the general assessment, validation, and summation process of *ask-acquire-appraise-aggregate-apply-assess*, noted earlier. Tacitly implied in this framing of EBP is the emphasis on SR of the available research evidence, which promotes a shift away from traditionally narrative reviews (commonly associated with academic research studies) and toward more systematic, context-sensitive, and summative research. Also tacitly implied in CEBMa's EBP approach is a soft *hierarchy of evidence* (also referred to as *levels of evidence*), which places results of SR (used here as a research methodology, rather than a general concept) and/or MA of empirical research studies at the top of the authoritative pyramid, followed by evidence obtained from reviews of empirically limited or qualitative research pools, and rounded off with evidence presented by single, non-corroborated descriptive or qualitative studies and, lastly, opinions of experts.

Interestingly, although the earlier cited sources of evidence encompass academic research as well as broadly defined organizational data (in addition to expert judgment and stakeholder values), the evidence sourcing, assessment, and amalgamation thrust of CEBMa's approach are decisively directed toward academic research. Thus, while making allowances for the type of evidence that is expected in an organizational context, most notably organizational data and expert judgment, CEBMa's overall approach remains rooted in its medical practice origins, which, at the very least, invites criticisms. Recalling the substantial differences between medical and management domains of academic research, most notably the rather obvious fact that the practice of medicine is built on biological sciences, whereas the practice of management is built on social sciences suggests that medical research can be characterized as convergent while management research as divergent. As a result, the practice of medicine enjoys far greater degree of epistemological consensus than the practice of management, which is all a somewhat technical way of saying that summaries of medical research are more opt to reveal universally true, practice-guiding insights. Perhaps even more importantly, constraining the definitional scope of managerial evidence to insights derived, primarily, from academic research studies effectively downplays the potential decision-guiding value of big data, which at the very least runs counter not only to current trends but also flies in the face of the core tenets that underpin the broad conception of knowledge economy.

Against Evidence-Based

Although EBP is gaining wider acceptance across private and public sectors, there are those who cast doubt on the appropriateness of applying EBP concepts and processes to applied contexts, ranging from public policy to policing to health care and, of course, organizational management. Arguments of those who argue against EBP can be grouped into two broad categories: (1) the quality and dependability of evidence and (2) the very idea of evidence-based approach to professional practice. The former can be seen as criticism of management-related theoretical/academic research, which, as noted earlier, has been the focal source of evidence. Those concerns are, to a large degree, reflected in the preceding overview of the EBP, and in fact contributed to the motivation to develop the Empirical & Experiential Evidence framework detailed in the ensuing chapters. The latter, on the other hand, is essentially a polemic against the advent of data-driven objectivism, and the perceived marginalization of intellectual pluralism and flexibility. Those arguments appear to be rooted in an implicit assumption that the embrace of objective evidence as a driver of the decision-making process somehow forecloses or at least foreshadows the decision-makers' openness to dialog and willingness to consider multiple perspectives. That particular line of reasoning is perplexing, to say the least, and thus it warrants a closer look.

Let us consider a simple yet common scenario: A risk manager for a large commercial business organization is trying to decide how much directors and officers liability (commonly referred to as 'D&O') insurance coverage to procure. Purchasing too little coverage could potentially expose organizational executives and members of its board of directors (the individuals for whose benefit that coverage is being purchased) to excessive risk while purchasing too much coverage might create an unnecessary drag on earnings, given that, from an accounting point of view, insurance premiums represent an expense with no residual value. Faced with that dilemma, the risk manager can either rely on his or her intuition and subjective judgment, or can make use of available external information, such as industry benchmarks, predictive models-generated likelihood and severity estimates, and other decision inputs. In a more abstract sense, the manager has a choice of managing by intuition or managing by evidence – frankly, it is difficult to imagine a situation where a rational individual motivated by the well-being of his or her organization would choose the former over the latter. In fact, it would be extremely irresponsible on the part of that decision-maker to not take advantage of the available objective data, and doing so in no way shackles his or her freedom to engage in constructive dialog or to consider multiple perspectives. Taking into account externally available evidence is not synonymous with surrendering one's decision-making-related freedoms or responsibilities – in fact, given that it is likely that different evidence might suggest somewhat different (D&O insurance purchase related) courses of action, managing by evidence may be seen as actually fostering decision-makers' willingness to consider multiple perspectives. Framing intellectual pluralism in contexts that abstract beyond the realm of organization-specific, environmentally and situationally shaped decision-making contexts renders such arguments meaningless, a yet another example of the academic-practice gap.

The Road Ahead

At its core, organizational management is about making choices under conditions of uncertainty, and judicious and explicit use of best available evidence offers the best hope of making the best possible choices. It is not a panacea, but by helping managers overcome the many potential mental prejudices and biases while also expanding their choice-pertinent knowledge base, it ultimately reduces the probability of making suboptimal, if not outright detrimental choices. In a sense, the value of EBP parallels the value of predictive modeling,[7] now widely used by marketers, risk managers, and other organizational decision-makers. For instance, contrary to common perception, predictive statistical models developed to estimate customer-specific probability of brand purchase are usually most beneficial not as customer selection, but rather as customer de-selection tools. The reason for that is largely methodological, and it comes down to the fact that, under most circumstances, those who are unlikely to purchase a particular brand tend to be easier to identify than those who are likely to purchase it. Filtering out the most unlikely brand purchasers effectively increases the proportion of likely brand purchasers in the remaining universe (really, sample), which ultimately translates into higher return on marketing investment (through higher conversion rates). In a similar vein, while making use of carefully vetted and compiled evidence may not necessarily always bring about the best possible outcome, it will nonetheless materially reduce the chances of making disadvantageous choice. Recall the blackjack card counting example discussed at the beginning of this book – all it does is to help the card-counting player (in reality, a team of players) to better the initially unfavorable odds, which often proves enough to generate almost disproportionately large benefits. In an organizational decision-making context, making fewer poor choices over a period of time will likely also produce equally disproportionately large benefits.

However, an approach to evidence-based management styled on the teaching or practice of medicine will likely fall short of that promise, though. Medical practice is largely based on natural sciences, and in natural sciences the bulk of new knowledge is created in what could be described as academy-centered research ecosystem. By and large, the new knowledge medical practitioners need is created and disseminated via formal processes which include the conduct, validation and dissemination of new knowledge, professional credentialing, and ongoing professional learning (also referred to as continuing education). With that as the foundation, the process of evidence discovery, assessment and amalgamation of primarily empirical academic research findings can be reasonably expected to produce better outcomes, in terms of the quality of medical care. The same process, however, cannot be expected to produce equally compelling results when applied to the domain of organizational management, which has little in common with medical practice, and rarely looks to academic research for guidance. The general approach to business education is far from standardized (something that even a casual review of a handful of business schools' curricula will quickly reveal), and the resultant lack of formal managerial credentialing translates into considerable cross-manager variability in foundational knowledge base, experience, and other qualifications. But perhaps most importantly, as so vividly illustrated by the much talked about academic-practice gap, comparatively little managerial know-how is derived from academic research. And while it would be a mistake to dismiss the possibility of worthwhile insights being produced by systematically reviewing or meta-analyzing applicable academic research studies, it would be an equally big mistake to conclude that making those means and sources the focal point of management practice-guiding evidence generation will blaze a viable path to significant improvements in the quality of organizational decision-making.

Thus, the challenge and the opportunity for EBP in management are one and the same: how to retain the spirit of evidence-based demonstrated by medical practice while also making it applicable to the considerably different practice of organizational management? The remainder of this book is focused on answering that question.

Notes

1 Sumer is a region in historical Mesopotamia, modern-day Iraq, and arguably the first civilization, around 4500–1900 BC (cuneiform script, the world's oldest extant writing system, was invented by Mesopotamians).
2 In the sense in which medical or law practitioners can be sued for professional malpractice; under the US tort law, certain organizational managers can be held accountable for their decisions under the *duty of care* doctrine, but are generally extended considerable leeway under the provisions of the *business judgment rule*.
3 Pfeffer, J. and R. I. Sutton (2006), 'Evidence-Based Management', *Harvard Business Review*, January, 63–74.
4 Other domains of practice such as education, policing, public policy, and social work also quickly joined the evidence-based movement although without having formed formal task forces as a way of promoting the new practice paradigm.
5 For example, within the domain of health care practice, the Preferred Reporting Items for Systematic Reviews and Meta-Analyses, or PRISMA standards spell out a process and the minimum set of items to help systematize the scope setting and the conduct of systematic reviews and meta-analyses.
6 Barends, E., D. M. Rousseau and R. Briner (2014), 'Evidence-Based Management: The Basic Principles', www.cebma.org
7 Broadly defined, it is a process that uses historical data to forecast future outcomes, such as the likelihood of product purchase.

5

THE ESSENCE OF EVIDENCE

Central to developing a sound understanding of evidence-based practice (EBP) is the very notion of 'evidence.' It is a widely used term, which means that it connotes a broad array of meanings. For instance, to an attorney, evidence can take the form of written or oral testimony, specific exhibits, documentary material, or demonstrations which are allowed to be considered by the trier of fact in a judicial process, whereas to a medical practitioner evidence can take the form of outcomes of specific diagnostic tests or results of scientific studies. In still other contexts, most notably, for organizational management, evidence can be usage- or situation-defined, which can even render the overtly objectively minded notion more argumentative than persuasive. All considered, the seemingly straightforward concept of evidence turns out to be surprisingly complex when examined from the varying usage perspectives which calls for conceptual and operational clarification, given that notion's central importance to the idea and practice of evidence-based decision-making.

The goal of this chapter is twofold: First, it is to offer a descriptive overview of the concept of evidence by means of capturing and summarizing its key sets of meaning and usage situations. Second, it is to propose an evidence classificatory typology, intended to serve as the foundation for meaningful identification and organizing of distinct types of choice-making-related informational inputs.

What is Evidence?

Immanuel Kant, one of the central figures in modern philosophy, argued that human mind creates the structure of human experience. Starting with that reasonable sounding assertion, when related to the idea of fact-based decision-making,

Kant's notion of human experience suggests that human sense of reality can be thought of as being comprised of three dimensions: (1) knowledge of facts, (2) sharing of the known facts with others, sometimes referred to as actuality, and (3) selection and contextualization of facts, or contextuality. Nested within that context is the notion of *evidence*, first addressed in Chapter 2, in the context of anecdotes.

Abstracting away from anecdotes, *evidence* can be defined as facts or other organized information presented to support or justify beliefs or inferences; the term itself is derived from Latin 'evident', or 'obvious to the eye or mind'. The concept of evidence is widely used in modern science to lend substantiation to theoretical postulates, in medical practice to help correctly diagnose and treat ailments, and in the practice of law to help settle disputes; as outlined in the ensuing chapters, it is also beginning to be applied in the context of organizational management. Since 'facts and other organized information' constitute a very broad, open-ended pool of possible insights, available and pertinent evidence may encompass a mixed bag of indicators, some supporting and others refuting a particular belief or proposition. Consequently, the totality of evidence is usually considered from the perspective of the degree to which the majority of indications support or not a particular argument. Within the confines of scientific and diagnostic settings, evidence is commonly framed using the notion of 'weight of evidence', whereas within the legal setting, the evidentiary plurality is captured in the notion of 'preponderance of evidence'.

Tacitly implied in the above-outlined conception of evidence is the notion's *external-to-self* aspect – to offer defensible corroboration of one's internally held beliefs or conclusions, any facts or information used to substantiate those beliefs ought to be derived from sources that are external to one's belief system. Presenting one subjective belief as proof of another subjective belief is not only tautological, but in the evidentiary decision-making sense it smacks of circular reasoning. Scientific theories, which as abstract ideas can be likened to one's internal beliefs, are validated with the help of externally produced empirical data, not other abstract ideas; similarly, in legal disputes, a party's claims are substantiated by independent (to that party) facts.[1] The external-to-self characteristic of evidence is critical to reasoning imbedded in the Empirical & Experiential Evidence framework described in later chapters, and it is also one of the key differences between that conceptualization and other evidence-based frameworks, such as the one advocated by the Center for Evidence-Based Management.

What about one's professional experience? The standard, dictionary definition of experience describes it as '...practical knowledge, skill, or practice derived from direct observation of or participation in events or in a particular activity'.[2] In that sense, one's professional experience clearly falls within the external-to-self framing of evidence, and as such could be considered a type of anecdotal evidence.

It should be noted, however, that there are other perspectives on the scope and the definition of what should be considered evidence. The socio-psychological perspective suggests that evidence consists of propositions and facts, and psychological states, including beliefs, experiences, and intuitions. Framed within that context is a four-category ontology of evidence: (1) propositions, (2) facts, (3) psychological states, and (4) factive psychological states, such as knowledge (which itself encompasses a broad array of ideas). As such, the socio-psychological perspective is notionally similar to *evidentialism*, a philosophical thesis capturing what it takes for one to reasonably believe in a particular assertion, which postulates that evidence can include not only empirical information but also prior arguments and subjective experience that can authenticate themselves as genuine grounds for belief. Conceptually ponderous, the socio-psychological/evidentialist premise effectively disregards the dangers brought about by cognitive bias, and other forms of self-deception. For instance, if, as a risk manager of a business organization, I believe that purchasing professional liability insurance coverage is unnecessary, and remain unconvinced by empirical evidence to the contrary, the only remaining belief authentication avenue is to wait until a professional liability related event actually occurs (at which point it would likely become expensively obvious that the initial belief was unfounded). In short, it is hard to foresee circumstances under which such posture would be beneficial within the confines of organizational management. Moreover, the all-in scope of evidentialism also leads to blurring of the distinction between a concept and its proof. If a particular idea and the empirical data generated by the application of that idea are both considered evidence, how could one be used to validate the other?

The same reasoning applies to other ontological, phenomenological, and similarly esoteric arguments for defining and delimiting the abstract notion of evidence in an all-encompassing manner. As a group, those arguments are unconvincing, and especially so when applied to practical problems of organizational decision-making. Business managers are constantly confronted with shifting markets, competitive pressures, and regulatory mandates, among others, which compel them to make choices in anticipatory manner, under conditions of uncertainty. When making a decision, an organizational manager can rely primarily on his or her intuition and judgment, and possibly also take advantage of convenience evidence in the form of whatever information might be available at that time – or that manager can rely primarily on carefully pooled, considered, and amalgamated decision-guiding insights that represent conclusive summaries of all available and pertinent data. That is the essence of how the notion of evidence, used as input into the decision-making process, should be framed. Moreover, that is the bottom line rationale for limiting the scope of the definition of evidence, as used in the Empirical & Experiential Evidence framework detailed in the ensuring chapters, to what is *factually* known and it does not encompass subjective feelings, opinions, or other not objectively corroborated (i.e., external-to-self) assertions.

The preceding discussion suggests that when limited to objective signals gathered from external, or exogenous sources, decision-guiding evidence can be grouped into two broad meta-categories of *empirical* and *experiential* evidence. The former encompasses knowledge derived from analyses of organizational data or

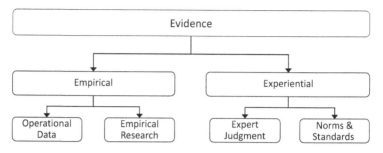

FIGURE 5.1 Evidence Tree Typology.

from findings of empirical research studies, whereas the latter embodies knowledge stemming from doing. Given its initially broad scope, empirical evidence can be further subdivided into *operational data*, derived from electronic transaction processing and communication exchanges, and *theoretical research*, which encompass observation- or experimentation-based scientific inquiries. Experiential evidence can also be subdivided into two distinct components of *expert judgment*, which are opinions and forecasts of highly qualified and practiced individuals, and *norms & standards*, which encompass recognized best practices and industry benchmarks. The resultant general *evidence tree typology* is graphically depicted in Figure 5.1.

Empirical Evidence

One of the intellectual foundations of the Western scientific tradition is the reliance on the *scientific method*, which is a set of procedures consisting of systematic measurement (by observation of experiment), and the formulation, testing, and modification of hypotheses, as the basis of knowledge creation. Testing of hypotheses using observation-or experimentation-sourced data is often linked to *empiricism*, which is the belief that knowledge is derived from sensory experiences (whee, any robust, applicable, external-to-self information could be considered empirical evidence). However, when considered from the standpoint of informational inputs into organizational decision-making, there are fundamental differences between empirical results of scientific research studies and analyses of organizational data. While some of those differences, such as the degree of organizational or decision specificity, might be self-evident, others, most notably those addressing the critically important issues of validity and reliability, require a closer examination.

Research Evidence

Although not nearly as amusing as a colorful anecdote, evidence gleaned from research studies tends to be more objective and more dependable than anecdotal insights. The reason for that is that while anecdotes are typically taken at face value, the conduct and subsequent publication of research findings entails rigor and open disclosure of means and methods, coupled with external review and scrutiny, all of which provide means of judging the trustworthiness of those findings.

Scientific research encompasses a wide and rich array of approaches and techniques, best summarized with the help of several dualities: theoretical vs. applied, quantitative vs. qualitative, exploratory vs. explanatory, and observational vs. experimental. Theoretical research, a staple of academic knowledge creation, focuses on building and testing of universal theories (hence the name), whereas applied research tends to have narrower-in-scope and more 'what works' focus. Quantitative research emphasizes objective statistical analyses of generalizable (i.e., sufficiently large and representative of the population) samples of already existing or specially captured data, whereas qualitative research makes use of ethnographic (in-depth investigation of human behavior) methods to discern deeper understanding of behavioral root causes of a typically small, nonrepresentative number of subjects. Exploratory research, nowadays often taking the form of 'data mining', represents an attempt to gain initial or further understanding of a particular phenomenon, whereas explanatory research, which encompasses predictive analytics, represents an attempt at establishing and assessing causal (i.e., cause-effect) connections. Lastly, observational research makes use of preexisting data, whereas experimental research is focused on capturing new data by manipulating some variables while controlling others, all to measure effects of interest. Overall, most research studies could be characterized in terms of those four dualities – for instance, a research study could be described as a theoretical, quantitative study of exploratory nature, leveraging observational data.

The multiplicity of research approaches together with a large universe of research-oriented institutions adds up to many and varied outcomes. In fact, even within a fairly narrowly defined domains, such as risk management, health informatics, or predictive analytics, the cumulative volume of past and newly published work can be nothing short of overwhelming.[3] Clearly, it is the problem of overabundance, quite unlike the insufficiency quandary associated with anecdotal evidence. It is also a problem of reconciliation, which stems from independent, incremental, and iterative character of research endeavors. Mostly independent (of one another) researchers pursue initiatives that reflect their interests, agendas as well as data and methodological preferences and capabilities – even if a group of researchers all happen to focus on the same research topic, such as the impact of prior beliefs on evaluations of product quality, they will likely approach the topic differently, in terms of data and research methods, ultimately generating individually framed outcomes. Hence, on one hand, there might be a wealth of results to consider, but at the same time the individual studies might be difficult to compare. Though not an insurmountable obstacle, it is nonetheless a substantial one.

Operational Data Evidence

Avid sport fans commonly speak in terms of the odds of a particular team winning an important match or a championship, and most of us almost habitually associate expected weather with probabilities of events such as precipitation. This shows that when used in certain contexts and when used colloquially, statistical evidence is naturally a part of the decision-making process, yet it may feel almost unnatural in some other contexts, which includes many business situations, in which biased and factually unfounded beliefs seem natural and trustworthy, whereas rational extrapolations can seem comparatively less believable. And yet, making use of statistical inferences drawn from data offers the only valid and reliable means of discerning the potentially (organizational) fortunes-changing patterns hidden in the torrents of transactional and communication data.

When considered from the perspective of knowledge creation, operational data can give rise to factual, or 'what-is', information, as well as probabilistic, or 'what might be', estimates. The former commonly takes the form of ongoing operational reporting, as exemplified by periodic sales summaries, while the latter tend to take the form of probabilistic inferences drawn from data, as exemplified by brand choice predicting statistical models. Both data usages are subject to data vagaries stemming from a wide array of data origination, capture, storage and manipulation processes and mechanisms, such as random coding errors, incorrect values aggregation, or poorly thought-out missing value imputation. Thus, in a more abstract sense, within the confines of decision-related sensemaking, data can be thought of as combination of *signal*, or informative elements, and *noise*, or informationless elements. And while the nearly inescapable and generally well-understood imprecision of organizational data impacts both the 'what-is' and 'what might be dimensions', the latter is also affected by the related, though comparatively poorly understood *compounding effect*. Simply put, though often almost excessively voluminous, data available to business and other organizations are, under most circumstances, explanatively incomplete, in the sense of being insufficient to fully explain observed outcomes of interest, in addition to also being predictively incomplete, in the sense that past patterns are imperfect predictors of future outcomes. For instance, when trying to discern consumer brand choices, the typically available data-sourced (e.g., past product purchases and purchase descriptors such as demographics, online product reviews, etc.) typically can only explain some of the cross-purchaser brand choice variability, simply because not all choice-determining factors are captured as data. Situationally emergent, ever-changing factors such as impulse, frame of mind, changing needs and tastes are just some of the potentially material but not available as data choice contributors, a limitation that is further compounded by the ever-changing relative importance and salience of choice-determining brand attributes. Thus effectively layering explanatory and predictive imprecision on the top of noisy data exacerbates, or compounds, informational limitations of operational data.

Not surprisingly, probabilistic usages of operational data invite skepticism, the bulk of which is rooted in the assertion that inferences drawn from imperfect data can only yield epistemologically[4] imperfect conclusions. And while that reasonable assertion may indeed render pure empiricism, which promotes the view that all rational beliefs are observational in nature, untenable, it is simply insufficient to merit an outright dismissal of operational data-sourced evidence (though it certainly warrants careful interpretation of data analytic insights). The reason for that is that if not all, then the great majority of knowledge claims, regardless of source, are tenuous. Scientific theories offer explanations that reflect the available information and the broader state of knowledge at a point in time, and as new information becomes available and the general state of knowledge advances so do the theoretical explanations; similarly, experience-based knowledge is also constantly remolded (recall the earlier discussion of brain plasticity) as new experiences update prior knowledge. In a more general sense, uncertainty of knowledge manifests itself more or less clearly across all dimensions of knowledge, and the probabilistic nature of statistical inferences drawn from operational data is merely more visible than the equally tenuous nature of other types of decision-guiding insights.

In practice, a wide range of important decisions are based on statistical inferences drawn from operational data. For instance, commercial and consumer credit decisions are made on the basis of past default rates of similar borrowers, and medical diagnostic is deeply rooted in the use of statistical correlation, a probabilistic measure of association between observed symptoms and the presumed ailment. And again, in aggregate, while offering only approximately correct insights, those and other examples of statistical inference-derived evidence routinely outperform intuition-inspired decisions.

It is also worth mentioning that not all statistical inferences are rooted entirely in historical data[5] – the widely used Bayesian probability estimation combines inferences drawn from historical data with prior knowledge, which can encompass a wide array of other sources, such as prior experience and expert judgment. In a sense, the idea behind the Empirical & Experiential Evidence framework makes use of similar reasoning of combining the best available information drawn from manifestly dissimilar sources.

An important set of considerations unique to operational data is the independence of data and data-derived insights. The majority of organizational data are by-product of the broadly defined transactional-informational electronic infrastructure, which captures, almost indiscriminately, any and all events and states as a part of its functioning, which stands in contrast to purposeful conduct of scientific research studies, or focused accumulation of experiential knowledge. Because of that, operational data need to be made to fit the particulars of knowledge those data are to yield, which entails a combination of data thinking, as well as computational and statistical thinking. *Data thinking* manifests itself in the ability to relate a particular informational need to internally (to the organization) or externally available data, and properly curating the data, especially in terms of appropriate feature engineering.[6] *Computational* and *statistical thinking*, on the other hand, manifests itself in the ability to analyze data, which may entail the use of the *scientific method*, which is a set of procedures consisting in systematic measurement (by observation or experiment), and the formulation, testing, and modification of hypotheses, or data mining, machine learning or other, more advanced (such as deep learning) artificial intelligence oriented tools. Thus, in terms of means of insight extraction, statistical and research evidence both are analyses-intensive and both produce probabilistic outcomes. The key difference is that sound research evidence is generalizable and replicable, whereas statistical evidence often is not, although it can still deliver robust insights. To be a source of sound decision-guiding information, however, statistical evidence needs to be carefully considered in terms of the validity of data used, the reliability of data analytic methods, and the dependability of the sensemaking or inference processes.

Experiential Evidence

The second of the two meta-categories of evidence, experience-based support or substantiation, is almost always less objective (than empirical evidence), and quite commonly it is also less context-specific. Broadly defined, experiential evidence encompasses suggestions or signs stemming from either commonly accepted standards and norms or experience-based opinions and forecasts of properly qualified and practiced experts. Although both stem from practical skills and involvement, there are numerous material differences between those two dimensions of experiential evidence; thus, a closer examination is warranted.

Normative Evidence

Recurring instances of a particular event may exhibit noticeable amounts of cross-time consistency. For example, the aggregate frequency of automotive accidents is relatively consistent from year to year, especially when adjusted for driving volume, as illustrated by the widely used statistic, Number of Fatalities per 100 Million Vehicle Miles Traveled, the value of which ranged from a low of 1.08 to a high of 1.15 during a five-year period from 2010 to 2015. When a recurring event shows such longitudinal stability, it often becomes enshrined in the form of an *industry benchmark*, or a standard point of reference against which more specific instances may be compared.[7] Given their aggregate foundations, benchmarks tend to be very general and slow changing which tends to limit their informational value when applied to a specific context. Nonetheless, being rooted in often considerable volumes of accumulated experience, those generalizations can offer sounds basis for face validity assessments.

It is important, however, to not lose sight of the colloquialism of industry benchmarks as those are, after all, informal, often word-of-mouth disseminated estimates. Given that, the source, applicability, robustness, or timelines of data that gave rise to a particular benchmark are often unclear, which should heighten the user scrutiny, though often that is not the case. It is certainly convenient to lean on a widely cited allusion, but unless the informational foundations and the applicability of that reference can be discerned and evaluated, it can be risky to do so.

Another widely used source of normative evidence is *best practices*, broadly characterized as solutions to recurring problems utilizing validated applied principles. Unlike the quantitatively minded benchmarks, best practices are qualitative and process oriented, aiming to single out and describe the best means of accomplishing a particular objective. Whether it addresses a fairly broad system, such as customer relationship management or insurance claim management, or a comparatively narrower process of identifying at risk of attrition customers or claims that exhibit heightened likelihood of adverse development, best practices can offer invaluable inputs into organizational decision-making. Still, there are dangers in over-reliance on such unchecked information, as illustrated by a fairly well-known meatloaf story, which goes like this: A man, let's call him John, with a great liking for meatloaf observed that every time his wife Mary made that dish she always cut off the ends prior to cooking it. When asked about it, Mary responded that she learned it from her mother. Not satisfied with that explanation, John then asked his mother-in-law about it, who told him that the cooking pan she was using for her meatloaf was quite small, and so she always ended up having to trim the ends. And so what her daughter internalized as being a part of the general meatloaf making ritual was a step that only made sense under specific circumstances. The point here is that it is important to critically assess the validity of any general practice to make sure it indeed reflects sound thinking, or that it stands on robust and sufficiently current and applicable informational foundation.

Expert Evidence

Anecdotes are brief, often amusing or humorous accounts of a person or an event – not surprisingly, *anecdotal evidence*, which encompasses just about any informal account or a testimonial, has considerable appeal. Anecdotal evidence tends to be limited to either a single case or a person, or a fairly small set of purposefully selected cases or persons, which frequently leads to usage that emphasizes substantiation of an already selected conclusion, rather than contributing to choosing a conclusion. The somewhat less visible consequence of that is that, when unchecked, reliance on anecdotes has the potential to amplify decision-makers' cognitive biases.[8] Thus while the value of anecdotal evidence should not be dismissed, it is difficult to overlook the unscientific (or pseudoscientific), nonrepresentative and conclusion-laden nature of that type of evidence, which is all too often used to lend credence to subjectively derived assertions. For centuries, aberrant examples have been used to substantiate out-landish claims made by charismatic political, spiritual, and business leaders, often as means of advancing their agendas. As elucidated by availability heuristic and other cognitive biases discussed in Chapter 1, rationality-warping pitfalls of human information processing abound and so it is easy to, for instance, over-estimate the prevalence of highly atypical events, and ultimately fall victim to compelling anecdotes.

This is not to say that anecdotal evidence should always be avoided as even the most bizarre cases, situations, or examples can yield worthwhile insights. Care and caution need to be exercised, however, to make sure the atypical examples are interpreted as just that – atypical, and not used to substantiate what might be a biased premise. Even the rarest, most unlikely events will eventually materialize and chances are will appear somehow bigger and more imminent – it is worthwhile to learn from such events, but at the same time remain cognizant of their outlyingness.

A somewhat distinct aspect of anecdotal evidence is *individualized evidence* (also referred to as 'epistemic accounts'), which encompasses expert judgment and professional experience. Unlike the typically external-to-self anecdotes, individual experiences are generally limited to the 'sample of one', but on the other hand commonly reflect learnings spanning many situations or long peri-ods of time. Thus, while subjective, individualized experience, properly sum-marized and cleansed (more on that later), can be a source of sound insights.

An obvious way of circumventing the subjectivity of expert judgments is to pool opinions of multiple experts, as exemplified by the Delphi method, a structured, systematic, and interactive forecasting technique relying on a panel of experts. Doing so allows the ultimate users of the resultant insights to retain the benefit of often deep experience and expertise of individual experts, while pooling opinions or forecast of multiple experts offers a measure of protection against the inescapably biased individual perspectives. Stated differently, seek-ing and amalgamating inputs from multiple experts will materially enhance the validity and reliability of expert evidence.

Internalizing Evidence

One of the foundational ideas underpinning the decision-making framework detailed in this book is that while, origin-wise, intuition is internal and data are external (to each decision-maker), within the confines of *evidentiary thinking* both intuition and data are internalized. What makes the end result different from the traditional or 'gut feeling' based reasoning are the two key enhance-ments: (1) conscious awareness of the instinct-warping impact of cognitive bias (discussed at length in Chapter 2) and (2) development of an intuitive un-derstanding of the logic, and limitations, of statistical inference. In a sense, it requires what amounts to a combination of some degree of objectification of subjective impulses with some degree of subjectification of objective data analyses derived insights. Both present difficult challenges to overcome because both require nontrivial resetting of natural tendencies or impulses, as exemplified by those that infuse cognitive bias into the decision-making process.

The idea of internalizing evidence appears to run counter the external-to-self characterization of evidence, although that is illusory. To internalize evidence is to fact-check and reset, when appropriate, one's subjective or impulse-driven beliefs or conclusions; it is to learn from carefully evaluated facts so that objective evidence helps to adjust or reshape prior beliefs. That does not mean memorizing every piece of information that a person comes across, which is clearly not realistic (technically, as discussed in Chapter 1, the human brain has ample storage space to store in memory every moment of a person's life – the problem is that without adequate refresh, the bulk of those memories cannot be retrieved). To be 'evidence driven', a decision-maker needs to resist the temptation to embrace a quick conclusion, to which human information processing is prone,[9] and instead thoughtfully and carefully consider the totality of all available indicators.

Using Evidence

Originally inspired by the prospect of material reduction in decision-making uncertainty, there is a substantial body of knowledge addressing systematic assimilation of evidence to practice, dating back to the emergence of evidence-based medical practice of early 1990s. Since then, the idea of EBP has been applied to education, more broadly defined health care, social policy, policing, and management. Interestingly, the focal point of EBP has been on systematic synthesis of scientific, largely academic research, and using the resultant insights to reduce decision ambiguity. Although the established EBP approaches do not exclude data generated for non-research-specific reasons, which describes the bulk of data available to business organizations, those approaches nonetheless offer little guidance to translating the ever-growing volumes of source- and type-heterogeneous data into usable – that is, decision-guiding – evidence. In view of that, the spirit of EBP can be seen as rooted in the traditional scientific paradigms (see the Four Learning Paradigms section in Chapter 1), most notably observational and theoretical paradigms, and to a considerably lesser degree computational, while almost entirely ignoring the rapidly emerging simulational learning paradigm. While that focus might be appropriate for hard science-based areas, such as medicine, it is clearly not appropriate for management because unlike diseases, which change slowly, if at all, competitive, environmental, and other factors impacting business organizations are highly variable. Combined with the big data, the current EBP-overlooked simulational learning paradigm can enable organizational decision-makers to leverage, rapidly and on ongoing basis, the ever-growing richness of operational data capture by more and more means, and in more detail. And when combined with other types of evidence, in an objective and sound manner, the totality of so-derived insights will arm organizational decision-makers with best available information, ultimately offering the greatest possible reduction in ambiguity, and the surest pathway to competitive advantage.

To be more explicit, the evidence-driven decision-making philosophy and approach discussed in this book is overtly and primarily focused on stimulating and enabling computational and simulational learning through systematic, on-going extraction of valid and reliable decision-guiding insights out of any and all data available to organizations. That emphasis is rooted in the belief that although generalizations established with the help of scientific research con-tribute an important dimension of managerial knowledge (and those sources of evidence are already fully described by the current frameworks), to make best possible choices managers have to make far better use of contextually specific and timely operational data. Rarely, if ever, will reviews of available scientific/academic studies produce such on-point, context, and timing wise in-formation, especially when modern organizational dynamics, where volatility is the new normal, are taken into account. Hence, one's ability to consistently reduce decision-making uncertainty is tied to being able to consistently lean on the totality of the available statistical, research, and anecdotal evidence, all consumed in the manner outlined in ensuing chapters. The timeliness and the acuity of evidence matter greatly, as that which was true yesterday may not be true today and it is even less likely to be true tomorrow. As evidenced, no pun intended, by the nearly frantic investments in data analytical capabilities, more and more organizations are beginning to realize that leveraging the informa-tional value of organizational data is no longer a race to the top – it is now at the center of organizational survival.

Evidentiary Thinking

Consider a case of two brand managers independently thinking about intro-ducing brand extensions to their brands. Further assume that the two brands are competitors, offering functionally comparable bundles of attributes, which amounts to two differently labeled versions of the same type of product. Both managers recently became immersed in EBP and are anxious to put those prin-ciples to work, thus are eagerly gathering evidence to help shape their brand extension-related decisions. For reasons that are beyond their control, one man-ager's key piece of evidence is characterized as 'purchase intention' containing results of survey-gathered prospective customers' interest in the proposed new product (brand extension), whereas the other manager's key piece of evidence is described as 'purchases', or actual sales of the new product experimentally introduced in a couple of markets. If those are the most informative pieces of evidence available to both managers, should either of the two decision-makers put more stock in his or her evidence?

It has been documented by numerous investigations that the aggregate de-mand estimates derived from surveys capturing buyers' intent to purchase a product are quite imperfect; thus, decision-guiding evidence derived from purchase intention estimates should not be considered as strong as evidence stemming from analyses of actual purchase patterns.[10] Self-reported intentions are subject to the same cognitive biases that afflict any other cognitive reasoning process, and so even when respondents are honest and forthcoming, they may be providing unreliable information. Actual purchases, even if collected with the help of a limited scale trial, are pure behavioral outcomes, free of self-deceit and other truth-warping influences, and as such offer more dependable decision-making basis.

In a more general sense, this simple illustration underscores a more general conclusion, which is that not all evidence is equally compelling or equally accurate. The *strength of evidence* is an important consideration when considering the available and decision-pertinent insights, and it is clearly recognized in the idea of *hierarchy of evidence* discussed in the previous chapter. However, the medical research-inspired hierarchy which places results of systematic reviews and/or meta-analyses of empirical research studies at the top of the pyramid of authority is not an appropriate template for prioritization of management evidence. The primary reason for that is because unlike medical research, which directly benefits the teaching and the practice of medicine, management research only contributes some ideas some of the time – certainly not enough to warrant most authoritative positioning. In addition, the medicine-derived EBP framework does not expressly address organizational – especially transactional – data, which by virtue of its coverage, accuracy, level of detail, and recency offers the most complete, on-time and on-point decision insights. After all, it is not a coincidence that the new 'commercial arms race' now takes the form of massive investments in data science, business analytics, and the related technological infrastructure.

However, just as overreliance on subjective reasoning amplifies cognitive bias leading to poor judgment, overreliance on data can amplify the ever-present data error[11] leading to seemingly sound yet unwarranted conclusions. One of the perhaps better known examples of overreliance on data analytic results is offered by the case of collateralized debt obligations (CDOs), and American Insurance Group's (AIG) accrual of huge and largely unfunded credit default swaps (effectively a form of insurance against CDO's price collapse), the combination of which helped to trigger the financial crisis of 2007–2008, known as the Great Recession. The same is true of overreliance on scientific research studies, as exemplified by well-known case of drugs developed to fight arrhythmia, an irregular rhythm of the heart. Arrhythmia drugs-related research showed that those drugs indeed stopped the irregular heart rhythm, which was heralded as a major breakthrough. However, subsequent investigations into life-saving, rather than just arrhythmia-stopping value of those drugs revealed that treatments did not actually save lives – in fact, it was shown that patients who received such treatments were actually about 30% less likely to survive. The conclusion is rather obvious: no single type of evidence is immune to bias, and thus no single type of evidence should be deemed informationally sufficient.

At the same time, there is a limit on how many distinct pieces of information a decision-maker can simultaneously consider, as captured in the earlier (Chapter 1) discussed notion of human channel capacity. Based on an older concept of channel capacity, originally introduced in the context of information theory to describe the information handling capacity of a communication channel, the concept of human channel capacity places a numeric limit of 7 ± 2 of discrete pieces of information an average human can hold in his/her working memory. Thus, merely piling on more and more information won't produce better decisions. In a manner that conceptually (only) resembles the logic of systematic reviews, available evidence needs to be screened and amalgamated in a conclusive manner. Stated differently, dependability of individual pieces of decision-related information needs to be assessed, following which potential differences need to be reconciled, all in the context of a sound foundation of probabilistic thinking.

Notes

1 More specifically, the US Federal Rule of Evidence calls for sufficient facts, sound methodology, and the use of applicable and accepted principles and methods when applying evidentiary facts to legal arguments.
2 Merriam-Webster dictionary.
3 A case in point: ABI/INFORM, a widely used repository of (mostly) academic published research keeps track of more than 5,000 publications.
4 Epistemology is a branch of philosophy concerned with questions about the nature and structure of knowledge, justification, beliefs, and the like.
5 Often referred to as the 'frequentist' approach to probability estimation.
6 This is a highly technical and context-dependent topic, but the general idea here is as follows: Because the vast majority of data is captured as a by-product of communication and electronic transaction processing, the manner in which data are structured and individual variables coded may need, at times considerable, amount of re-engineering to make it usable for the need at hand.
7 In this case, a simple five-year moving average could be computed to arrive at a single, smoothed 'national average automotive accident fatality rate' value, which then could be used as a point of reference by individual regions or states.
8 This is not to suggest that all subjective or even self-serving reasoning is inherently flawed or biased – after all, in business, science, and other aspects of life there are shining examples of mold-breaking reasoning and conclusions that were signs of genius, not bias; however, in a probabilistic sense, it seems reasonable to assert that flawed subjectivity is far more common than brilliance.
9 For more details, see D. Kahneman's 2011 book *Thinking Fast and Slow*, Farrar, Straus and Giroux, New York.
10 As detailed in J. Alba edited book, *Consumer Insights: Findings from Behavioral Research*, meta-analyses of data from 50+ research articles and a dozen industry data sets suggest an average purchase-purchase intention correlation in the range of 0.49–0.53.
11 It is important to distinguish between two quite different meanings of the term 'error', which in everyday language and in the context of subjective reasoning connotes a 'mistake', whereas in the context of data, or more specifically, statistical analyses of data denote 'estimation imprecision', or the difference between the estimated and actual values of a parameter.

PART III

The Empirical & Experiential Evidence Framework

6

PROBABILISTIC THINKING

Few mathematical concepts have as profound an impact on decision-making as the idea of probability. Interestingly, the development of a comprehensive theory of probability had relatively inglorious origins in the form of a 1654 gambling dispute which compelled two accomplished French mathematicians, Blaise Pascal and Pierre de Fermat, to engage in an intellectual discourse that ultimately laid the foundations of the theory of probability. For the next 150 or so years, however, probability theory was solely concerned with developing a mathematical analysis of games of chance, until another renowned French mathematician, Pierre-Simon Laplace began to apply probabilistic ideas to diverse scientific and practical problems, ultimately leading to formalization of the theory of errors, actuarial mathematics, and statistical mechanics. More than a century later, in 1933, Russian mathematician Andrey Kolmogorov outlined an axiomatic approach that forms the basis for the modern theory of probability. Today, it is hard to think of a domain of modern science that does not make extensive use of the ideas and mechanics of probability, and more and more aspects of everyday life are also being framed in probabilistic perspectives. It might even be reasonable to go as far as saying that nowadays, rational decision-making and probabilistic thinking are inseparable.

And yet, probabilistic decision-making is not as common as might be expected. The reason for that is encapsulated in subjectivity of sensemaking. Many individual and group decisions alike are 'personal' in the sense of being based on or influenced by personal feelings, tastes, or opinions; consequently, some alternatives or outcomes might be preferred to others. The important point here is that it is neither realistic nor necessary to set aside subjective beliefs – it is sufficient to simply use objectively derived probabilities as the basis for diminishing the impact of potentially biased beliefs. Of course just because a particular viewpoint is subjective does not necessarily mean that it is biased or otherwise flawed – that said, subjective beliefs also tend to lack corroboration, and it is that absence of broader validation that gives rise to the possibility of bias. Developing robust probabilistic thinking capabilities offers the most direct and effective pathway to circumventing the potential pitfalls of unfounded beliefs.

The focus of this chapter is on examining the interplay between the broad and general notion of probability and the idea of multi-source evidence amalgamation, evaluation, and synthesis. When looked at from a more practical or operational perspective, the goal of the ensuing analysis is to lay out a general rationale and the 'how-to' mechanics detailing the process that can be used to conclusively summarize the totality of dissimilar and divergent evidence.

Decision Uncertainty

Organizational decision-making commonly entails making choices under conditions of uncertainty, in which context objective evidence offers means of reducing choice-related doubts. Broadly characterized, *uncertainty* is a reflection of a general state of ambiguity regarding the future; it connotes a nonspecific opacity or insecurity regarding the future in general. From the perspective of a decision at hand, it is instructive to think of uncertainty in terms of *degree of knowability*, or the extent to which it can be reduced with the help of tangible facts or probabilistic estimates. In other words, a decision-maker's uncertainty can be a result of unfamiliarity with decision-pertinent information, or inability (or unwillingness) to make use of probabilistic inferences. For example, a brand manager contemplating introducing a brand extension may be unfamiliar with outcomes of similar efforts undertaken by other brands in the same sector, or that manager may not have access to customer analytics-based demand projections. In either case, the degree of knowability is a function of two somewhat independent factors: the scope of ambiguity and the availability of dependable ambiguity-reducing information.

Under most circumstances, more universal, or more broadly scoped uncertainties tend to be less knowable than those pertaining to more specific matters. For instance, during organizational restructuring it is easier to reduce uncertainty pertaining to the reaction of Employee X than the entire department or the entire organization because, in analytical sense, there are fewer factors to consider (i.e., only those that matter to Employee X) and no complicating interactions or systemic interdependencies need to be taken into account. The second of the two degree of knowability factors, the availability of ambiguity-reducing information, cannot be meaningfully surmised in the context of a simple yes vs. no assessment – what is needed is a deeper examination of organizational efforts and commitment to making the required information readily available. It is well known that factual 'what-is' type of information is generally preferred to probabilistic 'what might be' type insights, not only because the latter is more speculative but also because assimilation of probabilistic evidence requires greater reasoning acuity – simply put, it is more difficult to ground organizational decisions in statistical inferences. Hence, it is always possible that when probabilistic evidence is not readily available, it might be because it is indeed inaccessible, or it might be because making it available has not be pursued with sufficient veracity.[1]

Becoming a thoughtful and confident user of probabilistic evidence calls for rudimentary competency in three, somewhat distinct dimensions of *probabilistic thinking*: computational, inferential (or statistical), and evidentiary. *Computational thinking* is a reflection of one's understanding of general data sourcing, data feature engineering, and curation processes that produce what ultimately become the informational foundation from which probabilistic estimates are derived. *Inferential thinking* is a manifestation of one's familiarity with scientific means of extracting valid and reliable insights from data, which encompasses the overall logic of drawing inferences from data as well as the core tools, such as hypothesis testing, used. And lastly, *evidentiary thinking*, discussed in more detail in the prior chapter, is a reflection of one's ability to use analyses-derived insights as evidence in the decision-making process.

Although it is intuitively obvious why a user of inferences drawn from data should have a general understanding of the logic of statistical inference (inferential thinking) or the manner in which such information should be used (evidentiary thinking), it is reasonable to ask why the same user needs familiarity with data sourcing and curation processes (computational thinking). The short answer is believability. When data analytic results happen to be in alignment with previously held beliefs all is good, primarily because of the self-affirmation instinct (information that does not contradicts one's prior beliefs poses no threat to self-concept and thus is easily assimilated; it is indeed rare for people to question the validity of information that confirms their beliefs). However, when analytic results contradict one's prior beliefs distress ensues, which triggers defensive reactions, quite commonly taking the form of questioning the accuracy of data or correctness of inferences drawn from data. It thus follows that evidence that challenges decision-makers' prior beliefs stands better chance of being accepted and used (assuming, of course, that it is warranted), if the user has a basic understanding of the full process that produced that evidence.

As noted earlier, insights produced through analyses of pertinent organizational data give rise to probabilistic evidence, or substantiation that represents best available approximation of facts that may not be fully knowable. Probabilistic estimates are now ubiquitous, with perhaps no better example that weather forecasts, which have been expressing the possibility of events such as precipitation in terms of likelihood ranging from 0% to 100% since first introduced by the US National Weather Service in 1965. And although the notion of probability as exemplified by weather forecasts sounds quite simple and uniform, there are actually numerous critically important considerations that need to be taken into account to make proper and productive use of this important concept.

Probability as Uncertainty-Reducing Tool

Prior to the 17th century, the term 'probable' was synonymous with 'approvable' and was used in reference to opinions or actions reasonable individuals would hold or undertake. The more formalized, or mathematically explicit treatment of probability, known as the *probability theory*, can be traced back to the 16th century and the first attempts to analyze the games of chance.[2] The initial probability estimation work focused almost exclusively on the more mathematically manageable discrete events, and was later expanded to include continuous variables largely through work of Pierre-Simon Laplace; the modern probability theory is based on the seminal work of Andrei Kolmogorov.[3]

There are two distinct and dissimilar approaches to probability estimation: Bayesians and frequentist. The former, named after Thomas Bayes, an English clergyman and statistician who developed what is now known as Bayes' Theorem, relates conditional and marginal probabilities of two random events. Broadly speaking, Bayesian probability treats likelihood as measure of the state of knowledge, known and available to the decision-maker at decision time. As such, it is a function of largely subjective prior beliefs (of the decision-maker and/or decision-influencers) and past outcomes or objective data; it is particularly well suited to problems characterized by sparse or otherwise undependable or poorly projectable historical events, as exemplified by acts of terror.

Frequentist approach to probability estimation, as implied in the name, is a strictly observation-based, empirical method. Relying on objective data collected by means of experiments or recorded historical occurrences, frequentist estimation posits that the probability of a random variable reflects the relative frequency of occurrence of the observed outcome. Under the frequentist view, if 2% of publicly traded companies end up entangled in securities class action litigation on annual basis, on average, a given publicly traded company faces 2% chance of incurring this type of litigation. It follows that frequentist estimation is particularly well suited to problems characterized by abundant historical events and relatively stable longitudinal trends, as exemplified by annual auto accident counts.

In the everyday language of business, probability estimation is simply an attempt to predict unknown outcomes based on known parameters. For instance, weather forecasters strive to predict future conditions such as air temperature, the amount of precipitation, or the amount of sunshine, using historical trends and weather element interdependencies. Using statistical likelihood estimation techniques, forecasters can estimate unknown parameters based on known (i.e., historical) outcomes. That said, the users of the resultant estimates are rarely cognizant of which of the above two broad approaches was utilized, although the estimates can differ substantially based on the choice of an approach. The reason for that is that while the frequentist approach only leverages historical outcome data, the Bayesian method combines objective historical outcome data with subjective judgment, which can significantly alter forward-looking projections. As suggested earlier, when historical data are robust and cross-time trends fairly stable the frequentist approach is likely to produce more dependable probability estimates, whereas Bayesian approach is preferred when data are sparse and/or the phenomenon in question is highly variable. Estimation method notwithstanding, probabilistic inference can yield sound forward-looking predictions, which, in turn, can materially reduce decision-making uncertainty.

Business analysts tend to be concerned with three basic types of probability: marginal, joint, and conditional. *Marginal probability* is the probability of a given variable assuming a specific value, irrespective of the values of other variables; it is exemplified by the probability of an automotive insurance claim cost exceeding a specific threshold, such as $10,000. *Joint probability* captures the chances of two or more events occurring together, as exemplified by the probability of an automotive accident occurring in inclement weather conditions and involving two or more vehicles. And lastly, *conditional probability* expresses the chances that a given event, such as an automotive accident, will occur given that one or more other events, such as inclement weather or speeding, are also present.

Often overlooked by practitioners due to their esoteric character, frequency distributions are nonetheless essential to understanding the decision-making value of probability, because they offer elegant means of summarizing the spread of possible values that a random variable can assume. Although the practical task of compiling a frequency distribution is fairly simple, essentially entailing tabulation of events of interest described in terms of outcomes of interest, such as the cost of individual accidents, the underlying mathematical descriptions can be comparatively technical, possibly contributing to the reluctance to make better use of those tools. Still, those ultimately conceptually straightforward data analytic instruments offer succinct summaries of expected future developments of interest, which can offer an often-needed dose of empirical reality. It is worth noting that a possible simplification is offered by re-casting the raw probability distribution values in terms of more intuitive percentiles,[4] although a more in-depth exploration of the underlying mechanics falls outside the scope of this book.

Dependability of Probabilistic Evidence

'Chance favors the prepared mind' wrote Louis Pasteur, 19th-century biologist and chemist renowned for discovering the principles of vaccination, fermentation, and pasteurization (the last named after him). His words are timeless although what constitutes the 'prepared mind' continues to change. Early in the evolution of human civilizations, prepared mind was informed by description of natural phenomena, as exemplified by writings of Aristotle, which eventually (circa 17th century) gave rise to theoretical scientific knowledge, such as Newton's laws. As science and technology continued to advance, the prepared mind started to be informed by experimentally derived insights, best exemplified by the Large Hadron Collider experiments, and most recently data-intensive science where mining of vast quantities of multi-sourced data is the source of new knowledge. Turning to, well, more ordinary pursuits of organizational decision-making, the growing reliance on data as a source choice-guiding knowledge underscores the importance of recognizing that since practically all organizational data combine informative insights and informationless noise, all inferences drawn from data are potentially flawed. And so just as medical-practice-oriented EBP is highly concerned with critically appraising the soundness of scientific research findings, management-practice-oriented EBP should emphasize thorough assessment of the dependability of organizational data and insights derived from analyses of those data.

Generally speaking, there are three potential reasons for why data analyses produced information might turn out to be incorrect – those are problems with (1) data, (2) methods, and (3) interpretation. There are numerous reasons for data errors, encompassing how data are captured, retrieved, curated, and used; the specific reasons for data errors notwithstanding, prior to being analyzed all data need to be thoroughly reviewed and validated, which can be tedious and time-consuming. It is not just the sheer willingness to invest the requisite time and effort that matter – those conducting data due diligence have to have a way of knowing what constitutes an incorrect value for a particular data element, which can be a challenge, especially for poorly documented data sources. Should data pass the due diligence process, the possibility of analytic errors needs to be considered next to ascertain if data were analyzed using appropriate, vis-à-vis the expected outcome, methods, and if those methods were used correctly. Lastly, assuming data and methodological correctness, the possibility of erroneous or otherwise flawed result interpretation also needs to be considered. The following hypothetical example illustrates the potential pitfalls.

The dean of a business school wanted to estimate average earnings of the school's alumni who graduated within the past five years, and consequently requested his director of alumni relations to work to collect the needed information. Using several repeated waves of survey mailings targeting graduates, the school's director of alumni relations was able to secure employment and income data representing about 70% of the qualifying alumni pool (i.e., those who completed their degrees within the last five years). Upon the initial review of the available data, it was noted that range of incomes was very wide, largely due to a couple of outliers who reported exceptionally high incomes, several orders of magnitude higher than the next highest group. To the director's delight, the average income, computed using all available data and estimated using the mean statistic, was quite high, which in his view would help to further solidify the school's reputation. Should the dean of the school be concerned when using the average income information estimated in that manner?

At the first glance, it may seem that the evidence is indeed sound, as it used the actual data reported by the individual alumni. However, the presence of a small number of abnormally high incomes created the possibility of mean-estimated average value becoming upwardly biased, which would be particularly so if the underlying sample size was modest. The outlying values could have been left out of the analysis, or median rather than mean estimate could have been used. In addition, the nonresponse bias (i.e., the 30% of qualifying alumni who did not provide the requested income information) was not considered – were the nonrespondents a random subset of the initial sample, or were they skewed toward lower-income earners who chose not to report their earnings? Organizational data can be a source of powerful evidence, but it is essential to keep in mind that because data are almost always imperfect, insights derived from data can inform or mislead, and the difference maker can be one or two seemingly inconspicuous data usage choices.

Evidence Pooling

In many, if not most, organizational choice-making contexts, a decision-maker could plausibly take advantage of numerous individual bits of evidence, which would necessitate combining those pieces into a singular, conclusive whole. Paralleling the notion of construct validity used in behavioral sciences, particularly psychology and sociology, the task of joining together and reconciling distinct slices of evidence can be seen as the task of ascertaining *convergent validity*, or the degree to which multiple indicators (i.e., individual pieces of evidence) are suggestive of a similar choice. As such, this notion can be seen as data analytic operationalization of the concepts of preponderance of evidence and weight of evidence discussed in Chapter 5.

When considered from the standpoint of likelihood estimation, the process of amalgamating of available evidence should be geared toward estimation of *pooled probability*, defined here as the emergent possibility jointly suggested by the combination of available evidence. When appraising convergent validity of the resultant estimates, the two key concerns underpinning trustworthiness of pooled probability are the accuracy of, and confidence in, aggregation rules employed. Those rules, in turn, need to be considered in the somewhat homogenizing context of the three broad types of evidence: anecdotal, research, and statistical. Hence, the process of combining diverse bodies of evidence is comprised of two distinct steps: (1) within-type review and reconciliation and (2) cross-type amalgamation, as graphically illustrated in Figure 6.1.

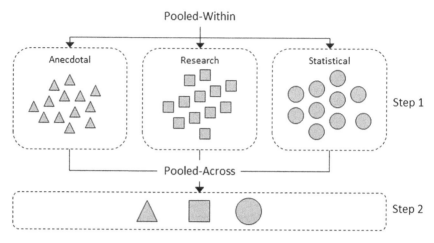

FIGURE 6.1 Two Stages of Evidence Pooling.

Anecdotal Evidence

Expert judgment is commonly viewed as one of the most dependable sources of subjective evidence because it allows decision-makers to tap into the tacit knowledge accumulated by those with considerable experience and expertise in a domain of knowledge. That said, it is generally not advisable to rely on a single expert's opinion because doing so precludes objective reliability assessment. When utilizing informational inputs from multiple subject matter experts, the question of combining those into a singular forecast arises. By far, the most common approach is to average their opinions,[5] as it has been shown that the accuracy of aggregated judgment increases monotonically as a function of the number of experts pooled, but at a diminishing rate that is tied to cross-expert similarity. The most common aggregation mechanisms make use of weighted or unweighted linear combinations of individual, that is, expert-specific, estimates, which is sometimes referred to as a *linear opinion pool*. Averaging pooled opinions also necessitate the choice of individual input weights – should all forecasts be equally weighted or should some be weighted more heavily than others? In general, when individual advisors are equally qualified and their forecasts relied on approximately equal number of decision factors, equal weighting is recommended; on the other hand, when there are material cross-advisor experience or decision factor differences, opinions of more experienced advisors and/or those whose forecasts were based on more explicit considerations ought to be weighted more heavily. There is substantial empirical support attesting to the benefits of linear opinion pools from fields as diverse as medicine, economics, weather, and psychology[6]; to assure best possible outcome, it is essential to make sure that the individual estimates are maximally diagnostic but minimally dependent on one another.

An alternative approach to opinion pooling can be characterized as *behavioral aggregation*. Here, an attempt is made to generate agreement among the experts through interactive sharing and exchange of knowledge and perspectives. Process-wise, it can be done in a focus group-like, face-to-face meeting, or remotely via a questionnaire, where several rounds of inputs are gathered from individual experts, aggregated and shared with the group after each round (formally, this is known as the Delphi method). A key limitation of behavioral aggregation is that those methods typically do not provide conditions under which the experts can be expected to reach agreement; it is not unusual for some experts to hold firmly to their individual forecasts, effectively disallowing the convergence of opinions.

An important, albeit a technical consideration is that of the magnitude of the amount of variability in a set of expert opinions (known as **variance** in statistics). Low variability is suggestive of high degree of cross-expert similarity, whereas high variability is indicative of potentially large differences across experts. Hence, it is important to not only consider the averaged opinion but also the degree of variability that is associated with that value. In general, pooled-across-experts estimates that exhibit low variability are more dependable than those that exhibit noticeably higher variability.

Another important and widely used type of anecdotal evidence is *industry benchmarks*, which offer standard points of reference against which some organizational choices may be compared. Almost always, those yardsticks are manifestations of collective, in the sense of representing a cross-section of opinions or experiences, and widely accepted norms, thus are conceptually similar to linear opinion pools. Although often representing fairly rough approximations, those metrics nonetheless offer sound decision evaluation thresholds in situations such as evaluation of the efficacy of marketing promotions or procurement of insurance coverage.

Not all anecdotal evidence, however, takes the form of expert opinions or industry benchmarks – illustrative cases, examples, and even hearsay are all used periodically as circumstantial substantiation or refutation of a claim or a point of view. Given the generally unscientific (or pseudoscientific), nonrepresentative, and conclusion-laden nature of that type of evidence, it is difficult to subject those claims to any type of averaging, or other forms of objectification. Not surprisingly, those often singular inputs should be used as sparingly as possible, if at all. Lacking corroboration, one-off anecdotes could not only be highly atypical – they could be an expression of the decision-maker's protection of a biased perspective. Consequently, such one-off supports should be placed at the very bottom of the hierarchy of evidence.

Research Evidence

Historically, reviews of scientific research were highly narrative and subject to individual reviewers' mindset and diligence (to be sure, that is still the case with individual research studies). The emergence of EBP in medicine, and the broader domain of health care, has led to the development of more thorough and more objective means of reviewing and synthesizing of topic-specific research outcomes. Known as *systematic review* (SR), those more structured, purposeful, and persistent efforts are perhaps best exemplified by the Cochrane Collaboration. A formally organized (in 1993) international cooperation aiming to facilitate SR of health-care-related research, Cochrane, as it is now known, offers a compelling case study in how large scale – in terms of the number of contributors – and focused – in terms of topics – can vastly enhance the accessibility and the value of scientific research to practitioners.

From the process point of view, SR comprises four steps: asking answerable questions, acquiring the research evidence, appraising the quality of the evidence, and aggregating the evidence. Implied in the SR process is the existence of distinct, objectively agreed on research topics, along with a considerable degree of topical convergence across individual research studies. In fact, one of the key reasons Cochrane has been so successful is that research in hard sciences, such as medicine, exhibits high degrees of epistemological consensus, along with an equally high degree of research convergence. Unfortunately, that is rarely the case in management and other soft sciences, such as management, where the efficacy of SR initiatives geared toward summarization and synthesis of distinct-but-related research streams has been questioned by researchers and practitioners alike. Skeptics argue SR is considerably less effective because management research output is not epistemologically mature, and it is also less cohesive. Consequently, while academic health care research is widely and commonly consumed by health care practitioners, that is not the case with theoretical management research, as evidenced by the earlier discussed, well-known academic-practice gap. Epistemologically inconsistent, in addition to also being seen as dismissive of practitioners and their needs, jargon-laden, overly mathematical and abstract, theoretical management research is simply a weak influencer of managerial decision-making.

Still, while the field of management has not seen Cochrane-like grass roots research compiling, assessing, and disseminating initiatives, there have nonetheless been some notable efforts aimed, at least in part, at spurring greater academic research convergence and practical applicability. For instance, some large-scale management research-focused data and research compilations, such as the Profit Impact of Market Strategies (PIMS) studies and database may be seen as notionally similar to Cochrane, though those research undertakings are methodologically substantially different from SR focused collaborations. Briefly described, PIMS is a comprehensive, long-term study of the performance of strategic business units of about 3,000 companies representing a cross-section of industries. Originally started at General Electric in the mid-1960s, briefly hosted by Harvard University in the 1970s, it subsequently morphed into a standalone nonprofit organization called The Strategic Planning Institute, which continues working on the development and applications of PIMS data. Although it has a broad appeal, PIMS database is not a research collaborative working to summarize and synthesize topic-specific empirical research but a proprietary source of data, and though it supports a wide range of research initiatives, itself it is not a repository of critically reviewed research outcomes.

However, even though theoretical management research is comparatively incohesive and epistemologically immature, there is still value in looking into applicable findings. It is not only because of the possibility of coming across thought-provoking insights, but also because when combined with anecdotal and operational data derived evidence, the resultant knowledge base can materially reduce the degree of decision-specific uncertainty. Moreover, decision-making prudence suggests that, looking past an entire category of decision inputs could possibly infuse the sensemaking process with bias. And so while academic research may indeed warrant the 'self-referential' label, excluding applicable (to the decision at hand) and critically reviewed findings of empirical research studies would effectively render managerial sensemaking self-referential as well.

Focusing on the actual conduct of management research summaries, it is important to note the key differences between SR and the more traditional *narrative reviews* commonly used in theoretical research studies. The latter tend to be somewhat opportunistic in the sense that they rarely entail systematic search of the literature, instead focusing on subsets of studies in areas determined by availability and author preferences, thus while informative, narrative reviews often include an element of selection bias. Those reviews can also be inconclusive, if not outright confusing, especially when similar studies have divergent findings and conclusions, and the primary motivation of those conducting narrative reviews is to lay a foundation for their own research, rather than to provide a complete assessment of the state of knowledge in a particular domain. Being built around a predetermined, detailed and comprehensive plan and search strategy, SR are expressly focused on reducing selection bias by identifying, reviewing, and synthesizing all relevant studies on a particular topic. Thus, unlike narrative reviews, SR are motivated by the desire to produce comprehensive, conclusion focused, and objective summarizations of the totality of empirical research derived, domain specific knowledge.

SR can also include a statistical assessment component in the form of meta-analyses, which make use of quantitative techniques to synthesize the data from several studies into a single numeric measure or a summary *effect size*. This is especially useful when applying the results of academic research studies to organizational situations. That is because academic research tends to equate importance with the notion of 'statistical significance', the goal of which is to assure non-spuriousness of observed associations or effects, but not necessarily 'practical significance', or materiality of research produced associations or effects. Thus the 'how large/strong is the difference/association' type of assessment associated with using effect size can be quite helpful when evaluating practical ramifications of scientific research findings. It should be noted that though meta-analyses can be used within a broader endeavor of SR, it is nonetheless a standalone methodology that can be, and is often, used on standalone basis.

Operational Data Evidence

Informational needs of organizational decision-makers continue to evolve. The invention of steam engine and the ensuing First Industrial Revolution created informational needs that did not exist earlier; a little more than a century later, electricity- and petroleum-fueled – figuratively and literally – Second Industrial Revolution presented organizational decision-makers with a new set of informational dilemmas. And more recently, the advent of digitization and automation, seen by many as the Third Industrial Revolution, is posing questions not asked before. However, in contrast to the earlier evolutionary industrial shifts, the Age of Digitization and Automation is also delivering torrents of informational raw materials, now commonly referred to as 'big data'. Continuously generated by the already vast yet still expanding data origination and interchange web of human-to-human, human-to-machine, and machine-to-machine interactions, data currently on-hand or otherwise available to business organizations hold the key not only to competitiveness of organizations, but also to their very survival. As often noted by management thinkers and practitioners alike, 'change is the only constant', and given the ever faster pace of change, detailed, timely, and accurate data generated by the modern transactional and communication infrastructure offer organizations an opportunity to infuse ongoing decision-making with highly context-, time- and choice-specific insights.

Based on acquisition and usage, organizational data can be divided into two broad domains: batch and streaming. *Batch data* can be thought of as legacy, best exemplified by the UPC[7] point-of-sales scanner data, first introduced in mid-1970s and now captured by virtually all retailers. Those data represent periodic (i.e., when, for instance, a store is open and an item is being purchased) recordings of states and events; are usually extracted and analyzed intermittently, hence the name 'batch', and their informational soundness takes the form of validity, reliability, and projectability. Batch datasets are predominantly numeric and structured, meaning easier to analyze, tend to be focused on specific types of interchanges, such as product purchases, and tend to suffer from relatively slow refresh cycles, which is a consequence of typically complex, multi-point origination, and processing flows. *Streaming data*, which represent far more recent addition to the organizational data universe, are a product of ongoing recording of states and events carried out by the seemingly ever-growing variety of always-on sensory and recording systems and devices, as exemplified by tracking data. Characterized by a combination of high volumes and velocity, and rich type and source variety, streaming data are central to many current and emerging automated and autonomous decision engines, thus the informational value of that diverse data category are accuracy, completeness, and timeliness.

The rich diversity of types and sources of organizational data is suggestive of a need for *metadata*, which somewhat tautologically defined, is data about data. Operationally, it is a summary view of the individual variables contained in the dataset expressed in terms of the key statistical descriptors, such as value ranges and the corresponding central tendencies, the average amount of variability, as well as the assessment of coverage and accuracy. Although historically more familiar to academicians than to practitioners, the concept of metadata is gaining popularity among the latter as the amount and diversity of data contained in corporate repositories continues to grow to the point of becoming overwhelming. In the world of corporate databases, even the well-annotated ones, that is, those accompanied by clear data model descriptions and comprehensive data dictionaries, are often just a hodgepodge of some well- and some sparsely populated variables or discontinued, definitionally amended metrics, with little indication as to what is analytically usable and what is not. Thus, when metadata information is not available, the task of finding the 'right' data can become riddled with time-consuming and confidence-shaking corrective re-work.

In practice, no data source can be analyzed in its entirety; thus, analyses of organizational data make extensive use of sampling, discussed in more detail in Chapter 2, which necessitates sample-to-population projections. In addition, since organizational data represent the past but organizational decisions look to the future, the now-to-future projections are also necessary. The combination of those two core considerations frames the context within which data are translated into meaningful information. Interestingly, drawing inferences from organizational data brings together scientific theory testing and applied knowledge generation, which not only gives rise to opportunities but can also spell out problems.

Although rarely compared side-by-side, theory testing and applied knowledge creation differ on some very important dimensions. Perhaps most importantly, theory testing aims to uncover universally true knowledge claims, whereas applied analyses focus on the delineation of drivers of competitive advantage. Both undertakings make use of hypothesis testing methods, especially tests of statistical significance (SSTs), which offer means of ascertaining the generalizability of sample-derived effects. (It is worth noting that although SSTs are widely used by theoreticians and practitioners, they are nonetheless widely criticized on methodological and practical grounds.[8] Of the multiple criticisms levied against SSTs, perhaps the most damning one is the tests' well-known dependence on sample size, commonly manifesting itself in a persistent correlation between the number of records used in significance testing and the likelihood of detecting statistically significant effects.[9]) Interestingly, practitioners' interest in SSTs is manifestly different from theoreticians' interest in those tests. The former are most interested in affirming the robustness or tangibility of competitive edge producing insights, while the latter are motivated by the search for universally true generalizations -those differences have, well, significant consequences.

One of the resultant and questionable practices is distinguishing between *statistical* and *practical* levels of significance. It has become a commonplace in industry applications to expressly differentiate between statistically significant findings that are also deemed practically significant and those that are not deemed practically significant, or stated differently, 'statistically significant results that should be acted on' and 'statistically significant results that do not warrant action'. Let us pause for a minute: Isn't there something unsettling about the manifestly objective, quantitative conclusions being effectively reassessed based almost entirely on subjective criteria? Consider the tendency to search for, interpret, focus on, and remember information in a way that confirms one's preconceptions (confirmation bias), or seeing as more immediate or relevant outcomes that occurred more recently (availability heuristic) – superimposing 'practical' over 'statistical' significance clearly opens the floodgates of cognitive bias. The essence of statistical significance tests is to infuse objectivity into the process of assessing the dependability of data analytic insights – using a judgment-based 'override' effectively nullifies those efforts.

Still, given their pass-fail character, when applied to a large sample size, SST will effectively deem very small size effects as significant as those that are considerably more pronounced (e.g., all effects that are significant at, let's say 0.05, are equally significant, their magnitudinal differences notwithstanding). Without getting tangled up in technically esoteric deliberations, SST are narrowly focused on estimating the probability that the effect of interest did not occur by chance, which means it does not represent a random, spurious event. Thus, as used in that context, 'significant' does not mean 'important' – it merely means nonrandom. Some nonrandom knowledge claims can be considered trivial if they do not address key aspects of the decision at hand – on the other hand, other nonrandom insights may shed new light on the decision at hand and thus be considered important. Consequently, even if adjusted for the inflating effects of sample size,[10] tests of statistical significance offer only a partial answer to the fundamental question of 'is the knowledge claim true (i.e., is it nonrandom), and does it matter (i.e., is it important)'? To fully answer that question, it is essential to combine the assessment of properly sample-size-adjusted statistical *significance* with an estimate of the *effect size*. A quantitative measure of the strength of a phenomenon, the effect size is typically expressed as a standardized metric, or one that re-casts absolute magnitudes in terms of the number of standard deviations (think of the z-score commonly associated with standard normal distribution). There are numerous computational variants of the effect size measure including standardized mean differences, weighted mean differences, or risk ratios, and the choice of a specific formulation is largely context- and data-driven. Depending on the type of comparison (e.g., a comparison of the quantity of interest to a benchmark or a comparison of two independent quantities), different effect size estimation formulas need to be used; interpretation-wise, effects smaller than 0.2 are generally considered trivial, 0.2 is considered small but not trivial, 0.5 is deemed to be medium, and 0.8 or higher is commonly considered a large effect size.

Cross-Type Amalgamation

Insights derived from anecdotal, research, and statistical evidence rarely easily fit together. Although there is a considerable degree of within-type variability, it is reasonable to characterize anecdotal evidence comprised primarily of pooled expert opinions and industry benchmarks, and research evidence comprised primarily of empirical academic studies as being substantially more general, in the sense of being non-context specific, than evidence derived from analyses of transactional and other organizational data. Although perhaps less visible, there are significant differences between conclusions drawn from scientifically unsubstantiated practitioner opinions or rules of thumb (anecdotal evidence), and scientifically validated but situationally vague, abstract research findings. And yet, in a decision-making context, those differences have to be overcome because to have decision-guiding value, all available evidence needs to be synthesized into a singular conclusion, as implied by the notion of preponderance of evidence. Stated differently, though individual informational inputs might individually suggest somewhat different courses of action, when considered jointly, *conclusive convergence* should be the goal.

What if the differently sourced evidence is persistently non-convergent? Starting from the base premise that not all evidence is equally informationally robust, a *hierarchy of importance* can be used as a way of resolving the non-convergence. Hierarchies are widely used in organizations, with the most obvious example provided by organizational governance, which almost universally use control structures where every entity in the organization, except one, is subordinate to a single other entity. Paralleling that logic, individual evidence types can be ascribed higher or lower levels of 'authority', which in the context of decision-making can take the form of weights assigned to different informational inputs, with evidence type weights representing credence ascribed to individual sources of insights. The basis for credence ascription can, in turn, be derived from assessing each general evidence source's objectivity and decision specificity – the more objective and more on-point a source the more credence it should be ascribed, ultimately manifesting itself in the form of a higher weight. The actual magnitude (of individual weights) estimation is more challenging, but in the absence of established, generalizable rules, the approach recommended here is to use what could be called a *doubling rule*, which is as follows: The individual types of evidence are rank-ordered from the least objective and decision-specific to the most objective and decision-specific, following which weights are assigned in the manner where each higher ranked type's weight is double of the lower ranked type, and all weights add up to about 100%. These ideas will be explored in more detail in the next chapter.

Notes

1 See Barends, E., D. M. Rousseau, and R. Briner (2014), 'Evidence-Based Management: The Basic Principles', www.cebma.org.
2 The earliest known contribution in this area is attributed to an accomplished Italian Renaissance mathematician, astrologer and gambler, Gerolamo Cardano (1501–1576).
3 Kolmogorov, A. N., *Foundations of the Theory of Probability*, 1950 (originally published in German in 1933).
4 Technically, that entails standardizing the original values, such as purchase amounts or insurance claim settlements, by converting ([value-mean]/standard deviation) each data point to a value that represents the number of standard deviations from the mean, known as z-score.
5 It can be accomplished by computing the arithmetic mean in situations in which the expert forecast addresses a continuous phenomenon (e.g., expected dollar cost), or selecting the most frequently chosen option in situations in which the forecast addresses a categorical phenomenon (e.g., 'high', 'medium', or 'low' threat level).
6 It has been suggested, however, that nonlinear, or more specifically beta-transformed linear pooling can improve accuracy although a more in-depth discussion of that methodology falls outside the scope of this book.
7 Universal Product Code, it is the barcode found on trade items, mainly used for scanning at the point of sale.
8 See Satake, E. (2015), *Statistical Methods and Reasoning for the Clinical Sciences: Evidence-Based Practice*, Plural Publishing, San Diego, CA.
9 This can be easily verified with the help of one of many online statistical significance calculators by fixing the estimation parameters while only changing the sample size from, let's say 300 to 3,000.
10 For more details, see Banasiewicz, A. (2005), 'Marketing Pitfalls of Statistical Significance Testing', *Marketing Intelligence and Planning*, 23(6), pp. 515–528.

7

THE 3E FRAMEWORK

It is widely known, though perhaps not as widely acknowledged that management is not a profession, but merely an occupation. Unlike professionals such as physicians, engineers, or attorneys, managers do not receive standardized education based on an agreed upon body of knowledge, nor do they need to be accredited to practice their craft. Moreover, the practice of management is also noticeably different from professional practices. An attorney, for instance, tends to deal with largely fixed sets of problems and constraints: A client in need of assistance, a problem that needs to be correctly identified and framed, an appropriate solution that needs to be identified, and the final resolution. Under most circumstances, as a subject matter expert, the attorney has high degree of control over the outcome and the process, primarily because the problem is contained and the final solution can be objectively assessed. The reality of managerial decision-making is considerably different: Behavior of organizational stakeholders is influenced by a combination of genetic, learned, and situational factors; moreover, in contrast to the controlled attorney-client interactions, organizational decision-making commonly takes place in a largely uncontrollable, often highly volatile environment. The resultant sensemaking ambiguity is a product of informational asymmetry, or the difference between what needs to be known and what is knowable at the decision time.

In fact, the reason that the original conceptualization of evidence-based professional practice was built around systematic reviews of pertinent scientific research was precisely because in that context (the practice of medicine), the bulk of practice-enhancing knowledge was, and still is generated and disseminated by the mostly academic research and publishing ecosystem. As discussed earlier, the same cannot be said about management practice, which only sparingly looks to academic research for knowledge. In fact, the scientific vitality of academic management research has been a subject of vigorous critique not only from practitioners but also from academicians. The former tend to see it as self-referential, jargon laden, excessively retrospective, obsessed with theory, and dismissive of practical considerations, whereas the latter lament the lack of intellectual coherence and highly disjointed nature of the overall research output, patterns of contradicting outcomes, and the lack of objectivity. In fact, the academic-practice gap is so wide and persistent that it constitutes its own area of academic discourse. Why then should management oriented conceptualizations of evidence-based practice keep at trying to emulate the informational scoping of evidence-based medical practice? It is clear why systematic research reviews benefit medical practice, and it is equally clear why the same informational scope will not deliver comparable benefits to management practitioners. The Empirical & Experiential Evidence (3E) framework it built upon that conclusion.

First and foremost, the 3E framework's logic is rooted in explicit recognition of organizational informational and decision-making realities, and the desire to retain the spirit of broadly defined evidence-based practice, manifesting itself in systematic identification and assessment of decision-guiding knowledge. Thus while retaining the spirit of the general six-step ask-acquire-appraise-aggregate-apply-assess evidence amalgamation process, the 3E framework departs sharply from the mindset that frames scientific research focused evidence-based medical practice. Building on the foundation of a comprehensive three-tier informational input classification typology dividing management-practice-relevant informational sources into progressively narrower categories, the framework offers operationally explicit means of identification, amalgamation, and reconciliation of often divergent insights. Its intent is to enable organizational decision-makers to make use of available and applicable empirical (i.e., operational data and academic research based) and experience-sourced insights in a manner that reconciles potentially conflicting insights to reach a singular conclusion.

Organizational Decision-Making

From 1980s till early 2000s, Circuit City was one of the most successful and best-known US retailers. Founded in 1949 as Wards TV[1] in Richmond, Virginia, selling television sets out of the front half of a tire store, the company grew rapidly, changing its name to Circuit City in the late 1970s, by 2003 rising to #151 on the Fortune 500 list of the largest, as measured by revenue, US companies. And yet by 2008, the once high-flying electronics retailer filed for bankruptcy protection, shortly thereafter shuttering all 567 of its stores and laying off all of its roughly 34,000 employees. All while, Circuit City's closest competitor, Best Buy, founded in 1966 as Sound of Music, grew into a global behemoth with annual sales (as of the end of 2017) of more than $40 billion from 1,575 stores worldwide.

In many regards, the two retailers were quite similar although the demise of one and the continuing success of the other can be traced back to significant differences in decision patterns of their senior managers. For instance, in 2001, Circuit City chose to discontinue selling appliances (Best Buy did not); in 2003, the company decided to eliminate its commissioned sales, firing, without notice, 3,900 of its highest-paid salespeople (Best Buy employed hourly associates from the start), and then spent almost $1 billion on stock repurchase between 2003 and 2007, paying on average $20 per share for stock that was worth only a bit over $4/share at the end of 2007 (which, by the way, was around the onset of what is now known as the Great Recession, a deep and prolonged economic downturn which forced retailers to rely on their financial cushions). The perspective of time, not to mention knowledge of outcomes, makes spotting and detailing bad decision patterns rather easy, and though volumes are often written about business organizations going from great to gone, there is ultimately little truly eye-opening knowledge in those accounts. Be it gone and mostly forgotten Circuit City, Radio Shack, Montgomery Ward, Borders Books or Linens 'n Things, or those considered on life support including the once-mighty Sears, K-Mart or JC Penney, are all unique case studies that are ultimately best understood in the context of key managers' decisions. What information, what evidence did Circuit City managers relied on in making their choices? Why were their choices so different from those of Best Buy's managers?

Evidence and Choices

The CEBMa's evidence-based management practice framework, outlined in Chapter 4, includes organizational stakeholders as one of the four sources of evidence (scientific literature, organizational data, and judgment of practitioners are the remaining three sources), which it broadly frames as 'the values and concerns of people who may be affected by the decision'. In the case of Circuit City, it was the company's shareholders who pushed its management into spending nearly $1 billion on stock buybacks (manifestly because stock buybacks tend to positively impact the value of outstanding, in this case held by Circuit City's shareholders, stock), which turned out to be a disastrous decision not only because of the aforementioned loss of value, but even more importantly because it depleted the company of its financial cushion, badly needed to survive the economic downturn that was about to ensue.

A single example certainly neither proves nor refutes a claim, but it raises an important definitional question: what should be considered 'evidence' in evidence-based decision-making? Building on an in-depth analysis of the meaning and the scope of that term, undertaken in Chapter 5, to be considered evidence, any input into the decision-making process has to be either objective or at least it needs to be objectifiable. Individual values or concerns do not meet that requirement as they are clearly subjective – in fact, individually held opinions or beliefs exemplify the very essence of subjectivity. Thus, to the degree to which evidence is meant to offer objective substantiation, subjective values should not be considered evidence. If differences of opinion exist, individually held beliefs are often the cause of those differences, and hardly ever a source of a potential resolution.

In addition, while the currently used (i.e., CEBMa's) framing of organizational stakeholders implies some degree of uniformity of values and concerns, that also tends not to be the case. There are at least five discernible groups of organizational stakeholders: shareholders, employees, regulators, customers, suppliers, and creditors; often, there are significant cross-stakeholder group difference in terms of salient values and concerns or goals and objectives. An illustrative case is offered, once again, by the demise of Circuit City: The company's shareholders were concerned with the falling value of the company stock and thus pushed for the share buyback program, whereas the employees were concerned about losing their livelihood and thus favored conserving cash to support ongoing operations. In this particular context, suppliers' and creditors', and to a lesser extent customers' concerns were more than likely aligned with those of employees, though creditors' concerns were also focused on the company's continuing ability to meet its debt obligations. In less narrowly defined contexts, such as organizational restructuring or mergers and acquisitions, not only are the values and concerns of different shareholder groups likely to diverge, they might be difficult to capture and express in an informationally meaningful manner. All told, it is difficult to see how such a diverse mosaic of largely self-serving values and considerations can yield objective decision-guiding insights.

The Empirical & Experiential Evidence Framework

The essence of evidence-based practice, be it in medicine, policy setting, or management, is that decisions should be guided by the best available evidence. What constitutes 'the best available evidence', however, is not, and should not be universally defined because of manifest differences across distinct domains of professional practice. For instance, in medical practice, the best available evidence is typically derived from empirical research, whereas in policy setting it tends to be experiential learnings, and in business management the best decision-guiding evidence arises out of operational data. Mirroring those differences, the challenges of identifying, assessing, and pooling together of evidence can also vary considerably across the distinct domains of practice, as, for instance, identification and synthesis of pertinent empirical research is procedurally and methodologically different from identification and synthesis of experiential learnings or operational data.

Evidence-based movement originated in the practice of medicine – as noted earlier, in that field, scientific research is, by far, the largest contributor of new knowledge that can be used to improve the efficacy of medical practice. In addition, research-derived insights are quite universal in the sense that most of new treatments addressing many general conditions are applicable to wide cross sections of patients. Moreover, under most circumstances, medical practitioners share in the common goal of working toward the best possible outcome for a patient. However, when applied to the practice of organizational management, those foundational tenets of medicine-inspired evidence-based practice do not stand up to scrutiny. As detailed in preceding chapters, not only is management-related theoretical research not the main supplier of new managerial knowledge, there is a well-documented schism separating theoretical research and managerial practice. Marked by more back-and-forth criticisms than meaningful and enduring collaboration, it is obvious to even a casual observer that management practitioners make very limited use of theoreticians' research. In addition, while medical practitioners tend to be united in pursuit of best treatment options, business practitioners are actively engaged in trying to outperform one another in what is commonly seen of a zero-sum[2] game of competing for scarce customers and resources. All considered, while the reasoning imbedded in medicine-inspired evidence-based practice is a source of tremendously powerful ideas, the 'as-is' adaption of that framework to management fails to recognize critical differences between those two domains of practice. That said, if properly re-framed to reflect the considerably different informational landscape of organizational management, evidence-centric decision-making can help managers move beyond biased, subjective decision mindset.

And so while retaining the key premise of evidence-based practice, which is that decisions should be guided by the best available evidence, the 3E framework posits that the core of organizational decision-guiding evidence should stem from inferences drawn from applicable operational data because of the unparalleled decision specific and timeliness offered by that heterogeneous and informationally diverse source of knowledge. For instance, UPC scanner data captured by virtually all retailers contains product purchase describing details of unequaled granularity and recency, which when combined with descriptive metrics, such as purchase incentives and demographics, can yield far more decision- and situation-specific insights than any other source of evidence. Moreover, reliance on UPC scanner data-derived insights promises the greatest chance of materially improving the efficacy of many brand management and marketing decisions, precisely because of the highly specific and timely nature of those insights.

Still, there are enduring generalizations that transcend the specificity of situational data, but can be discerned through carefully designed empirical research studies. Thus, while for reasons outlined above theoretical research should not be looked to as the primary contributor to evidence-based organizational management practice, it nonetheless can be informationally valuable. In a similar vein, practice-derived generalizations, commonly expressed as norms or benchmarks can also contribute worthwhile, objective insights, as can tacit knowledge of highly practiced and knowledgeable subject matter experts. All considered, while systematic exploration of organizational outcomes data should be the main informational driver of evidence-based managerial practice, no single source of evidence can entirely eliminate all decision-related uncertainty, which underscores the importance of jointly considering all available sources of decision-guiding insights.

It is just as important, however, to expressly acknowledge the relative informational credibility of the four distinct sources of evidence (operational data, empirical research studies, industry benchmarks, and expert judgment) in anticipation of potential cross-source insight divergence. Thus, individual informational inputs should be strength-weighted and evaluated in terms of their degree of concordance with the preponderance of evidence so that when conflicting inputs are encountered, the summary conclusion is shaped by rational evaluation calculus. When approached in that manner, jointly considered and efficacy-weighted totality of available evidence offers the best chance of materially enhancing outcomes of organizational decision-making.

Paralleling the two main dimensions of knowledge discussed in Chapter 2, explicit and tacit, the organizational-management-tailored evidence-based decision-making framework described in this book is built around a typology of evidence (see Chapter 5) that is grounded in clear differentiation between *empirical* (which parallels *explicit* knowledge) and *experiential* (which parallels *tacit* knowledge) evidence (hence the name: Empirical & Experiential Evidence framework). Furthermore, in a manner conceptually similar to other evidence-based practice conceptualizations, most notably the CEBMa's framework outlined in earlier chapters, the 3E framework is built around an implied progression of systematically identifying, evaluating, and making use of decision-related information. However, since the 3E conceptualization is uniquely focused on organizational decision-making, the framework is operational-data-centric, which represents a departure from other evidence-based practice conceptualizations. More specifically, the 3E process begins with three *within-source* steps: *identification* of distinct sources of evidence, *assessment* of the available and applicable data, and *aggregation* of type-specific evidence. The next part of the process encompasses three *cross-source* steps, starting with determination of relative importance *weights*, followed by *agglomeration* of source-specific evidence summaries, and *incorporation* of evidentiary conclusions into the decision-making process. Figure 7.1 offers the graphical summary of the 3E process.

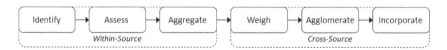

FIGURE 7.1 The 3E Process.

The within-source vs. cross-source distinction is intended to highlight the two-phased essence of the 3E framework, which draws attention to, first, judicious discovery and pooling of all similar, or type-specific data, and, second, thoughtful syndication of distinct types of informational inputs. Although within the organizational context operational data are the dominant source of decision-guiding insights, the 3E conceptualization is nonetheless expressly focused on distilling all pertinent insights into a singular, conclusive set of insights by means of expressly facilitating amalgamating distinct informational sources, and providing a priori resolution of potential informational divergence, which is accomplished through hierarchical importance rank-ordering.

One of the core practical obstacles to establishing a robust fact-based management practice can be characterized as informational over-abundance. From diverse and voluminous torrents of operational and related data, to research outlets numbering in thousands, to the diversity and subjectivity of expert opinions and industry benchmarks, the variety and the volume of potentially decision-pertinent information are overwhelming. Making meaningful use of what is 'out there' is contingent on developing a broad classificatory schema to organize the myriad of informational inputs into mutually exclusive and, at least somewhat, collectively exhaustive categories. The broad basis of such an organizational schema was in fact discussed in Chapter 5, and such general schema is also implied in the 3E process outlined in Figure 7.1.

Another key, and in fact foundational consideration is that, individually, all sources of decision-shaping information – operational data, empirical research studies, industry norms, standards and benchmarks, as well as individual-level experience – are singularly imperfect. Operational data are incomplete and noisy, empirical research methods are probabilistic thus yield only approximately true insights, industry benchmarks are often too generic and frequently outdated, and individual judgment is fraught with perception-warping cognitive bias. However, when the same or similar conclusion arises out of multiple sources of evidence, such cross-evidence type validation lends credibility to the conclusion in question. Broadly characterized as triangulation, such cross-validation is widely used in qualitative research to reduce data source-, researcher-, or theory-related bias, and it is implicitly used in a similar manner as one of the conceptual foundations of the 3E framework.

Informational Triangulation

When confronting routine or atypical choices, *informational triangulation*, or cross-source insight verification, enhances the efficacy of decisions by strengthening the credibility and dependability of available evidence. It tests the consistency of findings obtained through different data and analysis means, and increases the chances of controlling for the most pronounced threats to truthfulness of insights extracted from different informational sources. From the conceptual points of view, informational triangulation is framed in the context of 'what', or source of information, 'how', or means of drawing conclusions, and 'why', or the theoretical framework or logical rationale shaping the insight extraction processes.

The what-how-why evaluative context presents different set of challenges across the spectrum of potential sources of decision-guiding insights. In general, empirical sources of information, which include all manners of data available to organizations and results of scientific research studies, lend themselves more naturally to that three-pronged assessment, whereas experiential sources of information, best exemplified by industry benchmarks and practices, as well as individual-level, experiential knowledge, present far greater assessment challenge. That said, the ultimate point of informational triangulation is to arrive at evidence-derived conclusions that demonstrates the greatest degree of support, which in this case means the strongest degree of cross-evidence type congruence.

'All models are wrong, but some are useful' is an aphorism widely repeated by statisticians.[3] The essence of this assertion suggests that, individually, all sources of knowledge are suspect, but collectively can produce sound decision-guiding knowledge. This is one of the most fundamental assumptions underpinning the evidence assessment framework detailed in this book.

Typology of Evidence

Although the failure of once high-flying Circuit City cannot be attributed to a single cause, analysts tend to agree that the shareholders' push for stock buyback that drained the company's cash reserves heading into a severe economic downturn (the Great Recession of 2007–2008) was a significant contributor to its eventual demise. When considering their strategic options, should Circuit City's managers have factored in the company shareholders' desires into their decision-making process? Or stated more generally, should organizational stakeholders' subjective values and concerns be considered 'evidence', in the same way that data analysis or empirical research generated insights are considered evidence?

There are not many situations where a decision-maker is free of preexisting beliefs, expectations, or 'gut feelings' regarding the most appropriate course of action, primarily because organizational decisions tend to be made by those who are at least somewhat invested, interested, or otherwise connected to the decision at hand. Subjective beliefs and expectations, however, can stem from incomplete or skewed fact base, not to mention the reason-bending impact of numerous cognitive biases. And yet the primary decision-making value of evidence lies in the infusion of perception- or recall-untainted information that can enhance the rationality of one's sensemaking processes. To arrive at what will indeed turn out to be the best decision, the decision-maker needs external-to-self and dependable insights that can either shed new light on current knowledge or introduce an altogether new knowledge. It thus follows that the definition of evidence should be limited to objective and unbiased insights.

Those considerations were captured in the general evidence tree typology discussed in Chapter 5, which categorized organizational decision-pertinent evidence into two broad categories of 'empirical' and 'experiential', with the former further subdivided into 'operational data' and 'empirical research', and the latter broken down into 'expert judgment' and 'norms & standards'. Those still very coarse groupings are further refined into a three-tiered typology of evidence, summarized in Figure 7.2.

The overall evidence grouping logic is built around a nested three-tiered schema, where two broad meta-categories are each comprised of two narrower categories, each of which is, in turn, made up of several distinct subcategories. More specifically, the two meta-categories of evidence, *empirical* and *experiential,* are each comprised of two more narrowly scoped categories of *operational data* and *theoretical research* (empirical), and *norms & standards* and *expert judgment* (experiential).

Within the *empirical* meta-category, the *operational data* category is comprised of three distinct subcategories of *transactional details, communications,* and *descriptive attributes,* which are all still relatively broad types of data that are either directly or indirectly captured by business organizations.[4] For instance, as there

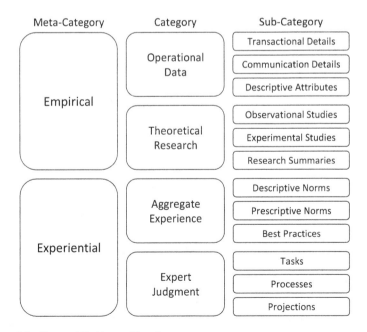

FIGURE 7.2   General Evidence Typology.

are numerous types of transactions that business organizations engage in, there are numerous sources of transactional data, such as product shipments, product purchases, promotional offer redemptions, and many others. Similarly, each of the distinct and different communication channels and modalities produces a unique communication data source and type, and there are copious sources and types of descriptive attributes, which are transactional entity characteristics, as exemplified by demographics or firmographics. Overall, the defining characteristic of operational data as a source of organizational decision-making inputs is that it encompasses a typically enormous varieties and volumes of raw data, which require a combination of vision, data analytical skill, and organizational commitment before it can offer decision-guiding value.

The second of the two categories nested within the empirical meta-category, *theoretical research*, contributes very different types of informational inputs – in contrast to raw materials supplied by operational data sources, theoretical research offers ready-to-use insights. It is important to note that while the domain of theoretical research is very broad, only those efforts that make use of explicit hypotheses tests or other confirmatory or exploratory analyses of observational or experimental data are considered here because those types of studies demonstrate the requisite external-to-self validation. As implied earlier, theoretical research studies can be *observational* or *experimental* – in addition, summarization-focused *research summaries*, which consolidate and reconcile similar types of outcomes from similar studies, are also taken into account. Overall, the defining characteristic of theoretical research as a source of organizational decision-making inputs is that it offers consumption-ready, but not necessarily application- or situation-specific insights.

Turning to the *experiential* meta-category, the *norms & standards* category encompasses several distinct, but similarly minded subsets, most notably *industry benchmarks*, which typically take the form of numeric yardsticks capturing activity or outcome-specific peer averages, *organizational norms,* which are internal (to the organization) expected activity or outcome-specific levels, and *best practices,* which usually describe tried and tested processes and means of accomplishing specific goals. Jointly, those sources of decision inputs can be considered a product of organization- or group-level practical experience, or insights that represent highly aggregate generalizations.

The second of the two experiential categories, *expert judgment*, captures the accumulated tacit knowledge of properly credentialed and practiced individuals. It can manifest itself as application-specific knowledge in the form of *select tasks,* as exemplified by one's knowledge and experience in a specific domain of practice, such as risk modeling, knowledge of *general processes,* as illustrated by familiarity with the process of commercial insurance procurement, and *future projections,* best exemplified by demonstrated expertise in forecasting outcomes of interest, such as frequency and severity of windstorms. In contrast to groupthink-sourced norms and standards, expert judgment is person-specific and thus those individual-level inputs can vary, quite considerably at times, across experts. For that reason, making use of judgment pooling techniques (see Chapter 6), such as the Delphi method, is often recommended.

Strength of Evidence

The previous chapter briefly addressed the idea of persistent evidence non-convergence, suggesting that robust *hierarchy of importance* could be used as a way of resolving such non-convergence. In an operational sense, individual evidence types can be ascribed higher or lower levels of 'authority', which in the context of decision-making can take the form of weights assigned to different informational inputs, with evidence type weights representing credence ascribed to individual sources of insights. The basis for credence ascription can, in turn, be derived from assessing each general evidence source's objectivity and decision specificity – the more objective and more on-point a source the more credence it should be ascribed, ultimately manifesting itself in the form of a higher weight. It was further argued that magnitudes of individual weights could be estimated using the *doubling rule*, according to which the individual types of evidence are rank-ordered from the least objective and decision-specific to the most objective and decision-specific, following which weights are assigned in the manner where each higher ranked type's weight is double of the lower ranked type, and all weights add up to about 100%.

It is reasonable to ask why doubling of importance? The reasoning behind that recommendation stems from the concept developed in the field of experimental psychology known as *just noticeable difference*, which represents an attempt at capturing the amount of change that is needed in order for that change to be detectable. In that context, while it proved to be difficult to derive a universal 'threshold of noticeability' rule, experience suggests that under most circumstances doubling of the starting value tends to be noticeable. It is also important to note the intent behind the introduction of the idea of hierarchy of importance, along with quantitative measures conveying differing levels of importance: It is to enable decision-makers to resolve the earlier mentioned evidence non-convergence situations – it is not to supply means of assessing universal value of evidence types.

Let us now consider some specifics. Using round values (it is an approximation after all), the doubling rule suggests that the meta-category of experiential evidence, which is deemed to be less objective and less decision specific of the two meta-categories, should have an overall weight of 33%, whereas the other meta-category of empirical evidence, which is deemed comparatively more objective and more decision relevant, should be assigned a weight of about 67%.[5] When considered in the context of the hierarchy of importance, the narrower types of evidence can be more difficult to rank-order as the informational efficacy of each source cannot be reliably generalized beyond situational contexts. That said, given that virtually all electronic commercial and personal activities are trackable and recordable, and the resultant data are captured on ongoing basis and a very granular level, it is difficult to imagine an organizational decision context where evidence stemming from operational data would not be deemed most objective and most decision-specific. However, the decision value, in the sense of relative rank-ordering, of the remaining three sources of evidence – expert judgment, norms & standards, and theoretical research – would likely vary across organizational decision contexts. It is important to note that the hierarchy of importance determination should be made following thorough and careful assessment of the informational content, and thus the anticipated decision-guiding value, of each of the three evidence types.

Numeric weights-wise, paralleling the process of pooling of subject matter experts' opinions, the aforementioned four different informational inputs can be amalgamated using a generalized form of the *weighted linear pooling* (WLP) approach (see Chapter 6). The particular rank-ordering notwithstanding, the weakest-to-strongest weight assignment that is suggested by the doubling rule (the weight of the next element is double that of the previous one, with the sum of all weights adding up to 100%) is as follows: 7% – 13% – 27% – 53%.

Assessment of Evidence

Although conceptual frameworks offer essential abstract guidance, it is the supporting operationalizations that ultimately determine the degree to which new behavioral guidelines are implemented. It is the proverbial 'where rubber hits the road', and it can also be seen as a test of the framework's utility – a compelling idea that lacks the 'how-to' details is of little value to organizational decision-makers because without the requisite operational details it cannot bring about the desired behavioral change (and better decision-related outcomes). Thus, the general evidence typology shown in Figure 7.2 calls for an explicit delineation of the analytic manner by which the raw materials that constitute the input into each subcategory will be transformed into decision-guiding insights. For example, the 'transactional details' subcategory of evidence will typically encompass diverse, and quite possibly voluminous pools of data which will require considerable analytical processing to yield meaningful insights; hence, it is necessary to delineate at least the general insight extraction approaches. Figure 7.3 shows the high-level summary of the most appropriate insight extraction approaches.

As graphically depicted there, each of the four categories of evidence calls for a methodologically distinct insight extraction approach, with cross-subcategory variability necessitating the utilization of multiple analytic techniques. Starting

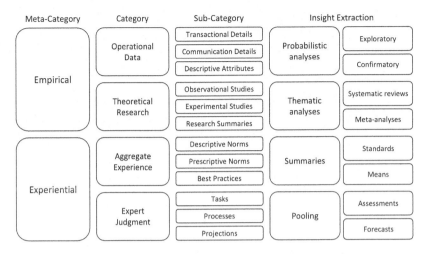

Meta-Category	Category	Sub-Category	Insight Extraction	
Empirical	Operational Data	Transactional Details	Probabilistic analyses	Exploratory
		Communication Details		
		Descriptive Attributes		Confirmatory
	Theoretical Research	Observational Studies	Thematic analyses	Systematic reviews
		Experimental Studies		
		Research Summaries		Meta-analyses
Experiential	Aggregate Experience	Descriptive Norms	Summaries	Standards
		Prescriptive Norms		
		Best Practices		Means
	Expert Judgment	Tasks	Pooling	Assessments
		Processes		
		Projections		Forecasts

FIGURE 7.3 General Evidence Typology with the Supporting Operationalization.

with the more general category – analytic approach linkage, broadly defined *probabilistic analyses* offer the most robust means of extracting decision-guiding insights out of diverse transactional, communication, and other data reservoirs. *Thematic analyses,* on the other hand, are best suited to the task of assessment and synthesis of applicable (to the decision at hand) findings of empirical research studies, which also includes research focused on reconciliation of findings of individual studies addressing a singular topic. The two experiential categories of norms & standards and expert judgment lend themselves to summarization and averaging of applicable insights. *Summarization* offers the most fitting means of amalgamating the applicable industry and the organization's own norms and standards, whereas *pooling* provides the most dependable means of drawing conclusions from often diverse opinions and forecasts of individual experts. A more in-depth discussion of each insight extraction approach follows.

Insight Extraction

Operationalization is the heart and soul of conceptual frameworks. There are multiple reasons for that, with perhaps the most important one being the ease of adoption, which is illustrated by some conceptually compelling ideas that nonetheless failed to deliver the anticipated benefits, manifestly because of lack of clear how-to. A case in point is the widely cited (in the field of risk management) COSO's Enterprise Risk Management framework, the goal of which, as implied in its name, is to offer organizations clear direction and guidance for managing the totality of internal and external threats. And while the framework puts forth compelling arguments in support of the desirability of individual risk level measurement, it offers no appreciable guidance regarding how that is to be done, which ultimately greatly limits the conceptualization's practical value. Though a glaring deficiency, the lack of clear measurement guidelines has a logical explanation in the form of situational risk invariance, the recognition of which likely compelled the architects of the framework to push the measurement specification responsibility onto users of the framework. When considered from that vantage point, the decision to not include explicit risk measurement details might seem quite reasonable, but since it led to undesirable outcomes in the form of diminished framework's usability, it was clearly a questionable choice.

As graphically depicted in Figure 7.3, the how-to of insight extraction is a key part of the 3E framework. Building on the earlier discussion of the within-meta-category, -category, and -subcategory communalities, and cross-meta-category, -category, and -subcategory distinctiveness, the goal of optimal measurement approach identification was to pinpoint methodologies capable of capturing the informational essence of evidence comprising the individual groups. In other words, at which of the three levels of evidence abstraction (meta-categories, categories, and subcategories) was an analytically singular measurement approach most appropriate?

The mix of evidence comprising the two broad meta-categories – empirical and experiential – is too diverse to lend itself to a singular analytical approach because while operational data require considerable curation, feature engineering, and analyses, theoretical research studies typically yield post-analysis findings. At the other end of the evidence categorization continuum, some of the multiple subcategories delineated in Figure 7.3 called for analytically non-distinct approaches (e.g., transactional details and descriptive attributes entail the same or comparable data analytic steps), whereas other ones required analytically distinct operationalizations, as was the case with research summaries and industry benchmarks. Ultimately, the four distinct evidence categories of operational data, theoretical research, norms & standards, and expert judgment were deemed to be most analytically cohesive.

Operational Data

Broadly defined, *operational data* encompass recordings of the routine functioning and activities of a business organization. As can be expected given the wide array of types and sizes of business entities, the makeup and the diversity of operational data can vary rather significantly across organizations. However, considering that all business organizations ultimately exist to produce and/or deliver products or services to customers, when abstracted beyond the specificity of an individual entity, operational data share some general characteristics: Those data usually include transactional details, descriptive and control indicators, flags and counters sourced from multiple electronic interchange systems and divided across numerous tables and files. When considered from informational point of view, operational data are generally captured as a passive (i.e., recording all manner of system details on ongoing basis) by-product of the modern electronic transaction processing and communication infrastructure, which just about guarantees that captured data are a mix of informative metrics (sometimes referred to as 'signal') and non-informative noise, which encompasses anything ranging from incorrect to meaningless details. Moreover, when considered from the point of view of decision-making, data-encoded past is not a perfect predictor of the future, in the sense that past behavioral patterns are only somewhat, though rarely, if ever, fully indicative of future behaviors.

When considered jointly, those two important characterizations of operational data suggest that evidence derived from analyses of those data is probabilistic in nature, as illustrated in Figure 7.4. When thought of as methodological means of extracting insights out of data, *probabilistic analyses* can be either *exploratory* or *confirmatory*. The former, often also characterized as data mining, encompass all analyses seeking to uncover potentially meaningful patterns or relationships, without being guided by any preexisting assumptions or beliefs. The latter encompass any analyses focused on testing preexisting beliefs, commonly utilizing a set of procedures falling under a general umbrella of the *scientific method*, consisting of systematic observation, measurement, and the formulation, testing, and modification of hypothesis.

At the point of insight extraction, both the exploratory and confirmatory analyses make use of *statistical significance tests* (SSTs), which are analytic tools designed to differentiate between material and spurious effects. Depending on the type of comparison (e.g., sets of frequency counts, such as the number of vehicular accidents, or mean differences, such as the average cost of vehicular accidents), SSTs utilize one of the distributionally defined statistical tests, such as χ^2, F-, or t-test, to determine whether observed differences (e.g., the frequency of accidents in Region A and Region B) are materially different, or if those differences are due to random fluctuations and thus not material, which means they are not expected to recur in the future. While the underlying statistical tests are themselves methodologically sound, the testing procedure suffers from consequential limitations, with sample size dependence being one of the more pronounced problems, at least in the realm of organizational data analyses. As noted earlier, the number of records used in analyses (i.e., the sample size) and the likelihood of detecting statistically significant effects are

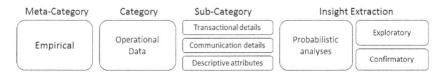

FIGURE 7.4 Extracting Evidence from Operational Data.

highly correlated, so much so that at a moderately large sample size even inordinately trivial differences can become statistically significant, while not being statistically significant at a smaller sample size (everything else being the same). In terms of detecting practically material insights, which typically entails a relatively large number of records,[6] tests of statistical significance are not able to meaningfully differentiate between practically material and trivial effects (see Chapter 6). This is indeed a worrisome limitation, especially considering that in the age of big data sample sizes tend to run quite large, and practically trivial but statistically significant effects are commonplace.

A yet another important consideration is somewhat more obtuse, manifesting itself in terms of *precision of estimates* and the *nature of generalizability*. Without delving into esoteric technical details, these two considerations embody the conflict between the business practitioners' informational needs and the methodological limits of SST, which are best illustrated using a simple example. Let us say that an insurance company's claim manager wanted to determine the magnitude of the difference between the average cost of an auto accident for Location A and Location B, and also wanted to ascertain that the said difference was statistically significant. Having compiled the requisite data, the manager then computed the average (mean) auto accident costs for each of the two locations, which we will assume were $2,995 for Location A and $3,405 for Location B, following which she selected the appropriate SST (in this case, the t-test) to assess whether or not the observed difference between the two means was also statistically significant.[7] The results suggested that the difference between the average cost Location A and Location B auto accidents was indeed statistically significant, based upon which the manager concluded that the observed difference of $410 ($3,405–$2,995) was material, that is, expected to recur going forward.

This is a fairly common example and it illustrates a rather common misuse of SSTs. The most glaring flaw in that reasoning is that statistical significance cannot be attributed to exact quantities, technically known as 'point estimates'. Again, without delving into technical details, SSTs have the power, subject to sample size limitations outlined earlier, to estimate whether the observed difference between two or more means or frequencies is greater than the difference that could be expected to arise by chance if, and only if, that difference is expressed as a range, rather than an exact value.[8] The reason for that is that the two location-specific averages were estimated using subsets or samples of all claims, and since all sample estimates are somewhat imprecise (which is captured in the statistical measure of 'standard error'), the degree of that imprecision needs to be factored into the estimate of the magnitude of the difference between the two means (the same logic applies to comparisons of more than two means and to frequencies). Given that, to be able to qualify the difference between the two location-specific average claim costs of $3,405 and $2,995, the originally point estimate-expressed quantity of $410 ought to be re-expressed as a range that accounts for the *standard error of the mean*, which is a statistical measure of the relative imprecision of sample estimated means. Assuming a standard error of $45, the commonly used 95% confidence interval would yield an estimated range of $321.8–$498.2, in which case the claim manager could conclude that there is 95% probability that the difference between average cost of auto claims was somewhere in the $321.8 to $498.2 range.[9] Clearly, it is less managerially compelling to characterize the difference between Locations A and B average auto accident costs in that manner, but only so-expressed magnitude can be ascribed statistical significance.

The sample size and confidence-level-related challenges point to a fundamental question of why is the notion of statistical significance important in the first place. While in applied business analytics it is often used as an indication of importance or attention worthiness of data analytic findings, statistical significance testing is merely a mechanism for attesting to non-spuriousness or nonrandomness of sample-derived estimates. Much like the term 'error', as in the earlier mentioned standard error, should be interpreted to mean 'deviation' rather than a 'mistake' in the context of statistical analyses, the term 'statistical significance' should be interpreted as conveying 'nonrandomness' rather than 'importance'. Additionally, the level of significance (with the three commonly used ones being 90%, 95%, and 99%) aside, tests of significance are strictly pass-fail thus are insensitive with regard to the 'degree of' significance (to be clear, that is the case within a chosen level of significance, such as 95%; using a higher level of significance, such as 99%, will result in a higher degree of significance). So, if 95% level of significance is chosen, all effects that pass that threshold are deemed equally statistically significant, regardless of any magnitudinal differences.

The above often compels analysts to draw a line of demarcation between the 'statistical' and 'practical' significance, as a way of differentiating between practically material and practically trivial findings. Let's pause for a minute: Isn't there something troubling about the manifestly quantitative SSTs having to be more or less subjectively qualified to become of value to users of the resultant insight? Though widespread, that practice stands on a shaky logical and methodological foundation. It is troubling that the manifestly objective task of differentiating between informationally worthwhile and trivial data analytic findings is ultimately subverted by largely subjective considerations, some of which are permeated by the very cognitive biases that objective data analyses aim to overcome.

It is important to keep in mind that while SSTs can and do serve an important hypothesis testing role, those tests are not always necessary, or even appropriate in applied business analyses. Unless it is important to show evidence of sample-to-population generalizability, significance tests may be plainly superfluous – sometimes the difference is what it is, and no generalizability validation is necessary. At the same time, when the use of those tests is warranted, it is important to make sure that they are used in the manner that leads to valid and reliable conclusions.

Exploratory Analyses

Any search for informationally meaningful patterns or relationships hidden in data falls under the broad umbrella of exploratory analyses. As a general rule, those methods are geared toward creation of new knowledge by means of uncovering previously unknown relationships; the earlier discussed SSTs play a pivotal role in those efforts, supplying means of differentiating between persistent and spurious findings. In view of the rich and continuously expanding diversity of data sources and types, there are numerous exploratory data methods that are available, ranging from classical descriptive statistics to automated data mining, with the latter encompassing numeric and text data mining tools.

Approach- and tool-wise, data exploration can range considerably from relatively simple analyses of small datasets to complex analytic undertakings encompassing large quantities of structured and unstructured source- and type-heterogeneous data. The former often make use of simple tools such as Excel to generate numerically expressed insights or Tableau to produce visual summarizations, whereas the latter typically utilize analysis-oriented programming languages such as R or Python, or sophisticated data analytic applications such as SAS or SPSS. Although the more in-depth operational coverage of the 'what, how, and why' of exploratory analyses falls outside of the scope of this book, the general process shared by different approaches is summarized in Figure 7.5.

The first step in any exploratory analysis is to carefully select data to be used. While that is rather intuitively obvious, in practice it may be more involved than one might expect because what constitutes appropriate – in view of the informational need at hand – data is not always clear due to factors such as knowing what data is available, how it can be accessed, etc. That can be particularly challenging in large organizations, many of which actively capture and store lots of different data but rarely invest in comprehensive, centrally

FIGURE 7.5 High-Level View of Exploratory Data Mining.

maintained data reference and access resources. Moreover, as organizations continue to struggle with finding the optimal data security vs. data access trade-off, the ever-present threat of unauthorized data breaches tends to push organizational data keepers to err on the side of tighter data security, which inescapably makes broader organizations 'getting to know' the available data more challenging. And so though conceptually trivial, the practical task of identifying the most informationally promising data can be far more involved than expected.

Once selected, data need to be reviewed for completeness and accuracy, with an eye toward correcting for any observed deficiencies. Broadly referred to as *data cleansing*, those activities encompass variable-by-variable value assessment and missing value imputation, data feature re-engineering which often includes variable re-coding, combination and indicator creation, and record aggregation, which is typically necessitated by 'one-to-many' data structures, as exemplified by customer purchase data where multiple records can reflect purchases of a single customer.[10] Moreover, data cleansing can be computationally and otherwise complex, requiring considerable data manipulation and programming skill, especially if data are pooled from multiple sources (i.e., there are multiple data files, each requiring separate processing, but ultimately expected to yield a single analytic dataset).

Given that the vast majority of operational data are captured as a functional by-product of modern electronic communication and transaction processing infrastructure, not all elements of an otherwise informationally appropriate data are themselves informationally meaningful. That typically includes the various system identifier values, but may also encompass names of entities, time stamps, or no longer used measures – those superfluous values need to be excluded to reduce the level of noise in data. In situations in which a relatively small subset of variables might be of interest, it might be easier to take an operationally alternative route of selecting only the a priori identified data features (i.e., variables) and simply dismissing the rest.

The efficacy of the final two exploratory data analytic steps – data mining and result interpretation – is highly dependent on the robustness of the preceding data preparation steps encompassing proper cleansing, restructuring, and filtering. Mining of analyses-ready data can be undertaken using what could be referred to as analyst-guided or automated means – the former makes use of descriptive statistics selected, deployed, and evaluated based on an analyst's judgment, whereas the latter leverages highly automated algorithms that sift through data using their internal logic. It should be noted that though the two approaches are operationally quite distinct, they nonetheless both make extensive use of the earlier discussed SSTs to identify attention-worthy relationships or outcomes, thus both are subject to the limitations of that broadly defined methodology.

It is important to not lose sight of the fact that the goal of exploratory analyses is to identify previously unknown patterns and relationships, which means that those efforts have uncertain outcomes and as such can have hard to foresee impact on organizational decision-making. New knowledge can provide some additional clarity by reinforcing the already known patterns of evidence, or can just as easily introduce evidence that contradicts or casts doubt on prior knowledge. In that sense, exploratory analyses can be likened to detective work insofar as both are focused on gathering evidence. The importance of new insights should not be over- or under-stated, and those insights should be evaluated in the context of the totality of all evidence, in the manner discussed in the Strength of Evidence section of this chapter.

Confirmatory Analyses

The central tenet of the scientific method is the formulation and testing of knowledge claims in the form of hypotheses; in the context of business analytics, those efforts frequently take the form of confirmatory analyses. Broadly characterized, *confirmatory analyses* make use of tools of statistical inference, significance testing, and confidence interval estimation to assess the validity of knowledge claims. In contrast to the earlier discussed exploratory analyses which can be seen as tools supporting evidence gathering detective work, confirmatory analyses can be likened to a court trial where the validity of evidence is tested.

The traditional means of conducting confirmatory analyses are rooted in dependence and interdependence families of statistical techniques. *Dependence* statistical methods aim to test the existence, and if so, the strength and the direction of causal statistical relationships between an outcome of interest (typically referred to as 'dependent' or 'criterion' variable) and one or more causal factors (commonly labeled as 'independent' or 'predictor' variables). Regression analyses, a broad family of statistical techniques including linear, logistic, and ordinal, to name just a few most widely used, are the best known examples of dependence confirmatory analyses. Using a dependence method, an analyst would be able to discern, for instance, which of potential influencers of consumer brand choice have statistically material impact on consumer choosing a particular brand, and would also be able to discern the direction (increasing vs. decreasing the likelihood of choosing the brand of interest) and the strength of impact of individual choice influencing factors. In the way of contrast, *interdependence* statistical methods aim to test the existence of more general, that is, causal or not, inter-variable relationships. The widely used correlation analysis is perhaps the best known application of interdependence statistical methods – those techniques[11] produce a more general numeric estimates of the direction and the strength of relationship that point toward some degree of co-movement or co-occurrence between pairs of variables, without addressing potential causality.

While the domain of confirmatory analyses is quite extensive and varied, the analytical process used to conduct those analyses is fairly general, as shown in Figure 7.6.

The overall confirmatory analytical process is comprised of seven distinct components, which are grouped into three explicit categories of Need Identification, Knowledge Creation, and Knowledge Dissemination. The goal of the Need Identification part of the overall process is twofold: First, it is to bring forth the agreed upon goals and priorities of the organization. To be clear, the focus of this step is simply on delineating – as opposed to deriving – the individual objectives that have been embraced by the organization; a common example is the goal of increasing customer repurchase-expressed brand loyalty. Second, it is to translate the delineated strategic objectives into specific informational goals, which in the case of brand loyalty could entail specific analyses-guiding questions, such as the assessment of repurchase incrementality of individual marketing programs. Implicitly, this step recognizes that a successful achievement of the organizational goals is, to a large degree, dependent on the attainment of a high degree of decision-making clarity. Hence, the overall objective of the Need Identification stage of the confirmatory analytical process is to distill the earlier delineated organizational goals into a clear set of informational needs.

The goal of the second broad stage of the confirmatory analytical process – Knowledge Creation – is to address the specific informational needs identified earlier, which encompasses a diverse set of data analytic activities starting with gathering and review of data, analyses of data, and translation of often esoteric data analytic outcomes into easily understandable – to nontechnical users –

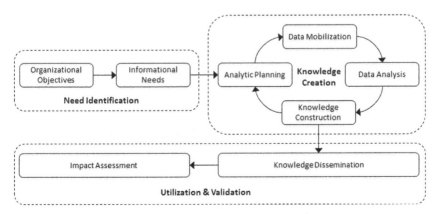

FIGURE 7.6 High-Level View of Confirmatory Analysis.

decision-guiding insights. That is both a tall order and a very broadly scoped endeavor. As graphically shown in Figure 7.6, it encompasses four distinct process-linked components: Analytic Planning, Data Mobilization, Data Analysis, and Knowledge Construction. It is an iterative process which continues to refresh data-derived knowledge supporting current goals, or generates new knowledge for updated or newly established goals; in a sense, this is the 'engine' of organizational data utilization.

Lastly, the confirmatory data analytical process culminates in the Knowledge Dissemination step, a deceptively simple, logical conclusion to the overall progression. It is, however, a very important conclusive step within the 3E framework where often technical outcomes of statistical analyses are translated into more universally understandable insights. This is also where the earlier discussed limitations of statistical analyses, such as the (statistical) significance inflating effect of sample size, need to be carefully addressed to make sure that the resultant decision-guiding insights exhibit the requisite validity and reliability.

The overview of confirmatory analytic approaches would be incomplete without at least mentioning *machine learning*. A subset of artificial intelligence (AI), which is a domain of knowledge focusing on development of computer systems that are able to perform tasks that normally require human intelligence, machine learning is an application of AI geared toward providing computers with the ability to learn (in a more narrowly defined sense than outlined in Chapter 1), in either supervised or unsupervised[12] fashion and without being explicitly programmed. Within the confines of confirmatory analyses, it is the supervised machine learning that can be used to perform, in the far more automated fashion, data analytic tasks that traditionally required human expertise. In fact, many of the commonly used classical statistical techniques, such as linear or logistic regression, discriminant analysis, or factor analysis are now readily available in machine learning systems. That said, it should be noted that the primary benefit of leveraging machine learning is to make use of more recently developed algorithms, such as support vector machines, ensemble methods or neural networks, that take fuller advantage of computational power of machines by leveraging mathematical optimization-based techniques which offer robust alternatives to classical statistical theory-based confirmatory data analytic approaches.

Theoretical Research

Recalling that the origins of evidence-based movement are rooted in the desire to make scientific research findings more easily and more immediately available to clinicians, it should not be a surprise that means of extraction of decision-related insights out of large pools of applicable scientific literature are well established. Leveraging prior work in that area, especially contributions

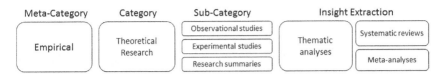

FIGURE 7.7   Extracting Evidence from Theoretical Research.

of the Center for Evidence-Based Management, the theoretical research aspect of the 3E framework makes use of those well vetted and widely accepted approaches. Consider Figure 7.7.

Although the scope of *theoretical research* encompasses conceptual as well as empirical work, as summarized in Figure 7.7, only the latter studies fall within the scope of the 3E framework, because only those research outcomes are objectively verifiable (due to being rooted in analyses of observational or experimental data). Purely conceptual research aims to develop new or refine the existing ideas, which renders those studies speculative and difficult to objectively verify. In fact, as illustrated by scientific theories, the efficacy of abstract ideas is typically validated by empirically testing hypothesis derived from those ideas, as illustrated by testing predictions stemming from a particular theory, which suggests that empirical research can be viewed as a mean of validating the efficacy of theoretical research.

As seen from the perspective of decision-supporting evidence, empirical theoretical research is comprised of three distinct subcategories of observational research, experimental studies, and research summaries. *Observational* research is rooted – primarily – in analyses of data captured as a de facto by-product of the functioning of electronic transaction processing and communication enabling systems, often supplemented by additional descriptive details, such as demographics or firmographics. In that sense, and within the confines of organizational decision-making, observational research generates new insights by exploring behavioral interdependencies hidden in transactional and communication data patterns, making use of exploratory or confirmatory approaches discussed in the context of operational data. *Experimental* studies, on the other hand, are means of testing hypotheses, which are yet unverified cause-and-effect beliefs. In contrast to observational studies which make use of independently (of the study itself) generated data, experimental studies produce data through execution of specific procedures aimed at gathering factual evidence to validate or refute a hypothesis of interest.

One of the often overlooked characteristics of observational and experimental research efforts is *distributed independence*. Multiple researchers, spread across many academic, commercial, governmental, and other research organizations, often work independently on the same or similar research questions. Their approaches, data selection logic, and data analytical methods are rarely exactly the same, which when coupled with the elusive character of many behavioral phenomena just about guarantees some degree of result dissimilarity. To the degree to which any single research study may produce atypical or otherwise non-generalizable outcomes, in situations in which numerous theoretical studies have been carried out focusing on the same underlying research question it is beneficial to synthesize their findings using *research summaries*, which is the third subcategory of empirical research.

There are two similar but distinct approaches to summarize applicable empirical research: systematic reviews (SR) and meta-analysis (MA). *SR* cast a fairly wide net to thoroughly search scientific literature for studies that address a specific research question, which are then critically appraised, and their findings are synthesized with the goal of drawing an overall conclusion regarding the current state of knowledge relating to the question at hand. The overall goal of SR is to enhance the thoroughness, objectivity, and reliability of (scientific) literature reviews that constitute a key part of the scientific research process. Whereas the traditional narrative literature reviews are highly subjective as individual researchers decide what studies to include in their review and what criteria to use to assess the content and outcomes of those studies, SR aim to reduce the review subjectivity through the use of explicit and transparent search and appraisal methods that can substantiate objectively defensible conclusions. In contrast to highly interpretive SR summaries, MA make use of quantitative statistical procedures as means of deriving quantifiable and generalizable conclusions from topically related studies. The goal of MA is to even further reduce interpretative subjectivity of research summaries by making use of numerically expressed estimates of pooled results, which often include explicit examination of result heterogeneity. However, the heightened scrutiny and objectivity come at a price in the form of more substantial informational demands placed on individual studies, which tends to reduce, at times considerably, the number of studies that can be meta-analyzed. And so it follows that while SR and MA are methodologically distinct, in the sense of offering two means of undertaking research summaries, the more rigorous and restrictive MA can be used within the less informationally demanding SR efforts.

Systematic Reviews

Leveraging the Cochrane Collaboration developed conceptual framing, SR can be more formally defined as an assessment of a clearly formulated question that uses systematic and explicit methods to identify, select, and critically appraise relevant research; it may include the use of statistical methods in the form of MA to analyze and summarize the results of the included studies. The stated goal of SR is to minimize reviewer bias by adopting a replicable and a transparent process, which also leaves an audit trail of reviewers' choices and conclusions. A key part of the 'systematic' aspect of those reviews is a general process, graphically summarized in Figure 7.8.

The seven-step SR process begins with carefully delimiting the research question of interest, followed by the selection of, first, databases to be used in literature search, followed by the selection of individual articles. The database selection step can be seen as a reflection of the size of the scholarly publishing universe and the resultant difficulty associated with clearly targeting search efforts, considering that some industry estimates count nearly 29,000 individual scholarly, peer-reviewed journals. And while most of those thousands of journals can be searched using curated databases such as Thomson-Reuters' Web of Knowledge, Elsevier's Scopus, ABI/INFORM, or SCImago, and typically only a small subset of journals might be of interest, the search may nonetheless yield large volumes of qualifying studies.

Once the focal databases have been selected, the more tedious and difficult process of finding individual articles ensues. Research articles are typically indexed based upon author-supplied keywords, and more open-ended database search operations tend to make use of simple bag-of-words text mining functionalities that disregard grammar, and even word ordering. Thus, results of literature searches tend to yield large volumes of 'raw' matches, out of which only a handful ultimately fit the search criteria. The search and selection aspect of the overall SR process can be further systematized by approaching it as a series of distinct decisions of *identification-screening-eligibility-inclusion*. Search-identified records are screened for duplicates and topical fit, then assessed based on reviews of abstracts, following which a more in-depth eligibility assessment is undertaken by examining the full texts of articles, ultimately arriving at the final set of records.

From the perspective of evidence gathering, the next two steps – extraction of data from studies and assessment of the quality of individual studies – constitute the heart of the SR process. The process is structured and it addresses review-related considerations, prior to delving into analyses of the content of selected studies. The former commonly includes an outline of the rationale for the review and the stated review objective, expressly addresses methods

FIGURE 7.8 Systematic Review.

used in the review process and points to protocols guiding the methods used, clearly spells out eligibility for inclusion, search, and selection criteria, as well as data collection processes, inclusive of methods used for assessing risk of bias of individual studies. Aiming to minimize reviewer bias, reviews of content of individual studies emphasize clear summaries of the main findings, the efficacy of the supporting evidence (e.g., statistical significance, goodness-of-fit, etc.) while also noting any limitations, considered at study and outcome level. Lastly, reviewers provide a general interpretation of results of each study while also pointing out sources of funding supporting the review process, along with the role played by fund providers. It should be noted that the analysis and assessment stage of SR can encompass MA, or the use of statistical techniques to integrate the results of individual studies, however, that is an optional, rather than a persistent part of the review process.

Rounding off the SR process is combining of data from individual assessment and review of so-agglomerated results. Those two distinct sets of activities emphasize the ultimate goal of those efforts, which is to distil numerous topically related research undertaking into generalizable knowledge that transcends idiosyncrasies of individual research studies.

Meta Analyses

MA can be defined as a set of statistical procedures designed to assimilate results of related empirical studies with the goal of deriving generalizable effect estimates. As a solution to the problem of pooling data across multiple related studies to reconcile differences across reported results, meta-analytic-like approaches were proposed in the early 1900s, but as a distinct and defined methodology, MA emerged in the mid-1970s.[13] The key premise of the newly proposed methodology was that past research in an area of interest could be consolidated by standardizing measures from individual studies and computing effect size across studies. Further work on meta-analytic methods offered means for combining probability values across studies to enable assessment of the overall level of statistical significance. Since then, numerous applications of MA showed that the systematic use of established statistical procedures to amalgamate results of individual research studies produces more valid and reliable estimates of observed relationships than would be possible by relying on singular studies. As used today, the general MA approach encompasses quantitative assessment of effect size and the level of statistical significance, in addition to also including methodological guidance on weighting of individual studies; as noted earlier, it can be conducted as a part of the broader SR initiative, or as a standalone project.

As is the case with most methodologies, to yield dependable outcomes, meta-analytic initiatives need to adhere to established procedures. Those include the following: (1) selection of studies to be included in the analysis, which need to be both representative and topically related, (2) validity of individual studies, all of which need to demonstrate adequate degree of empirical rigor (e.g., sample size, analysis, inferences), and (3) methodological homogeneity across studies, or the use of similar or comparable research methods and effect estimation approaches across studies.

Considering that MA can be nested within SR, the two process flows share some distinct similarities, as graphically depicted in Figures 7.8 and 7.9. Both begin with the same initial steps of defining research question, selecting of databases, and selecting of individual articles, and although the next step – extraction of data from studies – is also notionally the same for MA and SR, methodologically and procedurally it entails very different means and outcomes.

In contrast to SR which, even when highly structured, are still predominantly qualitative, MA is highly quantitative, and thus calls for well-defined numeric inputs. Key among those are each included study's reported *effect sizes*, which are quantitative measures of relationships or other phenomena, with common examples including correlation or regression coefficients. In general, the larger the absolute value[14] of the effect size the stronger the relationship, except when the quantity is expressed as an odds ratio (in which case, the interpretation is context-dependent). Implicit in combining effect sizes from different studies is the assumption of effect size estimation homogeneity – in other words, it assumes that effect sizes were estimated the same way across different studies. Testing of that assumption is a key part of the analysis stage of the MA process; if the assumption is shown to be valid, a single global effect size can be estimated, if it is not, the overall effect size should be expressed as a range-based average (mean plus the variance around the mean).

It is worth noting that while it offers a substantial improvement over comparatively more arbitrary and subjective means of summarizing quantitative results of research studies, MA is not a panacea. The earlier mentioned requirements of study selection, the validity of individual studies, and cross-study methodological homogeneity are also oft-cited criticisms of published meta-analytic research summaries, which suggests that those are indeed difficult goals to reach. Still, even if MA is imperfect, it nonetheless offers a notable improvement over the alternative means of pooling results of empirical research studies.

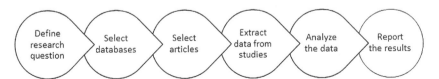

FIGURE 7.9 Meta-Analysis.

Norms & Standards

The first of the two experiential dimensions of evidence, norms & standards, encompasses a wide array of the 'tried and true' practical rules of thumb, demonstrated best practices, as well as quantitative and qualitative benchmarks. All those represent generalized, that is, group-sourced, knowledge developed in the course of engaging in specific professional activities and noting persistent patterns or similarities. Some are formally disseminated through industry co-operatives or trade groups, whereas others are informally shared on as-needed basis. As graphically depicted in Figure 7.10, the category of norms & standards is comprised of three types of applied informational sources: benchmarks, norms, and best practices.

Benchmarks are points of reference that can be used as basis for comparing or assessing outcomes of interest,[15] and as such are descriptive in nature, typically conveying past experience-derived, forward-looking expectations. Although not always, benchmarks tend to be expressed as generalized quantities – for example, an average publicly traded (in the US) company faces approximately 4% chance of shareholder litigation; on average, it is about four times as expensive to acquire a new customer as it is to keep the existing one. *Norms* are prescriptive standards, often mandatory, that spell out desired or acceptable behaviors; in a sense, they can be thought of as externally- or self-mandated organizational rules. Unlike the frequently quantitative benchmarks, organizational norms are typically expressed as sets of qualitative statements, as exemplified by the US Securities and Exchange Commission's insider trading standards. And lastly, *best practices* represent proven means of streamlining or optimizing of commonly performed tasks by means of embracing tested, accepted, and prescribed commercial or professional procedures, as exemplified by insurance companies' reliance on standard claim handling practices and procedures.

One of the dangers associated with relying on industry norms, particularly the informal benchmarks or best practices, is the difficulty in ascertaining their truthfulness or dependability. For instance, the Pareto principle, which states that for many events, roughly 80% of the effect come from 20% of the cases, is widely used in promotional planning, risk transfer, and numerous other business decision-making contexts, but in at least some of those situations the actual effect-cause relationship is significantly different. Needless to say, there

FIGURE 7.10 Extracting Evidence from Published Norms & Standards.

is no benchmarking equivalent to statistical significance tests which though imperfect, nonetheless offer objective evaluation means. Still, a set of normative evaluation rules can be used to assess the trustworthiness of practical benchmarks, rules of thumb, and best practices – the following four assessment rules are recommended:

1 Utility – what is the applicability of a particular norm or standard to the decision at hand?
2 Credibility – how sound and objective are the means used to compile the information?
3 Independence – is the applicable information free from undue pressure or influence?
4 Impartiality – is the applicable information unbiased?

Once reasonably assured of their appropriateness and soundness, applicable applied norms and standards need to be summarized into decision-relevant evidence. As illustrated in Figure 7.10, two general types of evidentiary outcomes can be produced: *standards* and *means*. The former, such as external (to the organization) or internal performance benchmarks (e.g., promotional response or prospect conversion rates) should be quantitative or quantifiable, whereas the latter, in view of their procedural nature, necessarily need to be qualitative, though should be encapsulated in the form of a template or an otherwise transferable sets of process steps. Lastly, it is important to not lose sight of the fact that the scope of otherwise diverse universe of norms and standards is constrained here to just those elements that fall within the broad characterization of decision-relevant evidence, as outlined in Chapter 5, which emphasizes objectivity and verifiability.

Expert Judgment

The second of the two experiential dimensions, expert judgment, encompasses opinions and forecasts of highly qualified and practiced individuals believed to have authoritative knowledge in a particular domain. As graphically depicted in Figure 7.11, within the confines of the 3E framework, expert judgment can take the form of expertise in distinct *tasks* and/or general *processes*, as exemplified

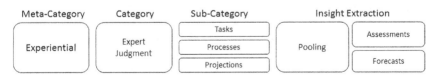

FIGURE 7.11 Extracting Evidence from Expert Opinions.

by highly experienced insurance claim adjustors, or making future *projections*, as demonstrated by weather or economic forecasters.

When considered from the standpoint of insight extraction, the general process of amalgamating available expert assessments and forecasts should be built around the idea of *pooled probability*, earlier defined (Chapter 6) as the emergent possibility jointly suggested by the combination of available evidence. More specifically, pooling of 'what-is' reflecting expert task and process assessments should be independent of pooling of 'what will be' reflecting expert forecasts; moreover, if either assessments of forecasts encompass multiple distinct task, process, or projection topical area, extraction of pooled evidence should be comprised of two operationally separate steps of (1) within-type review and reconciliation and (2) cross-type amalgamation. The within- vs. cross-type distinction addresses an important aspect of expert judgment, namely that it is not advisable to rely on a single expert's opinion because doing so precludes objective reliability assessment. In fact, it has been shown that the accuracy of aggregated judgment-derived insights increases monotonically as a function of the number of experts pooled, but at a diminishing rate, which means that adding more experts is beneficial – but only up to a point. A key consideration here is cross-expert similarity – as the number of pooled experts grows, the diversity of their backgrounds, experiences, etc., is likely to grow as well, which may manifest itself in increasing opinion divergence.

Estimation mechanics-wise, weighted or unweighted *linear opinion pooling* is the most widely used approach. A notable challenge associated with averaging pooled opinions is the choice of individual input weights – should all forecasts be equally weighted, or should some be weighted more heavily than others? In general, when individual experts can be deemed equally qualified and their opinions stem from approximately equal number of decision factors, using equal weighting is recommended; on the other hand, when there are material cross-advisor experience or decision factor differences, opinions of more experienced experts should be weighted more heavily.

An alternative approach to opinion pooling can be characterized as *behavioral aggregation*. Here, an attempt is made to generate agreement among the experts through interactive sharing and exchange of knowledge and perspectives. Process-wise, it can be done in a focus group-like, face-to-face meeting, or remotely via a questionnaire, where several rounds of inputs are gathered from individual experts, aggregated and shared with the group after each round (formally, this is known as the Delphi method). A key limitation of behavioral aggregation it usually does not expressly spell out conditions under which experts can be expected to reach agreement; it is not unusual for some experts to hold firmly to their initial, individual forecasts, effectively preventing the convergence of opinions.

Believability of Evidence

There are some very hard to believe facts associated with folding an ordinary sheet of notebook paper. First, regardless of the size of a sheet, no one has been able to fold a sheet of paper more than 12 times.[16] However, what is even more extraordinary about paper folding is the height of the resultant stack. Starting with an appropriately sized sheet of ordinary notebook paper, folding it seven times (the number of folds once believed to constitute the upper limit) will result in a stack approximately equal in height to the thickness of an average notebook. Extra three folds will result in the stack height about the width of a hand (thumb included), and additional four (for a total of 14 folds) would push the height of our stack to be roughly that of an average person. If one were able to continue to fold, the expected results would become very hard to believe: 17 folds would produce a stack of height of an average two story house; extra three folds (for a total of 20) would yield a stack reaching approximately a quarter of the way up the Sears (currently known as Willis) Tower, the landmark Chicago skyscraper. If folded over 30 times, then the resultant stack would reach past the outer limits of Earth's atmosphere, and lastly, if folded over 50 times, an ordinarily thin (albeit extraordinarily large in terms of area to allow a large number of folds) sheet would produce a stack of paper reaching … all the way to the Sun, which is roughly 94 million miles. Yet that is not all − a little more than doubling the number of folds, for a total of 103 total folds, would result in a stack of paper larger than the observable Universe, which, by the way, measures 93 billion light-years (and given the speed of light of approximately 186,000 miles per second, that translates into an unimaginable height of 5.4671216×10^{23} miles). Although the underlying math can be shown to be correct, are those conclusions truly believable?

Years of education tend to imprint human minds with a variety of abstract notions while also conditioning human psyche to accept as true a wide range of ideas. So long as those scientific and other truths do not contradict one's experience-based sense of reasonableness, most individuals are generally willing to accept even somewhat far-fetched ideas. However, when that is not the case, that is when a particular claim violates what one deems to be reasonable, the result is *cognitive dissonance*. Most find it difficult to accept an assertion as being true, even if the underlying rationale, and even the empirical method both seem acceptable and correct. It is simply difficult to embrace a conclusion that does not make sense, and that is precisely the case with the paper folding exercise. That particular example is an application of a well-known mathematical concept of *exponential growth*, which is a phenomenon where the rate of growth rapidly increases as the quantity (e.g., the above stack of paper) gets larger. Since it is a well-defined mathematical notion, its value can be computed without the need for physical measurements, which is the reason the paper folding example is estimable, though clearly practically impossible to execute. It is likely that most of the readers of this book have been introduced to the concept of exponential growth at one or more points in their educational journey. Moreover, it seems reasonable to assume that while learning that concept, most found the idea of exponential growth to be intuitively clear and reasonable. Finally, once properly explained, the computational logic and mechanics also likely made sense. Yet when put to a bit of an extreme test, the otherwise acceptable and reasonable idea now yields conclusions that many – the writer of this book included – find unimaginable, and impossible to grasp. It simply does not make sense that folding a thin sheet of papers a relatively small number of times could produce such a staggeringly high stack.

The above example underscores both the value and the challenge associated with using data analysis derived knowledge as the basis of decision-making. It is generally easy to accept findings that fall in line with one's existing beliefs, though quite often little incremental value comes out of such 'discoveries'. It is altogether a different story when findings contradict one's prior beliefs, which frequently prompts almost instinctive, doubt-ridden reactions. Is there a problem with the data? Is the approach flawed? Are there any computational errors? To be fair, data can be corrupted, an approach can be flawed, and logical, methodological, and other mistakes are always possible. But what if data, methods, and logic are all sufficiently robust? Doubts can linger, and truly provocative findings that could pave a new avenue for organizational thinking can instead join that dusty repository of insights that were just too far-fetched to be believable.

Yet taking the leap of faith and acting in accordance with objectively validated insights can be enormously beneficial. Consider the information technology that nowadays permeates professional and personal lives – the bulk of it is enabled by quantum mechanical principles; in fact, quantum theory is, in terms of the accuracy of its predictions, the most accurate scientific theory ever constructed. At the same time, it is also among the most bizarre, hard to believe scientific frameworks ever devised. In quantum theoretical world, objects can exist in two states or places simultaneously (a condition known as 'superposition'), in addition to which, objects are also instantaneously 'aware' of distant other objects (an effect known as 'quantum teleportation'). Although as far as it is known today, the quantum mechanical principles apply only to subatomic particles, translating those ideas into the familiar realm of human experience would create a world in which all people would be simultaneously alive and dead, and the act of looking would determine which state was true at a particular point in time. In addition, a person's physical existence would be entangled with consciousness of others, regardless of distance. Thus, in such quantum, world perception would create physical reality, and universal and instantaneous awareness of one another would link all humans. Does that sound believable?

To Einstein those were 'spooky interactions', which was a term he coined deriding quantum theory. In fact, the great scientist spent more time trying to disprove that theory than he did crafting his own theories of general and special relativity. But in the end, he failed. As much as it is hard to intuitively come to terms with the bizarre postulates of the quantum world, the equations describing its mechanics are extremely reliable. Microchip-powered computing devices work undeniably well because of the robustness of the underlying theory although it can be very hard to accept the bizarre picture painted by its postulates.

Obviously, this is not a text on quantum mechanics or paper folding trivia. However, those two examples point to an interesting observation: The believability of analytically derived insights is not a sufficient, or even a necessary condition of decision-guiding value of analytically derived evidence. To parallel the famous Arthur Conan Doyle phrase, 'Once you eliminate the impossible, whatever remains, no matter how improbable, must be the truth'. Even the most deeply held beliefs should be re-assessed when objective evidence is made available.

Notes

1 The founder's name was Sam Wurtzel – Wards was an acronym for his family's names.
2 Each competitor's gain is exactly balanced by the loss of other competitors.
3 It is generally attributed to a noted statistician, George Box.
4 For example, a consumer packaged goods firm may directly capture product shipment or web browsing data, and indirectly – that is, through retailers – also captures product sales data.
5 33% + (2 × 33%), total rounded to 100%.
6 While there is no universally accepted threshold for what constitutes a 'large' sample size, in practice, sample sizes comprised of several thousand records or higher would be considered large, insofar as the statistical significance effects are concerned.
7 We are abstracting away from the level of statistical significance, or the so-called Type II error, for the sake of illustrative simplicity, but one can assume that the manager used the 95%, or $\alpha = 0.05$, level of significance.
8 Briefly, the essence of the underlying reason is that, as mentioned earlier, data are noisy and thus all parameters estimated using imperfect data are only approximations.
9 Lower confidence interval = \$410 − (\$45 × 1.96); upper confidence interval = \$410 + (\$45 × 1.96). The '1.96' factor represents the number of standard deviations away from the mean (known as the 'z', or standardized value) that corresponds to 95% confidence interval (for the two other commonly used confidence intervals, 90% and 99%, the z-score values used in the confidence interval formula would be 1.645 and 2.576, respectively).
10 Under most circumstances, each record in a data file should constitute a distinct and separate entity, such as a customer. In situations/systems in which data are captured at the level of individual transactions, as exemplified by retail point-of-sales data, some records may represent multiple purchases by a single customer, in which case those records need to be aggregated into a single customer record.

11 While the Pearson's product-moment, or Pearson's r correlation is by far the most widely used correlation technique, it is only appropriate to use with continuous variables and thus it is just one of several correlation methodologies; when variables are not continuous (i.e., are nominal or ordinal), other correlation methods should be used such as Spearman's rho and Kendall's tau for ordinal or ranked variables.

12 If not outright misnomers, those labels are at least somewhat misleading: Supervised learning takes place when a computer is provided with labeled inputs (e.g., 'good' vs. 'bad' outcomes expressly labeled in the input data), whereas unsupervised learning takes place where no such labeled inputs are presented – beyond that single difference, both machine learning processes operate independently of any explicit human guidance or supervision.

13 The term 'meta-analysis' was coined by G. Glass in his 1976 article titled 'Primary, secondary and meta-analysis of research', published in Educational Researcher journal (vol. 5, pages 3–8).

14 Absolute value is the magnitude or a real number without regard to its sign; for instance, the absolute value of correlation or regression coefficients of 0.5 and −0.5 conveys the same effect size of the otherwise not equivalent values.

15 The term 'benchmark' originates from the chiseled horizontal marks that surveyors made in stone structures, into which an angle-iron could be placed to form a 'bench' for a leveling rod, thus ensuring that it could be accurately repositioned in the same place in the future.

16 The 12-fold threshold was reached using a very long stretch of thin paper, resembling toilet paper, using what is known as 'single direction folding'. A number of people, however, questioned the validity of that outcome, believing that a proper folding approach entailed folding a sheet in half, turning it 90° and then folding it again – under those constraints, a single sheet of thin paper can be folded 11 times, with the first eight folds accomplished manually and the remaining three folds with the help of mechanical equipment (a steam roller and a fork lift).

8

SOURCING & ASSESSING

Operational Data

Much of organizational decision-making takes place in highly uncertain, volatile environment, where the need to make a decision can arise at any time, and the resultant need to act is often urgent. Decision-makers typically seek information that might help to reduce choice-related ambiguity, but to be of value, decision-aiding insights need to be as recent and as specific as possible. Arguably, the best source of such information is the modern electronic transaction processing and communication infrastructure, which generates vast quantities of diverse and detailed data that record and describe an ever-expanding array of outcomes and outcome-precipitating factors. Broadly characterized here as *operational data*, it encompasses any data generated during performance of various organizational activities such as product shipments or sales, customer interactions, marketing communications, and many others.

When considered from the standpoint of evidence-based managerial practice (EBMP), operational data should be viewed as the core source of decision-guiding insights. The criticality of operational data is the key difference between EBMP frameworks modeled on the rationale derived from medical practice and the Empirical & Experiential Evidence (3E) framework detailed in this book. It is important to note that the centrality of organizational data is not idiomatically assumed by the 3E framework's logic, but rather is a direct consequence of glaring differences between the practice of medicine and managerial practices. As noted earlier, the former is a profession governed by formal standards and legally framed responsibilities, whereas the latter is an occupation with no formal standards (one does not need a license to be a manager) and no legally framed responsibilities (managers cannot be sued for malpractice). The differences are equally glaring in the context of the actual discharge of duties. Medical practice, characterized by largely controllable and collaborative physician–patient interactions[1] in which scientific research-derived knowledge plays a vital role, is starkly different from managerial practice, characterized by largely uncontrollable and competitive interactions in which choices are usually only tangentially shaped by knowledge derived from scientific research. All considered, medical practitioners need valid and reliable – that is, tested and proven to be true in sufficiently generalizable manner – scientific facts, whereas organizational managers need timely and specific – that is, as recent and as situation specific as possible – insights. Consequently, scientific research is central to medical practitioners' abilities to fulfil their professional responsibilities, and operational data are central to organizational managers' abilities to make the best possible decision under conditions of uncertainty.

This chapter takes on the challenge of making sense of the totality of available and applicable data in the broader context of multi-source and multi-type decision-aiding evidence. Framed in the context of probabilistic thinking, general types and sources of organizational data are reviewed, along with distinct challenges and opportunities associated with utilizing different types of data. Lastly, an explicit, application-minded overview of exploratory and confirmatory analyses is presented, as potential tools within the broader endeavor of evidence gathering and validation.

Data, Research, and Decision-Making

Many organizations continue to treat decision-making as an inherently human endeavor. And considering that organizations are essentially groups of people joined together in pursuit of common objectives, that mindset seems indeed reasonable when framed in abstract terms. However, such one-answer-fits-all conclusions become harder to defend when the topic of decision-making is considered in the context of decision type, the disruptive impact of rapidly proliferating and maturing artificial intelligence (AI) technologies, and the mechanics of human decision-making. Is predicating decision-making on human reasoning indeed the most, well, reasonable stance, especially when looked at from the perspective of organizational choice making?

Some decision situations are highly uncertain, characterized by unknown number and nature of potential consequences, and unpredictability of what constitutes a 'good' or 'desirable' outcome – many of the organizational strategic deliberations fall into that category. At the same time, numerous other decision situations are characterized by a predetermined range of outcomes, and relative clarity of what constitutes a 'good' or 'desirable' result; many everyday operational decisions fall into that category. In a more general sense, high degrees of choice and outcome uncertainty are emblematic of decisions that aim to anticipate the future, whereas comparatively lower degrees of choice and outcome ambiguity tend to typify decisions focused on reacting to past developments. Thus, the former conjures up images of large, dynamic and complex organizational systems tackling system-wide problems while confronting previously not seen events or developments, and struggling with unpredictability of the future efficacy of today's choices. The latter, on the other hand, brings to mind a seemingly endless array of tactical, often daily decisions precipitated by recurring matters, such as those associated with ongoing management of insurance claims or marketing programs. In many such situations, human expertise can be reduced to a set of simple 'if-then' rules: the same set of symptoms treated with the same remedy will frequently bring about the same, expected outcomes. And so while it is self-evident why human creativity and problem-solving abilities are necessary to deal with the highly uncertain and speculative nature of strategy-type decisions, it is difficult to see why the same talents are necessary to tackle problems the solution to which is nearly fully contained in the past occurrences.

Taking that line of reasoning a step further, routine choices characterized by known range of outcomes and data-rich setting lend themselves to decision automation, which becomes even more apparent when the mechanics of human decision-making are taken into consideration. Recalling the discussion of cognitive biases in Chapter 1, the rationality-warping effects of cognitive biases working in tandem with the input capacity-limiting effects of channel capacity (which suggests that an average person is able to simultaneously process in attention only about 7 ± 2 informational 'chunks') can effectively deprive a decision-maker of the benefit of truly considering all available and pertinent information. Stated differently, there are decision situations in which unchecked shortcomings of human information processing can produce logically or empirically flawed choices.

This is not a new idea – intrigued by numerous accounts of irrational choices, behavioral economists have been studying the impact of circumstances, location, time, emotional states, societal influences, and other factors on human choice-making for decades. A diverse and convincing body of scientific research points to choice-making processes as being governed by two distinct systems: System 1, which can be seen as a manifestation of involuntary, non-deliberative, and experience-based thought processes, and System 2, which manifests itself through purposeful, controlled, and analytical choice evaluation processes.[2] Even more laconically summarized, the former is highly instinct- and emotion-driven, whereas the latter tends to emphasize rational thinking, ultimately suggesting that System 1 requires less mental effort than System 2. As a result, in many routine decision situations, System 1 functions as the default decision engine, which explains many diverse and common behavioral phenomena such as impulse purchases or prejudice. It is all a long way of saying that making fuller use of data-enabled decision automation in situations characterized by routine choices and predictable outcome sets can not only save time and effort, but it can also yield better long-term outcomes.

There are numerous examples of data-enabled automated, even autonomous decision engines currently in use. The earlier discussed famed chess dual of IBM's Deep Blue supercomputer with the then-reigning world champion Gary Kasparov that took place more than two decades ago (first in 1996, followed by the 1997 re-match) can be seen as the earlier and more visible manifestations of advantages of the now ubiquitous *AI* systems. Broadly characterized as computer systems able to perform tasks that normally require human intelligence, AI applications are behind such familiar systems as Apple's Siri, Amazon's Alexa, or ridesharing applications such as Uber. Nested within that broad informational technology category are *machine learning* (ML) applications, which provide computers with the ability to learn without being explicitly programmed; the ubiquitous speller correction and web page classification systems, as well as newer applications such as Airbnb search rankings now take advantage of ML technologies. An even more informationally evolved subset of AI is represented by *deep learning* (DL) algorithms, which are able to surmise the meaning of multilayered data representations to power such familiar applications as Google's voice recognition or Amazon's search engines. It is worth noting that DL technologies are also a key component of the emerging *cognitive computing* systems, perhaps best exemplified by IBM's Watson, the present-day embodiment of Deep Blue, the chess playing supercomputer discussed in Chapter 1. Ironically, although not many users of those data-driven systems expressly acknowledge, or even realize it, AI applications help to make many routine decision more rational. In a more general sense, the ability of AI systems to quickly access and evaluate the often staggering number of competing choices makes the various embodiments of those technologies highly effective in routine, finite choice situations.

It is important, however, to remember that these applications learn from data; thus, their efficacy is closely tied to data quality, in particular the completeness and accuracy of data, as well as the degree of historical data – current situation concurrence.[3] Hence, it follows that when historical data can be considered reliable, and the decision at hand can be categorized as routine, data-driven, automated decision engines can not only equal but also even surpass the efficacy of human decision-making. At the same time, when historical data are not dependable, creative human reasoning will likely yield more credible outcomes. And since even the more advanced, DL applications ultimately depend on pattern recognition – abstract reasoning, which is required to make a previously unknown situation at least somewhat understandable, is still a largely human domain, as are decisions made under conditions of high degree of uncertainty.

As could be expected, many important organizational decision scenarios are indeed characterized by a high degree of uncertainty and outcome fuzziness, and in those situations, the marvels of modern information technology can become relatively ineffective. It is essential to note, however, that it is not the underlying data that lose their decision-guiding value, but rather it is the automated algorithm-encapsulated decision engines that become comparatively ineffective, typically due to outsized decision scopes. Data that are sufficiently robust and accurate to yield reliable insights in defined and routine decision contexts will remain equally robust when used in more ambiguous decision settings – it is the manner in which those data are used that needs to be changed. For instance, when used by an insurance carrier, automotive accident trends data are equally robust when used as input into auto claim frequency forecasts, as when used as input into broader forecasts of the total (i.e., including automotive and other lines of insurance coverage) number of claims. The difference is that in the narrow context of auto claim forecasts, past auto claim data are a reliable indicator of future auto claim frequency because automotive accident trends tend to be fairly stable across time and thus historical data can be expected to yield dependable future auto claim count estimates. At the same time, the same auto claim data are not as reliable as a predictor of future trends when used as an indicator of all insurance claims because those data only account for one of several factors that determine the expected total future claim counts. The old warning to not 'throw the baby out with the bathwater' seems particularly appropriate here – it is advisable to rethink how data are used, but keep using the pertinent data.

Yet quite commonly when choices are not well defined, circumstances uncertain, and decision parameters poorly understood, those entrusted with making organizational choices tend to retreat to the perceived safety of intuition. Some are unaware, and others are wilfully dismissive of perception- and conclusion-warping effects of cognitive biases, channel capacity limitations, and other sensemaking inhibitors although as documented by numerous experimental studies,[4] relying solely on unaided human choice-making can yield irrational or economically unsound outcomes. For instance, poorly informed decision-makers tend to assume more risk to avoid potential loss while being more conservative at locking-in profits, and tend to show preference for relative, or percentage based, rather than absolute magnitudes when evaluating cross-option differences. Both reasoning traps can be easily avoided, provided the decision-maker is armed with the requisite knowledge, which in the case of the first of the two examples is encapsulated in the notion of 'risk aversion' while the idea of 'just-noticeable difference threshold' captures the reasoning flaws illustrated by the second example. Just as the now ubiquitous AI applications make many consumer choices easier to rationalize, understanding the many pitfalls of unaided human reasoning can lead to vastly improved choice-making outcomes.

Decision Automation

Apple's Siri, Amazon's Alexa, IBM's Watson, and numerous other embodiments of ML and DL applications are all examples of *decision support systems* which, in a very simple sense, are software tools designed to offer automated support for various, largely routine decisions. Those tools are distinct from *decision automation* tools which are also computer software tools, but are actually capable of making decisions, instead of just offering information to humans who then make decisions. Although their architecture and logic are typically quite complex, broadly characterized, decision automation systems make choices based on preprogrammed business rules, which often use probabilistic Bayesian logic (which uses the knowledge of prior events to predict future events). It thus follows that decision automation systems usually learn from patterns of successes and failures, which means that those technologies are well suited to areas where the same or similar decisions need to be made repeatedly, and where there is a predetermined range of good outcomes and good outcomes are predictable, as is the case with routine manufacturing, health care, or financial decisions.

Decision automation technologies can be seen as a natural evolution in the general mechanization and automation of work that started with the introduction of steam-powered engine in the latter part of 18th century. Progressively more advanced – mechanical at first, then electric, followed by electronic, and soon to be quantum-based – technology continues to relieve human workers of many difficult and dangerous tasks. And so long as the activities that were being taken over by machines were largely manual in character, there was little-to-no hesitation in embracing work automation innovations. However, that is not the case with decision automation tools, which are overtly aimed at replacing humans at what is one of the human-most of all tasks – thinking. The self-driving, or autonomous cars now under development by auto manufacturers such as Tesla, Ford, and BMW, technology companies such as Apple, Google, and Uber, not to mention a plethora of lesser known startups such as FiveAI or nuTonomy, illustrate not only the technological challenges associated with that undertaking but also the extent of societal consternation. Can human passengers trust that computer algorithms correctly interpret situational stimuli and make a correct choice? The earlier mentioned widely used AI applications offer some still early, though clearly encouraging evidence. Still, while countless crashes of human-piloted vehicles occur each day, with many, if not most due to human operator error, it is the comparatively rare instances of machine-piloted vehicular accidents that receive a very disproportionate amounts of coverage and scrutiny.

Concerns like those will soon begin to disappear as the advantages of new automation based on quantum mechanical principals become more commonly known. For instance, advanced sensors built using a quantum principle of 'entanglement'[5] will enable autonomous vehicles to 'know' sooner of obstacles in their pathways, and quantum superposition[6] powered onboard computers will be able to much more quickly determine the most appropriate response. Though at least some of the principles that underpin those emerging advanced decision automation technologies will indeed be hard to accept (many of the theoretically and experimentally proven quantum mechanical principles are incredibly weird when contrasted with everyday human experience[7]), those ideas already power some seemingly simple devices. The humble noise-cancelling headphones react to regular and constant noise surrounding users by playing the exact opposite sound that cancels annoying noises, such as those produced by jet engines – that seemingly obvious and simple solution is an application of quantum principle of 'quantum superposition'.

Systematic Immersion

The wonders of modern science notwithstanding, human sensemaking is a marvelous mechanism. It is, however, not perfect, as evidenced by the dozens of cognitive biases. Also, although the human brain's storage capacity is immense (current estimates suggest it could be as much as 2.5 petabytes, or enough to record every second of one's life, or roughly 300 years of nonstop TV programming), the ability to recall the stored information is quite a bit more limited. Thus as elucidated in Chapter 1, the process of ongoing learning is beneficial not only because it adds new information but also because it spurs reactivation of previously added (i.e., learned) information, and retrieval of earlier stored information from long-term to active memory leads to strengthening of one's ability to access, or remember, stored information. But that is not all: As captured in the notion of brain plasticity, each subsequent experience prompts the brain to subconsciously reorganize stored information, reconstitute, and update its contents, ultimately making what is commonly referred to as 'knowledge' not only more accessible but also more current. Hence, the widely used characterization of learning as the 'acquisition of knowledge' is not only an oversimplification – it also misses the point in terms of what actually happens when new information is added into the existing informational mix. Rather than being merely 'filed away' and stored in isolation, any newly acquired information is instead integrated into a complex web of existing knowledge. And so it follows that ongoing and systematic immersion in new information systematically reprograms decision-makers' intuition, to the degree to which the latter is, at least within most domains of professional practice, driven by knowledge stored in long-term memory.

It is important to note that although the earlier discussed decision automation is built around (typically) large volumes of detailed operational data, the ongoing informational immersion calls for far more 'processed' or summarized inputs. There are distinct challenges and processes that frame the manner in which raw organizational data and outcomes of empirical research are assimilated into the decision-making process, both of which are discussed in more detail in the remainder of this chapter.

Probabilistic Analyses of Organizational Data

In the age of data, one of the arguably greatest challenges confronting organizations is that of extracting value out of the ever-expanding volumes and varieties of readily available, and potentially informationally valuable data. The familiar 'data-rich but information-poor' adage is perhaps more true today than it ever was in the past, as business and other organizations seem to be almost besieged by torrents of data. Most habitually capture and store transactional, communicational, and other details, though the prevailing mindset is storage-, rather than usage-focused, as a result of which the manner in which data are stored is not conducive to analyses. A case in point is offered by relational databases, which are still the most common organizational data storage and management structures. A typical such database is comprised of multiple data tables, or standalone data files, linked together by a unique identifier, such as 'Customer ID'. Each table usually contains somewhat unique data (e.g., a 'master' table may contain customer demographic data, 'purchase' table may contain individual customer purchases, etc.) and thus the structure and the level of aggregation are reflective of the type of data. Thus, before meaningful analyses can be attempted, an often considerable amount of data restructuring is required. More specifically, individual variables of interest need to be identified within individual tables, each variable's accuracy and completeness needs to be assessed, any within-data-table record duplicates eliminated, and lastly selected content of different data tables needs to be amalgamated into a single data file. It should be noted that amalgamation of data culled from different data tables frequently entails resolving one-to-many cross-table record alignments that characterize many transactional databases, in which a single 'master record', such as 'customer', is usually attributed with multiple, non-duplicate attributes, as exemplified by purchase transactions or promotional responses (i.e., a single customer with multiple purchases or promotional responses). In a large organization where data are spread across multiple databases, and where each database encompasses large numbers of often poorly documented tables,[8] the task of pulling together complete and well-structured analytic datasets can be daunting. In fact, the explosive growth in the demand for data scientists, an occupation that emerged within the past decade or so and embodies skills necessary to wrangle large volumes of heterogeneous and noisy data, clearly attests to both the importance and the difficulty of systematic consumption of organizational data.

Making organizational data analytically usable is only one of the impediments to broad data utilization. Organizational data usage is also hampered by security considerations, often exacerbated by highly publicized data breaches, as exemplified by the 2017 breach of about 143 million of Equifax consumer credit records or roughly 80 million of Anthem health insurance records. Unauthorized data access is a threat faced by virtually all business and other entities and it is at the center of the struggle that is a consequence of organizations trying to balance the ease of access to data with a reasonable assurance of data security. On one hand, making data easier to access by a wider cross section of users is a key step toward infusing data-derived insights into organizational decision-making, but on the other hand, wider and easier data access also tends to increase the danger of unauthorized data access. Without a doubt that is a difficult challenge to overcome, but that difficulty can be significantly lessened by taking a few relatively operationally simple steps. First of all, it is important to recognize that the aspects of data which are the ultimate source of risk are also the aspects of data that are, from the analytical point of view, information-ally trifling. More specifically, personally identifiable information (PII) is the ultimate source of concern from data security point of view, and it also happens to be of little-to-no analytic value. Given that essentially all analyses of data are focused on the identification of patterns, record-unique PII attributes such as names, social security, or financial account numbers contain no analytically useful information; thus, there is no reason for those attributes to be included in data to be analyzed (the record identifying function of PII can be easily replicated using replacement identifiers that are meaningless when used for true entity identification purposes, and thus pose no identity disclosure threats). It thus follows that while the threat of data access may remain the same, the threat of unauthorized data usage can be significantly reduced by creating usage-oriented data files where sensitive, PII is replaced with system-generated data record identifiers, whereas the informationally valuable data are retained and made readily available for usage by organizational stakeholders.

The second risk-reducing step that organizations can take is to make *feature-engineered*, rather than the original or source data available for wider organizational consumption. This requires an ongoing, systematic, and thoughtful preprocessing of raw organizational data in a manner that anticipates future utilization, in more tangible terms, re-coding original values and/or creating new variables (out of existing ones – e.g., 'customer spend' could be used as the basis for creating customer value indicators, such as 'high', 'average', or 'low' value). Doing so is further necessitated by the growing diversity of data sources and data types which challenges the ability of individual organizational constituents to find, access, and ultimately make use of data that may be available, but in a difficult to use format and spread across numerous systems.

A relatively common example of retail purchase data illustrates some typical challenges. The original, UPC scanner data are typically captured and stored at the individual transaction level, framed in the context of what (a product), when (date), where (location), who (buyer), and for how much (price). Thus, the resultant data file is comprised of a series of records, where each record contains details of what product that was purchased, along with the afore-mentioned purchase-describing attributes (e.g., price, location, purchaser, etc.). Consequently, such data file is a collection or a mix of records of items purchased by the same buyer, as well as items purchased by other buyers. When used as basis for buyer-level analyses, so-structured data need to be restructured into buyer-level aggregates,[9] which requires two separate actions: (1) re-coding the original transaction-level (i.e., 'purchaser as product attribute') into buyer-level (i.e., 'product as purchaser attribute') and (2) aggregating of any multiple product purchases made by the same buyer into a single purchase record. Though usually not challenging to a skilled data analyst, such data restructuring requirements may, and often still do hamper wider utilization. As expected, the broadly defined data feature engineering capabilities have even a more profound impact on the ability to engage in more analytically involved data mining initiatives, as exemplified by the often talked about '360° customer view'. In addition to the within-data-file feature re-engineering efforts, the development of 360° customer view also requires cross-data-file amalgamation, which is usually accompanied by additional challenges stemming from structural to systemic data file level differences. All considered, while challenges are a plenty, many, if not all, of structural data obstacles can be overcome if thoughtfully and skilfully approached.

However, even if all of the many data wrangling, curation, and re-engineering challenges are surmounted, the resultant analytic inputs are still likely to be somewhat informationally imperfect, in the sense of containing some degree of imprecision. In addition, although analyses of the past patterns and outcomes are meant to inform organizational choices focused on the future, behaviorally speaking, the past is an imperfect predictor of the future. And lastly, the various methods of extracting decision-guiding insights out of data, including classical statistics as well as machine learning methods, are ultimately means of arriving at empirically valid approximations. Thus, as discussed in the previous chapter, analyses of organizational data yield *probabilistic estimates*, which means that the resultant insights should be considered approximately true, and interpreted accordingly.

Looking beyond transactional and other organizational databases, it should be noted that the notion of *data* encompasses more than just details of transactions and communications. The Merriam-Webster dictionary defines data as 'facts about something that can be used in calculating, reasoning, or planning', a definition that clearly includes any known or estimated quantity that can be used as input into the decision-making process. Thus, within the realm of decision-making related sensemaking which is at the center of the 3E framework detailed in this book, the notions of 'data' and 'evidence' can be seen as synonymous, really as two dimensions of the same phenomena. More specifically, the former can be seen as reflecting the 'what is it' of informational inputs, whereas the latter can be conceptualized as echoing the 'how it is used' aspect of decision-related inputs.

Given the above and recalling the evidence typology summarized in Figure 7.2, when considered from the broadest possible perspective, data can be either empirical or experiential. Within the realm of empirical domain, data can be further subdivided into operational and theoretical research outcomes, whereas within the experiential domain data can take the form of either general norms & standards or expert judgment. As posited by the 3E framework, each of the resultant four broad categories can be further subdivided into three more narrowly defined subcategories, ultimately giving rise to operationally specific 'insight dozen', representing 12 distinctive sources of potential decision-making inputs. However, when considered from the standpoint of informational raw materials, the four general categories of operational, theoretical research, norms & standards, and expert judgment represent the most informationally distinct groupings, thus each is described next in the context of the key decision-making usage-related analytic considerations.

Operational Data and Databases

Although the term 'database' is usually associated with modern computer applications, as repositories of facts databases existed long before the advent of modern electronic computing. In a strictly definitional sense, the once ubiquitous telephone books that were a staple in nearly every US household for decades were every bit as good an example of a database as are now Google's, Facebook's, or Amazon's mega cloud systems. Hence, a database can range from a simple listing of one's friends' phone numbers written down on a single sheet of paper to a large corporate or governmental computerized system.

Definitional considerations aside, in a practical organizational management sense, the notion of a *database* conveys a certain level of utility and technical sophistication that is typically not associated with just any pool of information. Hence, in a more formal sense, an organizational database could be defined as an electronically stored collection of facts requiring its own management system, typically referred to as 'database management system' (DBMS), in conjunction with specialized query and analysis tools, all of which requiring specialized skills for ongoing reporting and knowledge extraction. There are multiple ways of describing organizational databases: by data type, purpose, content, organizational structure, size, hardware and software characteristics, etc. From the standpoint of informational content, the most pertinent aspects of a database are as follows: (1) scope, which considers differences between data warehouse and data mart, (2) content, which specifies the form of encoding, which can be text, multimedia, or numeric, and (3) organization, which spells out the basic organizational structure of a database.

Scope

Even limiting the database definition to business applications, database is still a very general designation. To make it more operationally meaningful, business databases can be grouped into the following two categories: data warehouse and data mart. *Data warehouse* is a comprehensive data repository encompassing enterprise-wide data from across many or all operational areas, such as sales, marketing, service. Those repositories tend to be subject-oriented (e.g., claimants, customers), time-variant (i.e., capturing changes across time), and cumulative or non-updatable in the sense that new data are added to the old (i.e., periodically refreshed with a new batch of data). Data warehouses are usually data, rather than task oriented, application independent (i.e., can be hierarchical, object, relational, flat file, or other), normalized or not (database normalization is a reversible process of successively reducing a given collection of relations to a more desirable form) and held together by a single, complex structure. Data analytical initiatives typically source their data from a data warehouse, but the analysis itself almost always takes place outside of its confines.

Data mart is usually a specific purpose data repository limited to a single business process or business group. Data marts tend to be project, rather than data oriented, decentralized by user area and organized around multiple, semi-complex structures. An example is a claims data mart holding current (open) and past (closed) workers' compensation claims, containing claimant's contact details, accident and injury-type information, medical, indemnity and other costs, insurance coverage information, adjustor activities, and treatment history and related details. Usually, a data mart contains a subset of the contents of a data warehouse, which makes it informationally more homogenous and considerably more application-ready. Data marts can serve as just data repositories or, in conjunction with business intelligence applications, can support ongoing performance dashboarding.

The term 'database' is sometimes used to denote a data warehouse, other times a data mart, which confuses often substantial usage utility differences. Even worse, it is not uncommon for an organization to expect data mart-like functionality from a data warehouse, simply because in view of some, a database is a database. Yet in the knowledge creation sense, there is a vast difference between these two general types of databases. A data warehouse is a storage-oriented repository of data, inspired by an idea that it is both more cost-effective and more convenient to store large volumes of data in a single storage facility. A data mart, on the other hand, is usually focused on predetermined subset of data and predetermined functional utility, which emphasizes not only storage of data but also easy retrieval and manipulation.

Content

Content-wise, there are a number of different types of databases, comprising several distinct categories, including bibliographic, full text, multimedia and hypertext, and numeric. Bibliographic and full-text databases are traditionally associated with library informational services, such as ABI/Inform or LexisNexis, containing summaries or full texts of publicly available published sources, such as newspapers, professional journals, conference proceedings, etc. In a business sense, they offer a referential source of information rather than ongoing decision support. Multimedia and hypertext databases are one of many Internet and the World Wide Web related informational innovations that tend to be used more as businesses communication (i.e., promotional) vehicles, rather than sources of decision-guiding insights. Although at this point in time (2017–2018) these types of databases offer limited informational utility, the gradual emergence of the Semantic Web is slowly changing that. The last of the four broad types of databases, numeric, is the primary decision support engine of organizational decision-making, primarily because numeric data naturally lend themselves to all manner of analyses. The content of numeric databases, such as the earlier described transactions, behavioral propensities, or basic descriptors, coupled with the easy to analyze coding makes these databases both statistically analyzable and informationally rich.

Organization

Business databases that are designed to store event-tracking and augmenting data are almost always explicitly or implicitly numeric (i.e., the initially non-numeric data can be appropriately recoded). The information they contain can be organized in accordance with one of several data organizational models, which tend to fall into the three general categories: entity-relationship, relational, and object-oriented. The entity-relationship is the most basic data model, built around parent-child hierarchical typology; it identifies basic organizational objects, such as customer, age, gender, product, and specifies the relationships among these objects. It is the simplest and the oldest of the three models, which means it is relatively easy to set up, but at the same time offers limited usability. The relational data model represents facts in a database as a collection of entities, often called tables, connected by relationships in accordance with predicate logic and the set theory. While the relational model is more supportive of automated, templated report generation, it is also more restrictive as the relationships need to be specified and programmed in advance. As suggested by the term 'relational', individual tables are linked to each other, which means that adding new data tables requires fitting of those additions into the existing network of interconnected tables. Lastly, the object-oriented data model is, in many regards, the most evolved data organizational model, but it is also least analytically flexible. The data structure is built around encapsulated units – objects – which are characterized by attributes and sets of orientations and rules, all of which can be grouped into classes and super classes. Although the individual objects exhibit a significant amount of usage flexibility, their preparation requires a considerable amount of programming.

Database types and data model differences certainly contribute to the level of difficulty associated with developing a solid level of understanding of the informational value of organizational data. However, although these considerations have a significant impact on the database's querying and reporting capabilities, they exert only a relatively marginal impact on more advanced analytics. The primary reason for that is that querying and reporting are conducted within the confines of the database itself with the help of the DBMS, whereas data analytics is usually carried out outside of the database. Thus, from the standpoint of utilization of available data, the organizational structure of the database is of interest only insofar as the identification and proper classification of the available data.

Getting Started with Operational Data

In the vast majority of instances, data needed to shed light on a particular question are scattered across multiple data files and/or databases which necessitates extracting data elements of interest and amalgamating all into a singular analytical dataset. An *analytical dataset* is a subset of all available data, properly structured, organized, and cleansed. Its importance is often overlooked, and all too often haphazardly selected analytic datasets are used in analyses. This problem also tends to be compounded by a combination of poorly documented organizational data assets spread across numerous data storage systems, and a frequent use of outside data analytical service providers who have little-to-no familiarity with the 'what' and 'where' of organizational data. And yet, the efficacy of data analytic insights is ultimately rooted in the quality of the underlying data.

The overall task of pulling together analyses-ready datasets is comprised of two broad, but distinct sets of endeavors: picking the 'right' data, followed by carefully cleansing and structuring the selected dataset. Given the importance of those steps, an in-depth discussion of each follows.

Picking the 'Right' Data

The often bewildering size and informational diversity of modern organizational data reservoirs is a topic that received a considerable amount of attention, both from practitioners to academicians. In fact, the overwhelming volumes and varieties of data available to organizations are, ironically, among the main contributors to many organizations' inability to truly leverage the informational value of data. One of the frequently seen mistakes is what could be called an 'upside-down' approach to organizational data consumption: All too often, data users approach the task of data utilization from the standpoint of 'what can I do with the data I have', rather than 'how can I use the data I have to help me answer the question at hand'? Whereas the former often leads to proliferation of endless reports that try to capture and convey every detail contained in the available data (recall the earlier discussion of the difference between informative 'signal' and informationless 'noise'), the latter forces data users to critically evaluate the available data elements, select those that appear to be in some way related to the question at hand, and analyze the selected data within the confines of the question at hand.

An altogether different consideration is that of sample size and composition. Many operational data systems capture numerous outcome measures across time, often resulting in a very large number of records, some dating back many years. Even if those particular measures are directly related to the stated question, large sample sizes have a potentially skewing effect on the robustness of statistical parameters and tests, with data 'recency' and 'size' being the two main culprits. In general, the more recent a behavior, the more indicative it is of future behaviors, from which it follows that including excessively old data may actually reduce predictive efficacy of analytic conclusions. The impact of sample size is a bit more esoteric; thus, it can benefit from more in-depth explanation.

Central to the estimation of many statistical parameters is the notion of standard error (SE), which is an estimated average deviation of a particular statistic (it is computed by dividing data-estimated standard deviation by the square root of the sample size). Abstracting away from technical details, SE is one of the key inputs into the earlier discussed statistical significance testing, the goal of which is to determine whether the observed effects (e.g., differences between means, coefficient estimates, etc.) have informational substance or are spurious, meaning, not real. Given that SE is a quotient of standard deviation and sample size, as the magnitude of sample size increases the value of SE decreases, resulting in the ever smaller, eventually trivial, differences being deemed statistically significant, even though their small magnitudes may render them practically insignificant. In more general terms, excessively large sample size artificially deflates the size of the SE estimates which, in turn, increase the likelihood of false-positive findings, or ascribing an informationally meaningful or a factual status to practically immaterial magnitudes. Needless to say, that can have an adverse and considerable impact on the quality of the resultant information.

Cleansing & Structuring

Working with operational data, it is reasonable to anticipate various degrees of imperfection which necessitates numerous data preparatory steps, with data cleansing and normalization being the two most important ones. Data cleansing can be broadly defined as the process of repairing of the contents of an extracted dataset, whereas data normalization is the process of identification and removal of unusual or outlying and thus potentially result-distorting values, as well as correcting for undesirable distributional properties.[10]

Data Repairing

One of the key criteria for evaluating the initial analytic quality of database extracts is the degree of completeness, which is usually expressed at an individual variable level. For instance, if 1,000 individual records were extracted, with each containing 100 individual variables, what is the proportion of missing to non-missing values for each of the 100 variables across all 1,000 records?

Frankly, it is rare for an extract data file to be 100% complete, and though organizations vary in terms of their data capture and maintenance proficiency, even those that excel in that area still need to contend with the inevitable missing value challenges. Factors such as human error, occasional technical glitches, inapplicability of some measures to some of the records, or imperfect data capture methods virtually guarantee that all data types exhibit some de-gree of incompleteness. Many data analytic techniques require missing value resolution – in some cases, the analyst needs to make a specific imputation choice, in other instances records containing missing values are systematically eliminated (a process often referred to as pairwise or listwise deletion). Those unintended and unaided deletions of missing data-containing records can be particularly troublesome from the standpoint of maintaining an adequately rep-resentative, and possibly sufficiently large analytical dataset. Even if missing values are randomly scattered throughout the extract dataset, due to a condition termed 'missing completely at random', the analysis sample may become pro-hibitively small. Still worse, unchecked elimination of records containing one or more missing values can lead to systematic bias, which is particularly likely if the missing value problem is concentrated in certain subsets of data.

An important consideration that arises in the context of *missing value imputation* is that of the degree of the problem. More specifically, at what point – that is, the proportion of missing values – is a given variable is no longer usable? There is no agreement among analysts or among theoreticians, for that matter, as to what such a threshold should be, and as a result, what might be deemed reasonable might vary across situations. Still, it is desirable to have at least general guidelines in that regard, and the one recommended here is as follows. Starting from the premise that it is reasonable to assume that a missing value metric is a continu-ous, randomly distributed stochastic variable that could be examined within the notion of standard normal distribution, it thus seems reasonable to conclude that basic distributional properties of the normal distribution can be used as bases for identifying an objective missing value evaluation threshold. In particular, the proportion of all observations accounted for by the set number of standard deviations away from the mean seems particularly appropriate, as it expresses the probability of the actual value falling within a certain range. Still, the decision of how many standard deviations away from the mean should constitute the outlier line of demarcation will always remain, at least somewhat, arbitrary.

Consider the idealized depiction of the standard normal distribution shown in Figure 8.1. Roughly two-thirds of all observations can be accounted for within ±1 standard deviation away from the mean which increases to about 95% of all observations within ±2 standard deviations and more than 99% within ±3 deviations away from the mean. Although 95% or even 99% would be the ideal standards, in practice, setting the threshold at such a high level could lead to the elimination of the vast majority of individual metrics. At the same time, recent analyses suggest that any variable which has fewer than 32% of its values miss-ing can still be 'repaired' without significantly affecting its basic distributional

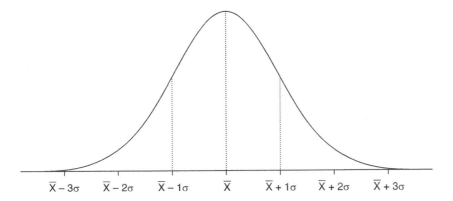

$\overline{X} - 3\sigma$ $\overline{X} - 2\sigma$ $\overline{X} - 1\sigma$ $\overline{X}$ $\overline{X} + 1\sigma$ $\overline{X} + 2\sigma$ $\overline{X} + 3\sigma$

FIGURE 8.1   Standard Normal Distribution.

properties, hence variables which have more than roughly one-third of their values missing should be excluded from further analysis.

Imputation technique-wise, there are several available replacement options, which include cold deck, mean, regression-based, and probabilistic imputation. Cold deck imputation is perhaps the simplest approach to missing value imputation as it uses an externally derived constant as a (missing value) replacement. However, because a single value is imputed into numerous cases, this approach will lead to an artificial reduction in the variability of data, which is likely to bias coefficient estimates, ultimately diminishing the explanatory or predictive validity of findings. In a manner similar to cold-deck imputation, mean imputation replaces missing values with the commonly used measure of central tendency (arithmetic mean), estimated with non-missing values. Its main advantage is the conceptual and operational ease; however, it has numerous disadvantages. First, the true variance in the data might be understated, thus reducing the reliability of subsequent analyses. Second, the actual distribution of values is likely to be distorted, and third, cross-variable relationships might be depressed because of a constant being added to numerous cases. Overall, both cold deck and mean imputation methods are likely to produce results that are inferior to regression or model-based methods discussed below.

Regression-based imputation is the first of the two methodologically more complex methods. It finds the best fitting substitute for the particular missing value based on the relationship of the missing value variable with other variables in the dataset. Since the approach makes a better use of the available data, it is relatively efficient (able to yield unbiased coefficient estimates while also being easy to implement), but it has several distinct disadvantages. First, it is considerably more complex as it requires the calibration of a multivariate statistical model; second, it reinforces the relationships already in the data; third, it diminishes the variance of the distribution unless stochastic values are added to the estimated values (which increases complexity); lastly, it makes an assumption that the missing value variable is highly correlated with other variables. Ultimately, empirical assessments of the efficacy of regression-based imputation suggest that the approach may deliver suboptimal results.

Probabilistic imputation is perhaps the most methodologically complex method, but has been found to yield the most robust replacement values while also being most efficient. There are two distinct variants of this general method: The first utilizes maximum likelihood estimators which make use of all available data to generate the correct likelihood for the unknown parameters. Although there are numerous maximum likelihood computational methods, in general, they are all based on the assumption that the marginal distribution of the available data provides the closest approximation of the unknown parameters. The good news is that the most popular statistical analysis systems and languages (e.g., SAS, SPSS, R, Python) already implemented the maximum likelihood methods for missing data; the bad news is these methods are quite computationally intensive. The second variant of probabilistic imputation uses Bayes theorem to estimate the conditional and marginal distribution for missing data. Computationally, it is based on a joint posterior distribution of parameters and missing data, conditioned on modeling assumptions and the available data.

Data Normalization

From an analytical point of view, outlier identification remediation is one of the most important data cleansing steps, where *outlier* is a value that falls outside of what is considered to be an acceptable range. Some outliers are illustrative of data errors, but others might represent accurate, though abnormally large or small values that are extremely rare. Depending on the size of the dataset (i.e., the number of records), outliers can be visually identified by means of simple two-dimensional scatterplots, or can be singled out by means of distribution scoring, which is the process of flagging of individual records whose values on the variable of interest fall outside of the statistically defined norm, such as ±3 standard deviations away from the mean. The goal here is to, ultimately, identify individual values that exert excessive and analytically undesirable (in the sense of potentially distorting data analytic conclusions) degree of influence, typically captured by the estimation of leverage, which is an expression of outlyingness of a particular value. In more operationally clear terms, it is the distance away from the average value – the further away from the mean a particular value is located, the more leverage it has.

Admittedly, outlier identification is a vexing undertaking that can yield imperfect outcomes, unless approached with care. For instance, while using the aforementioned degree of outlyingness sounds reasonable, the approach can potentially mask some outliers. That is because it uses all data points, including any outliers, to compute a mean, thus it is possible that some of the less extreme outliers will be masked by an artificially inflated mean values (since that approach is used as the basis for outlier identification, any mean estimates have to use all available data points). Those challenges, however, can be overcome using a relatively easy fix: Prior to computing the mean of a variable, all data records to be used should be rank-ordered, following which the lower and upper 5%–10% of the records should be excluded, prior to calculating the mean. Doing so will prevent any potential outliers from affecting the mean and thus eliminate the masking problem outlined above.

What remains is the setting of an outlier threshold – at what point an otherwise normal, in the sense of being correct, value becomes an outlier? In thinking about this issue, consider the goals of the planned analysis and the general inner workings of statistical methods to be used. Statistical parameters are commonly evaluated in terms of their level of statistical significance. The commonly used 95% significance level expresses the validity of an estimated parameter in terms of the likelihood of it falling within ±2 standard deviations away from the mean. Why not calibrate the acceptable value range to the anticipated level of precision? Using such a simple yet objective benchmark, only records falling outside the standard deviation-expressed range of allowable departures from the mean should be flagged as abnormal. This rationale can be translated into a simple four-step process:

Step 1: Compute the mean and the standard deviation of the variable of interest.
Step 2: Select the desired allowable limits, that is, 2 standard deviations away from the mean = 95% of the values, 3 standard deviations away from the mean = 99% of the values, etc.
Step 3: Compute the maximum allowable upper values: mean + upper allowable limit and the maximum allowable lower values: mean – lower allowable limit.
Step 4: Flag as abnormal records falling outside the allowable range, both above and below.

Exploring Operational Data

The idea of 'data exploration' suffers from a bit of identity crisis, as it can be used to convey somewhat different activities across usage situations, largely because data can be explored in great many ways, ranging from the very casual perusing of simple summaries (e.g., a sales manager reviewing period sales reports) to complex analyses of large volumes of raw outcomes data (e.g., an analyst conducting customer value segmentation analysis). Moreover, data exploration can be, well, *exploratory*, in the sense that it represents a journey of discovery, or an open-ended search for not-yet-known patterns or associations; at the same time, data exploration can also be *confirmatory*, which is when preexisting beliefs are tested using available data. While the exploratory-confirmatory duality may often be lost in the everyday conversational usage of the data exploration idea, it is actually quite important when the 'how' of data exploration is contemplated because it points toward very different method-ological approaches, first discussed in Chapter 7.

Broadly characterized, *exploratory data analysis* (EDA), also referred to as *data mining* entails sifting through new or previously not analyzed data in search for informationally meaningful patterns or associations. Exploratory analyses can take on varying degrees of complexity and sophistication, and typically make use of statistical tests as bases for establishing the validity and reliability of its conclu-sions. Process-wise, data exploration can be analyst-driven or automated. The former requires an analyst to 'manually' select individual variables and desired outcomes, in addition to also choosing analytic techniques or tests to be used for analyses; the latter, on the other hand, makes use of specially designed computer algorithms and software applications to sift through all selected data in search for any patterns or relationships. The significant process differences notwithstand-ing, both the analyst-driven and automated EDA approaches are geared toward numeric assessments, which encompass producing numerically expressed associ-ations as exemplified by correlation matrices or tests of difference.

An increasingly popular approach to exploratory analysis takes the form of *data visualization*, which takes advantage of specially designed, stand-alone software applications which aim to express data patterns and associations using graphical means (e.g., histograms, trend lines, etc.). Process-wise, data visualization tools can be seen as a hybrid of the aforementioned analyst-driven and automated means of carrying out numeric EDA analyses as those applications require an active participation of the part of analysts, to specify variable sets and visualiza-tion types, but then produce sophisticated visualizations in a highly automated manner. The main appeal of data visualization is that those applications can re-place some of the obtuse and frequently misinterpreted (and misunderstood) nu-meric tests with more intuitively meaningful visual representations of patterns found in data, which ultimately makes data analytic results easier to consume by non-technical users. After all, a picture is worth a thousand words (or numbers).

The second of the two data exploration avenues is *confirmatory analysis*, the goal of which is to assess the truthfulness of prior beliefs, which can encompass anything from hypotheses derived from established theoretical frameworks to subjective suppositions. Thus, in contrast to the search for new knowledge that drives exploratory analyses, confirmatory analyses are focused on substanti-ating current knowledge, using the tools of statistical inference, significance testing, and confidence interval estimation. To put that difference in a more illustrative context, exploratory analyses can be seen as evidence gathering de-tective work, whereas confirmatory analyses can be portrayed as a court trial where the validity of evidence is tested. Method-wise, confirmatory analyti-cal techniques can be grouped into dependence and interdependence statistical methodologies. *Dependence* statistical methods aim to test the existence, and if so, the strength and the direction of causal statistical relationships between an outcome of interest (typically referred to as 'dependent' or 'criterion' variable) and one or more causal factors (commonly labeled as 'independent' or 'predictor' variables). Regression analyses, which is a broad family of statistical techniques including linear, logistic, ordinal, ridge, and several other techniques, offer probably the best known example of dependence confirmatory analyses. An analyst could use dependence methods to, for instance, delineate and impact-assess the strongest influencers of outcomes such as consumer brand choice or the likelihood of adverse development of insurance claims. *Interdependence* statistical methods, on the other hand, aim to validate the existence of relationships that are believed to exist among variables. As such, interdependence confirmatory analysis are conceptually and methodologically reminiscent of exploratory analysis, so much so that the difference between the two is primarily that of the initial purpose: looking for new (exploratory) vs. validating current (confirmatory) relationships. Not surprisingly, some of the same techniques, such as correlation analysis, can be used by both.

The type of analysis notwithstanding, it is important to keep in mind that though the mention of 'data' can imply numeric or number-like[11] values, an estimated 90%+ of data captured nowadays are non-numeric (after all, as illustrated by Facebook, Twitter, Snapchat and other social media platforms, words, images, and video are the primary means of human communication). That said, from the information processing standpoint, those torrents of structured and unstructured, numeric and non-numeric data ultimately need to be reduced to somewhat conclusive trends, patterns, relationships, and other outcomes that can inform one's decision-making process. And although there are numerous methodological and technological means of accomplishing that goal, that diverse set of data analytic tools can be grouped into two broad sets of approaches: statistical and visual data exploration. The key difference between those two data exploration methods lies in 'how' data are analyzed as quite frequently – though not always – the same data can be explored using either of the two approaches.

As suggested by its name, *statistical* data exploration is built upon the use of mathematical tests, best exemplified by tests of statistical significance, as means of identifying non-spurious patterns or associations. The overriding goal of statistical exploration is to use objective, quantitative methods as guides for finding valid and reliable insights; as such, that general approach is particularly well suited for drawing generalizable inferences from sample-based analyses. *Visual* data exploration, on the other hand, makes use of a wide array of graphing and charting means of capturing emergent trends, distinct patterns, and persistent associations. In contrast to the implicitly 'pass-fail' spirit of statistical data exploration (i.e., a given association is either statistically significant or not), visual data mining emphasizes the 'degree of' manner of sensemaking by leveraging the simplicity of visual cues (for instance, a cross-time customer attrition trend line just captures what-is, without qualifying it as being significant or not). Inherently summarization-focused, visual data exploration lends itself especially well to mining of huge volumes of what is now known as 'big data'.

Although both data exploration approaches have a number of distinct advantages and limitations, a more in-depth discussion of their respective merits and demerits falls outside of the scope of this book. The underlying data usage related considerations, however, are of fundamental importance to the evidence-based decision-making process outlined here, and thus are addressed in more detail next, in the context of a generalizable EDA process.

Exploratory Data Analysis

At the most general level, the purpose of EDA is to disclose patterns in sets of data, as described by a simple formula where Data = Smooth + Rough.[12] The 'smooth' is the relationship between two or more variables, whereas the 'rough' are the remaining residuals, or what is left over after all patterns have been extracted from a dataset (earlier also referred to as 'noise'). The essence of exploratory analysis is not just to simply extract patterns and discard residuals in a single step, but to first extract the initial patterns (the 'smooth', in the above formula), then examine the residuals for additional patterns (i.e., analyze the 'rough' in search for additional 'smooth'), extract any new patterns that can be found, and finally discard the final residuals containing no more discernible patterns.

When looked at from the standpoint of statistical analysis, the EDA process can be portrayed as an open-ended search, the goal of which is to pinpoint any and all relationships between variables. It is important to keep in mind the roots of that approach, which was empirical social science research conducted in the 1970s, characterized by small, in terms of both record and variable counts, datasets; in that context, exploring available data for any patterns was both conceptually reasonable and operationally manageable. It plainly is not so now (ca. 2018), and given the projected data growth trajectories, it will most certainly not be so in the future. Applying the 'search for any relationships' EDA process to the staggering volumes, and particularly varieties (i.e., variable counts) of data will most certainly produce equally staggering numbers of statistically significant relationships.[13] Thus, it follows that to produce manageable volume of insights, the general EDA approach needs to be constrained to specific informational needs stemming from the decision at hand. Additionally, though perhaps less self-evident, to minimize the preponderance of chancy associations, prior data analytic results should also be taken into account, as a mean of finding longitudinally stable or persistent relationships.

The so-amended and framed EDA process can be broken down three general phases: review of previous findings, examination of data quality, and analyses of data. The first of the three phases offers an opportunity to 'take inventory' of earlier analyses and assess their potential contributions to the current informational needs, the second phase calls for a critical and thorough examination of the value of the data assets vis-à-vis the stated analytical objectives, whereas the third and the final phase is focused on extraction of new insights out of the available data.

Phase 1: Review of Previous Findings

Knowledge creation is a cumulative process, which means that even the most eye-opening and revolutionary insights ultimately exist within the realm of other, previously created knowledge. This is a particularly important realization when the goal is to build a comprehensive reservoir of decision-aiding insights. It is so because unless proper steps are taken, past data analytic learnings can become nothing more than collections of unconnected, random pieces of information lacking collective power. Thus, the knowledge creation process outlined in this text emphasizes a purposeful and systematic accumulation of learnings derived from analyses of data conducted at different points in time, which, in turn, stipulates that each additional insight contributes something new to the already-in-place knowledge base, with the so-expanding set of insights giving rise to more time-invariant or generalizable themes.

The general MECE (*m*utually *e*xclusive and *c*ollectively *e*xhaustive) principle can be used as an intellectual guide to the development and maintenance of such a knowledge base. Its basic premise is that the best way to approach an analytical (but not necessarily quantitative) problem is by identifying – within the confines of the scope of the analysis – all independent components in such a way as to provide a maximally complete coverage or an explanation while avoiding informational redundancies. Hence, the principle stipulates that each element of knowledge should be informationally non-overlapping with other ones while the totality of all knowledge elements should yield informationally exhaustive insights. Meeting those rather lofty goals demands unambiguous explanation of the meaning of individual insights, along with the detailing of their measurement properties (e.g., continuous vs. discrete, the unit of analysis, acceptable value ranges, etc.) all with the goal of reducing interpretational ambiguity. In a more operational sense, it also requires an assessment of the appropriateness of individual variables, as well as the determination of sufficiency of coverage of the combined variable set.

At the most disaggregate level of individual variables, an appropriate variable is one that exhibits the desired value availability (i.e., the proportion of non-missing and correct values), scaling (i.e., the type of measurement), distributional (i.e., the shape of the frequency distribution), and interpretational (i.e., meaning) characteristics. The intent behind such detailed assessment is to ascertain that individual contributors to a particular insight are statistically as well as contextually sound. More specifically, a single variable can be deemed analytically appropriate if it meets the following criteria:

1 The proportion of its values that are missing is within the objectively allowed limits – that is, the previously discussed norm of not exceeding about one-third of the total number of observations.

2 Its measurement scale is appropriate given its anticipated usage – in practice, that tends to amount to assuring that variables that are expected to be

continuous or indeed continuous (remember that continuous variables can always be re-coded into discrete values, but discrete values cannot ever be converted into continuous ones).

3   Its frequency distribution meets the requirements of the statistical techniques to be used, or the desired properties can be brought about through an appropriate transformation.

At the same time, a given variable can be deemed informationally appropriate if its meaning falls within the general scope of the stated informational needs, and the measured quantity or quality is valid and reliable. Moreover, individual variables that are deemed informationally appropriate also need to contribute incrementally to the explanatory power of the entire variable set, as posited by the *principle of parsimony*, or Ockham's razor.[14] One commonly used operationalization of parsimony is the statistical concept of *collinearity*, loosely defined here as the degrees of explanatory redundancy. One of the more common uses of collinearity is in explanatory analyses, where the variability in an outcome of interest, such as product repurchase, is assessed with the help of numerous potential predictors of that outcome. In that context, collinearity acts as a de facto filter for evaluating the incremental – that is, denoting measurable positive or negative change – explanatory power of individual predictors under consideration.

Phase 2: Assessment of Informational Quality

When assessing the informational value of available data, it is important to look beyond 'what is'. Quite commonly, informational needs pose analytic questions that seem to go beyond the currently available metrics, suggesting current data insufficiency. Yet, it might be possible to either re-express (as new variables) the currently available measures or derive altogether new ones by combining two or more of the existing variables.

Indexing is a process of re-expressing raw metrics as more immediately usable markers, as exemplified by value or attribute indicators (e.g., high, medium, and low value). It usually is a product of data usage logic – for instance, a 'high-value' indicator can be created by evaluating the available 'annual spend' field in relation to organizational norms (e.g., if a particular retailer considers anyone with, let's say, $1,000+ annual spend to be a high-value customer, then any customer record with 'customer spend' of $1,000+ would have its 'high-value' indicator set to 1, otherwise it would default to 0). It is also common to derive target variables for predictive modeling in that manner – for instance, in the context of insurance claim analyses, one of the first steps in the threat of claim litigation modeling is to create a binary (yes vs. no) modeling target, which is usually accomplished by re-purposing an existing 'litigation date' field, typically included in historical claim data, into a newly created 'litigation' (0–1 or no-yes) indicator.[15]

A yet another variable set enhancement step is to combine two or more existing measure into a new one. Such broadly defined *interaction effects* are also usually products of conditional logic – for example, creation of a 'current high-value customer' field entails an assessment of two distinct states: current vs. lapsed, and high-value vs. not high-value customer. Another possibility is entailed by derivation of higher-order measures from more disaggregate raw components, as exemplified by summing up individual purchases to period (e.g., annual) sales.

An altogether different, though equally important aspect of informational quality assessment is a review of statistical robustness of all, which means the original as well as any newly created, variables. Of particular importance here are variable *validity* and *variability* considerations. The former is quite straightforward as it pertains to truthfulness of values comprising each variable, whereas the latter has a more obtuse meaning as it is an expression of changeability of values of a particular metric across records in the analytic dataset. To that end, a measure that exhibits little variability is one that would assume the same or very similar value for a large number of records, as exemplified by a situation in which the vast majority of respondents to a particular promotion are females, or a situation where the vast majority of, let's say, an airline frequent flyer program are college graduates. The challenges posed by invalid measures are quite obvious – problems associated with low degrees of variability, however, are somewhat more opaque. Without getting wrapped up in often confusing technical statistical considerations, let is suffice to say that measures that exhibit low variability have comparatively limited explanatory (and predictive) value, precisely because they assume the same value in large number of cases. In a way of a simple illustration, if the majority of those enrolled in the earlier mentioned airline frequent flyer program are college graduates, then 'education', as a descriptor, would have reduced informational value because it would be unlikely to point toward meaningful differences across any subsets of the frequent flyer program members.

Assessment-wise, the typically easiest and most meaningful approach to reviewing the key aspect of data's informational value is data visualization. Again staying above numerous technical considerations, numeric data can be broadly grouped into *categorical* or *continuous* measures.[16] The former encompass all quantities comprised of distinct groups, such as 'males' vs. 'females' for gender or 'freshman', 'sophomore', 'junior', 'senior', or 'graduate' for college student classification, and thus is comprised of a finite, and typically manageable number of discrete categories. The latter, on the other hand, includes all quantities measured on a scale that has, at least in theory, an infinite number of possible values, as exemplified by time, age, or income. The categorical vs. continuous variable distinction is one of the most fundamental considerations in virtually all aspects of data analyses – within the confines of data visualization (and, ultimately, the assessment of individual variables' informational value) that distinction implies the use of different visualization techniques. For example, bar or pie charts are commonly used to portray the relative frequency of categorical groups, whereas histograms or density plots are often used to convey notionally similar information about continuous quantities.

Phase 3: Data Exploration

Although visual means of data exploration can quickly and easily highlight interesting trends and patterns in data, those methods are prone to considerable subjectivity, not only in terms of how results are used but also in terms of how they are prepared. The sample visualization depicted in Figure 8.2 highlights the most salient points of that assertion.

Shown are two line graphs of the same hypothetical stock price – the only difference between the two graphs is the scale granularity, with the graph on the left showing a more 'zoomed-in' view (scale ranging from $18.50 to $23.50), whereas the graph on the right depicting a more 'zoomed-out' view (scale ranging from $10 to $30). As can be seen by more careful examination of that example, the individual stock price values are exactly the same between the two representations, yet when viewed individually, the zoomed-in presentation clearly suggests more price volatility than the zoomed-out view. Which view is correct? Both, since the underlying data are identical, and yet depending on the often arbitrary choice made by the analyst conducting the analysis, materially different implied conclusions can be communicated.

This not to suggest that data visualization is inherently ineffective, as that is not the case. But because it can be heavily influenced by arbitrary and subjective presentation and interpretation choices, its overtly easy-to-use character can obscure the kinds of problems that are exemplified in Figure 8.2. The alternative to visual data exploration – statistical exploration – is not a panacea, but has the potential to help mitigate some of the challenges associated with data visualization. To be sure, the tools of statistical analyses are imperfect, as exemplified by statistical significance tests' sample size dependence discussed

FIGURE 8.2   The Skewing Effect of Visual Presentation.

earlier, but those tools are also consistently imperfect (meaning, could potentially be viewed as random error rather than systematic bias), and their imperfections are well known. And so it stands to reason that consistent cross-time and cross-situation use of transparently imperfect tools is likely to yield more valid and reliable knowledge claims than analytically vague means. And hence the importance of relating new outcomes to past ones, as discussed in Phase I: Review of Previous Findings.

Another critical consideration is the choice of statistical analysis tools. Very broadly characterized, the available means of statistical data analysis can be divided into two segments: (1) analyst-driven syntax + menu applications and (2) automated data mining/ML tools. The former encompass open-source computational programming languages such as R or Python, as well as commercial syntax + menu-based systems such as SAS or SPSS, whereas the latter range from general open-source data mining libraries such as Scikit-Learn or TensorFlow, to commercial object-based applications such as SAS Enterprise Miner or SPSS Modeler. The core difference between those two general means of extracting insights out of data is that the analyst-driven approaches rely on analyst choice throughout the analytic process, which is in sharp contrast to automated data mining systems, which function largely as 'black box' systems in which within-process (of data analysis) human choices are replaced with pre-programmed, algorithmic logic. The numerous computational and technical differences aside, given their manifestly transparent analytic processes, results produced by analyst-driven approaches lend themselves to process validation, thus any anomalous or unexpected outcomes can be rationalized in terms of the fundamental 'why' and 'how' questions. That is not the case, however, with automated data mining produced findings, which tend to be produced by complex computational processes that cannot be reduced to easily understand logical steps (meaning that, under most circumstances, the efficacy of the underlying data analytical processes cannot be reviewed). In the end, both means of analyzing data have merit and both can produce valid and reliable insights, provided that sufficient data preparatory work was done, and those doing the work have the requisite knowledge and experience, but automated data mining outcomes may require more willingness to believe the unexpected and unexplainable, which can be challenging, especially in an organizational setting permeated by a web of preexisting beliefs.

Looking beyond the general approach related considerations, the task of exposing patterns in sets of data entails numerous contingencies, data manipulation steps, and result interpretation. Although some of the more technical details fall outside of the scope of this book, other data exploration considerations can be meaningfully described in more general terms. While some of those considerations are highly technical and thus fall outside of this overview, a few of the more general cogitations are outlined next.

Univariate Analyses

The first of those considerations addresses the nature of exploration, which can be either *univariate*, meaning a single variable focused, or *multivariate*, meaning focused on relationships between two or more variables. The purpose of the former is to describe an outcome or a characteristic of interest, such as the average product repurchase cycle or buyers' gender breakdown, whereas the goal of the latter is to identify any relationships between two or more variables (e.g., the relationship between the gender of product buyers and product repurchase cycle). Univariate analysis is typically the first EDA step because a thorough understanding of properties of individual variables is of key importance not only to correctly interpreting the information contents of individual variables but also to what is typically the next step, which is the analysis of relationships between two or more variables or multivariate analysis. Of central importance here is individual variables' measurement scale, or more specifically, whether a particular variable is categorical or continuous.

Categorical variables assume only values that represent discrete and distinct categories, and can be either nominal (i.e., unranked labels, such as 'male' and 'female' values for gender) or rank-ordered (i.e., relative magnitude or position implying designations such as 'small', 'medium', and 'large' for size). From data analytical standpoint, it makes no difference if the actual values are encoded as numbers, such as '1', '2', and '3' for 'high', 'medium', and 'low', respectively, or as so-called 'strings' (words or alphanumeric values, which represent a combination of letters and digits) – either set of values is ultimately treated as labels for individual categories comprising a particular variable. In the vast majority of applied business situations, categorical variables have a finite, often relatively small number of values. *Continuous* variables, on the other hand, can assume an infinite number of possible values, usually bounded by two extremes,[17] and have to be encoded as numbers. Those variables can represent any numerically measurable property, with common examples including age, weight, income, or job satisfaction (if measured using a continuous scale, such as Likert).

Implied in this very brief overview of the two general variable types is the fundamental difference in their mathematical properties – the 'label-only' or 'ordered-group' encompassing categorical values permit far fewer mathematical operations than the 'any value between the two extremes is possible' continuous variables. Thus in an informational sense, the former are informationally poorer than the latter, a fact that manifests itself in the availability of value-describing statistics (this is also why continuous metrics can always be re-coded into categorical ones, but the reverse is not possible). The practical consequences of the impermissibility of some basic algebraic operations, such as division, required to compute average values, can place rather severe limitations on the informational value of categorical data. More practically significant, however, consequence of the categorical-continuous variable schism is that univariate (as well as multivariate, as discussed later) analyses require different statistical techniques for each variable type. In general, categorical variables are described using counts and frequencies, whereas continuous variables are best characterized with the help of measures of central tendency (e.g., the average), variability (e.g., variance or its derivative, the standard deviation), and the spread (e.g., the range); under most circumstances, due to fewer possible mathematical operations, univariate analyses of categorical variables are more straightforward to execute and understand.

Approach-wise, being comprised of finite, and at times relatively small number of groups, categorical variables naturally lend themselves to visual descriptions, with basic tools such as histograms offering an easy-to-interpret way of conveying relative frequency counts of individual categories. However, just because the number of categories is finite does not mean that it is small. For instance, descriptors such as 'address' or 'location' can yield a very large number of distinct values, which when graphed might produce visually and otherwise incoherent representations (it should be noted that when summarized statistically, in a frequency distribution table, the results might be equally difficult to interpret). An easy corrective step is to create meta-groupings of categories, which, while reducing the specificity of information may ultimately make the data more meaningful. An added benefit of taking that step is that it will also likely reduce the amount of noise in the data (i.e., the earlier mentioned 'rough' part) since low-frequency categories contribute disproportionately more to the 'rough' in data than they do to the 'smooth'.

Delving into continuous variables is almost always more involved. In theory, a variable measured on a continuous scale can assume a different value for each individual data record, and though that rarely happens in practice, almost always the number of different values is quite high, which necessitates the use of different tactics for describing contents of individual continuous variables (i.e., univariate analysis). Again, due the possibly very large number of random (i.e., not known ahead of time) values that an individual continuous variable can assume, the most informative tactic for describing such a variable is to do so in the context of three related but distinct measures: (1) the typical, or *average*, value, (2) the expected *deviation* from the average or typical value, and (3) the observed *range* of values, or the difference between the smallest and the largest value. It thus follows that continuous variables lend themselves more to statistical data exploration, largely because the aforementioned three parameters used to describe their distributions are essentially mathematical artifacts that are simply easier to interpret as numeric values than as graphical images. For instance, while one could certainly graph the average customer age of, let's say, 46.7 years or the average product repurchase lag of 2.4 weeks, arguably, little would be gained by recasting those straightforward numeric estimates into visual representations.

The three core descriptors of continuous variables – the average, deviation, and the range – are conceptual, rather than operational expressions of value distributions, which means that their discussion would not be complete without addressing some additional, methodological considerations. The familiar-sounding notion of the 'average' is commonly used in everyday business vernacular to denote the 'mean', and more specifically, the 'arithmetic mean'. There are two key problems with that, well, habit: First, there are three distinct mathematical expressions of the 'average' – mean, median, and mode – and the mean is not always the most appropriate statistic to use; in fact, as discussed below, quite often it is an inappropriate statistic to use. Second, there are several distinct mathematical variants of the mean statistic – in addition to arithmetic, a mean can also be weighted, geometric or harmonic. And again, although the 'arithmetic mean' may end up being the appropriate variant to use in a particular situation (assuming that the mean is an appropriate statistic to use in the first place), there are numerous practical instances where one of the other formulations might be more appropriate.

Turning back to the more general idea of which of the three aforementioned measures of central tendency (the mean, median, and mode) can be expected to yield the most robust estimate of the average, there is a general tendency to over-use the mean, which is probably due to a combination of the statistic's simplicity and the general familiarity with it. Under some very specific circumstances, most notably when the distribution of the variable of interest is perfectly symmetrical (i.e., the so-called standard normal distribution), all three estimates of central tendency will yield the same value, which, in turn, will render choosing one over the others a moot point. However, those instances are extremely rare – some would even argue that they can only be found in statistics textbooks. A fairly typical, on the other hand, situation is one where the distribution of an outcome or a phenomenon of interest is asymmetrical, which is usually a consequence of more cases clustering toward either of the two ends of the underlying value continuum. For instance, considering customer value to a brand, virtually all brands have a lot more 'low'- than they do 'high'-value customers; similarly, there are significantly more trivial than severe automotive accidents, there are considerably more people living in poverty than those living in opulence, and the list goes on. In fact, it is hard to think of a practical business outcome measure that is symmetrically distributed – the elegant standard normal distribution makes for a handy statistical concept teaching aid, but that is where its usefulness ends. And so in the vast majority of practical situations, the values of the mean, the median, and the mode will diverge, ultimately leading to a dilemma: Which of those numerically different estimates of the 'average' offers the most robust approximation of the 'typical' value? Under most circumstances, when describing either positively or negatively skewed variables,[18] median tends to yield the most dependable portrayal of the typical value. The reason for that is rather simple: Median is the center-most value in a sorted distribution, with exactly half of all records falling above and below it[19]; it is also unaffected by outliers since it is an actual, rather than computed value. The far more frequently and often erroneously used mean tends to yield biased estimates of the average because it is a computed (by summing all values and dividing the total by the number of cases) estimate whose magnitude is directly impacted by outlying or extreme cases. Lastly, in theory, the mode can also yield reliable depiction of the average (like median, it is also an actual, rather than a computed value), but in practice there are often multiple modes, especially in larger datasets, which ultimately diminishes the practical utility of that statistic.

The second of the three core continuous variable descriptors is the *deviation*, which can be seen as a complement to the earlier discussed average. It is simply the measure of variability, or the amount of spread of values of a variable around the estimates average. So although the 'average' paints a picture of the most typical, single value that can be used to characterize an entire set of data, the deviation speaks to the typical degree of departure from the average. In a sense, it can be seen as a measure of heterogeneity of individual records with regard to the value of a particular variable – the higher the deviation, the more diverse (in terms of values) a dataset.

While conceptually a bit more abstract than the notion of the average, operationally it is more straightforward as it is operationalized using a single metric of *standard deviation*. There is a caveat, however: Standard deviation is a property of the mean (as it measures the spread of value around the mean) thus it can only be used with the mean, not the median or the mode. Given the inappropriateness of using the mean as a measure of the average for non-symmetrical distributions, the practical utility of standard deviation is thus considerably reduced. A methodologically sound alternative is offered by a comparatively lesser known statistic of *average absolute deviation* (also referred to as *mean absolute deviation*), which is a generalized summary measure of statistical dispersion that can be used with any measure of central tendency – the mean, the median, and the mode.

The third and final continuous variable descriptor is the *range*, which is simply a measure of dispersion of values, operationalized as the difference between the largest and smallest value of a variable in a dataset. While conceptually similar to standard deviation, it is computationally quite different as it only takes into account two values – the maximum and the minimum – and ignores the rest (whereas standard deviation is computed using all values). While useful as an indication of how spread out the data are, range can produce unreliable or even unrealistic estimates when outliers are present. An obvious remedy would seem to be to simply recommend filtering out extreme values, but doing so is both difficult and problematic. It is difficult because there are no standard, objective outlier lines of demarcation, and while it might be relatively easy to pinpoint some outliers in some situations (e.g., Bill Gates or Warren Buffett would certainly stand out if compared to others in their respective high school graduating classes in terms of income), it is quite a bit more difficult to do so in other situations (e.g., insurance claims or customer brand spending). Moreover, it is problematic because, after all, outliers are actually valid data points and excluding them from analyses can introduce downward bias. For instance, when measured in terms of economic damage, hurricanes Harvey (2017), Katrina (2005), and Sandy (2012) are, as of early 2018, the three costliest storms in the US history – when compared to a median cost of hurricane caused damage, Harvey, Katrina, and Sandy were each more than 50 times costlier, which makes all three of those storms outliers. Given that, should those storms be excluded from any damage forecasts and related estimates? It is a difficult question to answer because while those are real and important data points (the argument against exclusion), those three data points will likely exert disproportionately large, and potentially distorting influence on at least some of the estimates (the argument for exclusion).

Multivariate Analyses

A natural extension of univariate EDA is to assess relationships among variables. For example, the analysis of 'customer spend' almost naturally suggests looking into possible associations between that outcome and various customer characteristics, such as 'age'. Is there a material relationship between customers' age and their spending level?

A word of caution: As postulated by the Simpson's paradox, the direction or strength of empirical relationships may change when data are aggregated across natural groupings that should be treated separately. In the context of the above example, assessment of a potential relationship between 'age' and 'spending' should contemplate the possibility of natural data subsets, such as gender-based ones. In that case, a search for an overall (i.e., both genders combined) relationship might yield no discernible age-spending association while within-gender investigations may reveal statistically significant relationships.

As implied by the above example, the assessment of between-variable relationships is, at its core, a pairwise comparison although numerous such relationships may be examined concurrently. And once again, the categorical vs. continuous, variable-specific level of measurement plays a pivotal role, as it determines how individual pairwise relationships are assessed. From the methodological perspective, pairwise comparisons coupled with two levels of measurement yield three distinct contrast scenarios: (1) two categorical variables, (2) two continuous variables, and (3) one categorical and one continuous variable.

Relationships between two categorical variables are most commonly assessed using contingency table based cross-tabulations (abbreviated as cross-tabs) with χ^2 (chi square) test of association. In a statistical sense, χ^2 is a non-parametric test, which means that it places no distributional requirements on the sample data; however, to yield unbiased estimates, the test requires the sample to be random, data to be reported as raw frequencies (not percentages), and the individual categories to be mutually exclusive and exhaustive and the observed frequencies. The underlying comparisons are conceptually and computationally straightforward: the analysis simply compares the difference between the observed and expected (i.e., calculated using probability theory, in this case by multiplying the rows and columns in the contingency table, and dividing the product by the total count) frequencies in each cell to identify patterns of co-occurrences that are more frequent than those that could be produced by random chance (i.e., are deemed to be non-spurious). It should be noted that the underlying comparison is binary – that is, it may suggest the presence of relationships, but yield no information regarding the strength of the association. A different statistical technique, Cramer's V, can be used to assess the strength of the relationship for associations earlier determined to be statistically significant.

Relationships between two continuous variables are most often examined using *correlation analysis*. In the definitional sense, correlation is a concurrent change in value of two numeric variables, which represents the degree of linear relationship between those variables. Due to the fact that correlation examines relationships between continuously scaled variables which can be subjected to wider range of mathematical operations, it produces richer informational outcomes. Hence, correlation-expressed assessment of pairwise relationships yields information addressing not only the presence of statistically significant association, but also both the direction and the strength of individual associations. The former can be either positive, where an increase in one of the two variables is accompanied by an increase in the other, or negative, where an increase in one variable is accompanied by a decrease in the other, while the latter is captured in a standardized metric ranging from 0 (no association) to 1 (perfect association). Both informational dimensions are summarized in correlation coefficient, which expresses the strength of the relationship between two continuous variables as ranging from +1 (perfectly positive correlation) to −1 (perfectly negative correlation) and centered on 0, which denotes a lack of relationship.

There are several important considerations that need to be addressed in the context of the fairly generic overview of correlation analysis sketched out above. First, correlation-based assessment of relationships between variables is limited to only the simplest possible association, which is linear, which means that a change in one variable is always proportional to change in the other variable. For example, if the relationship between the earlier mentioned 'age' and 'spending level' yields a correlation coefficient of 0.5, the implication of that estimate is that for every 1 unit increase in age (1 year), there will be a corresponding increase of 0.5 units ($.5) in spending, and that relationship will remain unchanged, in theory, into infinity. Second, and perhaps even more importantly, correlation analysis cannot detect nonlinear associations, which means that a lack of statistically significant correlation should not be interpreted as the absence of association, but merely as only the absence of linear association. Unfortunately, given the common and loose usage of the term 'correlation' in formal and informal business communications, that important distinction is often overlooked.

Moreover, there are two main types of correlation coefficients: Pearson's product-moment correlation coefficient and Spearman's rank correlation coefficient (the earlier general overview of correlation analysis implicitly assumed the former, which is by far more commonly used). The correct usage of correlation coefficient type depends on variables' distributional characteristics, most notably the shape of each of the two variables' distribution. Pearson's correlation is appropriate when variables being studied are normally distributed (i.e., symmetrical), and relatively outlier-free, as the presence of outliers may exaggerate or dampen the strength of relationship. Spearman's correlation, on the other hand, is appropriate when one or both variables are skewed; it is also worth noting that its coefficients are largely unaffected by outliers.

The last of the three measurement scale based variable pairings are mixed-scale relationships, which are those between a categorical and a continuous variables. The underlying logic of assessing those relationships is noticeably different from that of assessing like-scaled variables' associations, which essentially considers different expressions of co-occurrence. When a categorical and a continuous variables are related to each other, the relationship takes the form of contrasting average values of the continuous variable across the categories comprising the categorical variable. In the simplest case scenario, the relationship between a categorical variable comprised of two distinct categories, for example, 'males' and 'females', and a continuous variable, for example, 'product spend', would be examined by comparing mean 'product spend' values for 'males' and 'females' using *t-test*, which one of the tests of difference discussed earlier. If the difference between the two means was statistically significant, then that would be taken as an indication of non-spurious relationship between the continuous variable 'product spend' and the categorical variable 'gender'. It should be noted that the t-test can only be used for comparisons of two means – if the categorical variable is comprised of more than two categories (e.g., 'male', 'female', and 'other'), a different test of difference, the *F-test*, needs to be used. Although the general rationale underpinning the F-test conceptually parallels that of the t-test, the result interpretation can be fuzzier. The reason is that the statistically significant F-test is an indication of some statistical mean inequality among all means being compared. Stated differently, statistically significant F-test only attests to the conclusion that all means being compared (for instance, comparing 'average spend' across numerous store geographies could easily result in 10 or even more individual mean contrasts) are not equal. And 'not equal' means that all could be different or that only one could differ from the rest (with the rest being statistically the same), or any number of in-between possibilities. Given the relative non-specificity of the F-test, a number of post hoc tests (conducted after the initial F-test) were developed to address the problem of identifying where the differences occurred between groups; some of the more commonly used post hoc tests include Tukey's honestly significant difference (HSD) and Games Howell test.

Confirmatory Data Analysis

Recalling the in-depth analysis of the essence of what constitutes 'evidence' presented in Chapter 5, it is fact or other organized information presented in support of or justification for beliefs or inferences. In view of that relatively broad definitional scope, available and pertinent evidence may encompass a mixed bag of evidentiary signals, some supporting and others refuting a particular belief or inference. For instance, the organization's past marketing results may offer 'mixed evidence' regarding benefits of temporary price reductions, leading to obvious decision uncertainties regarding the future usage of that promotional tactic. In such a situation, it is important to not dismiss any mixed signs as inconclusive, but rather to treat those as starting point for further knowledge development. More specifically, closer examination of past results may reveal associations between situational factors, such as the depth of temporary discounts, and outcomes in the form of the resultant benefits, which, in turn, may lead to the formulation of specific past outcomes-based hypotheses framing the potential promotional value of temporary price reduction. Confirmatory data analysis can then be used to test those prior experience-based hypotheses to produce unambiguous insights regarding the value of temporary price reduction as a marketing tactic. Thus, when considered from the standpoint of knowledge creation, the overall aim of confirmatory analysis is to assess and substantiate the truthfulness of what is currently believed, using the tools of statistical inference.

It is important to note that, ideally, confirmatory analysis is used as means validating knowledge claims initially derived using the earlier discussed exploratory analysis. The standard clinical trial process offers perhaps the most compelling illustration of the 'exploratory-then-confirmatory' progression: Phase 1 of clinical trials typically *explores* the safety and side effects of a new treatment, which is followed by Phase 2, which further *explores* whether the new treatment is effective in improving a health condition, and lastly Phase 3, the goal of which is typically to *confirm* the efficacy and safety effects in larger, carefully planned studies with prespecified methodology. In general business analyses, however, the distinction between exploratory and confirmatory research is rarely that procedurally systematic and operationally clear, and the distinction is more often framed in the more nebulous context of data mining/ insight generation (exploratory research) vs. hypothesis testing (confirmatory research).

Considered as a standalone data analytic endeavor, confirmatory analysis is most commonly used as a mean of providing evidence supporting or refuting specific effects, such as the impact of sales incentives on product purchase, or more generalized relationships, such as the association between price and aggregate sales. It is rather common, however, for results of such analyses to yield ambiguous conclusions, which is typically due to uncertainty in the methods or the underlying rationale (or more formally, the theory utilized in the research process), or low statistical power.[20] To avoid such problems, confirmatory analyses should use data from valid to reliable sources, sample size that has been calibrated to detect the minimum effect size of interest (which in practice means statistical power of 0.90 or higher), clearly spelled out inference criteria (i.e., conditions for accepting as true or rejecting of individual hypotheses), and a carefully thought out data analytic methodology. In even more operationally clear terms, the following considerations need to be addressed prior to delving into data analytic work:

- what transformations or adjustments, if any, are to be applied to the data,
- what criteria are to be used for excluding or deleting data,
- what specific statistical tests are to be used for hypothesis testing,
- whether the test should be one-sided (e.g., A > B) or two-sided (i.e., A ≠ B), and
- what specific inference criteria, such as p-value (Type I error, or false positive, denoted by α) magnitude ($\alpha = 0.05$ being the most often chosen value) should be used for accepting evidence.

The process of delineating valid and maximally complete confirmatory data analytic insights also hinges on the notion of *informational domain specification* (IDS). Broadly characterized as the expression of informational sufficiency of available data, this simple sounding concept hides surprising amounts of complexity. That is because the intent behind IDS is to outline a conceptual blueprint of the formally or informally stated analytic model, which entails clearly spelling out all hypothesized relationships, not only at the abstract concept level but also at operational level of individual variables. In view of the importance of that confirmatory analysis preparatory step, coupled with potential operational ambiguities, a more in-depth overview of IDS is offered next.

Informational Domain Specification

In an applied sense, IDS is a process by means of which analysts select and arrange specific (raw) data elements to form a conceptual model, based upon which specific (statistical) analyses and tests are to be carried out, all with the goal of delineating the sought after evidentiary insights. In more abstract sense, IDS can be seen as a summary construct of several key analyses-shaping considerations: First, selected data need to match the stated informational objectives (e.g., to analyze customer purchase behavior, customer-level purchase details need to be included among the selected data); second, the selected variables need to be non-redundant and operationally comparable (i.e., variables that are to be related to each other on the same plain of abstraction need to be expressed at a comparable level of aggregation); and third, the analytic model, or the totality of all hypothesized relationships, needs to be parsimonious, which is to say that it needs to offer the greatest possible depth of insight while using the fewest variables. The seemingly ever-expanding variety of data sources and types puts a particularly bright spotlight on the parsimony aspect of IDS. Throwing every available data element into the data analytic mix is undesirable from statistical as well as interpretational perspectives, as introducing redundant and/or spurious metrics tends to confuse the task of identifying knowledge-building insights.

In terms of the outcomes of the IDS process, the informational domain can be just-, over-, or under-specified. Ideally, an informational domain is just-specified, which is accomplished when a sufficient number of nontrivial explanatory variables are available. As might be intuitively obvious, arriving at a 'sufficient' number of variables is not an easy task, particularly given that objective benchmarks are rarely, if ever, readily available. A general rule of thumb that can be used here is to deem the number of explanatory variables to be sufficient when the selected variables together yield a statistically robust results[21] while the variable set is small enough to be practically actionable.

An under-specified informational domain is one that yields too few nontrivial variables resulting in diminished explanatory power and predictive validity. It is a direct consequence of insufficiently small amount of variability in the data being explained by the combined variable set, or more formally, the model; in practice, it tends to manifest itself in incomplete explanations or inaccurate predictions. On the other hand, an over-specified domain is one that encompasses excessively large number of somewhat related but trivial factors, resulting in cumbersome explanatory outcomes and unreliable predictions, where small value changes produce drastically different outcomes. Under-specification is most often a function of data sparsity, which can be difficult to overcome, whereas over-specification is usually a function of flawed variable retention and usage rationale, which under most circumstances can be rather easily rectified by means of more careful variable selection, aggregation, and transformations.

Variable Selection

Sometimes, there is simply too much data available. Data over-abundance frequently leads to indiscriminate use of all that is accessible, a tendency made worse by the advent of powerful ML applications capable of quickly processing vast – record- and variable-wise – quantities of data. The ability to process what is available does not, however, eliminate the 'garbage-in, garbage-out' problem. Given the widespread usage of statistical significance tests in classical statistics and ML/data mining applications alike,[22] coupled with the well-known (discussed earlier in Chapter 2) dependence of those tests on sample size, analyses of large, that is, a few thousand records and larger, datasets containing a random mix of variables will almost inescapably yield a mix of information-ally meaningful and illusory effects and associations, all deemed 'statistically significant'. Making use of the often recommended but poorly thought out reasoning of subsequently differentiating between 'practically important' and 'practically not important' often worsens the initial problem, as it re-introduces the possibly biased subjective evaluations that were to be kept at bay by objec-tive analyses of data.

The idea here is not to only select variables that one expects to matter, but rather to de-select those that have no conceivable connection to the informa-tional need at hand. Considering that much of the organizational data emanates from the various transaction processing and communication systems, individ-ual data files quite commonly contain numerous redundant and analytically meaningless measures that reflect the mechanics of how data are captured while offering little-to-no informational value. There is no one-size-fits-all template that could be used to single out variables that should be excluded because those choices reflect a combination of data at hand and anticipated data analytic out-comes, thus a careful study of both should precede data analytic work.

Variable Aggregation

The totality of organizational data is almost always a mix of variables exhibiting various degrees of aggregation, or specificity. For instance, marketing-related data might encompass point-of-sales derived, purchase-level transactional de-tails, customer-level promotional responses, and geography-level, typically clusters of nearby households, demographic estimates. To be pooled together, those distinct and differently structured files need to be homogenized with respect to individual metrics' levels of aggregation, which can easily turn into a computationally involved task. It is, nonetheless, a necessary precondition of deriving deeper insights out of the available data, thus reconciling variable-level aggregation differences needs careful and skillful consideration.

Variable Transformations

A yet another manifestation of type, form, and format heterogeneity of a mix of variables that might be available and applicable to the stated informational needs is captured by the relatively technical dimension of individual variables' measurement and distributional properties, which become particularly im-portant in the context of methodological choices. For example, the widely used Pearson's correlation imposes normality requirement on all variables to be correlated, which means that the distribution of each variable has to be ap-proximately normal (i.e., it has to resemble the familiar bell-shaped, symmetric curve). Yet, many commonly analyzed outcomes, such as 'customer spending', tend not to be normally distributed as there are typically far more low than high spending customers (which results in an asymmetrical or skewed distribution); when non-normally distributed variables are correlated using Pearson's correlation, the results are not robust, which simply means that there is no reasonable assurance of efficacy, or validity of the resultant correlation estimates. Variable transformations, broadly defined as the application of a deterministic mathematical function, such as the logarithm, to each data point, can be used to bring individual variables' distributions into closer alignment with assumptions of data analytical techniques.

★★★

Turning back to the discussion of confirmatory data analysis, that broad knowledge creation endeavor can be broken down into sets of statistical methodologies: *dependence* and *interdependence*. The former, which encompass a rich array of distinct techniques including regression and discriminant analyses, structural equation modeling, and analysis of variance, are used to test the existence, and if so, the strength and the direction of relationships between an outcome of interest, typically designated as the 'dependent' (or 'criterion') variable, and one or more potential predictors of that outcome, typically designated as 'independent' (or 'predictor') variables. The latter, which commonly takes the form of factor analysis, cluster analysis, or multidimensional scaling, purport to examine the relationships that are believed to exist among variables of interest, without differentiating between outcomes and their predictors. As implied by this very general contrast, the difference between dependence and interdependence methods and analyses hinges on the notion of *causation*: Dependence analysis can be seen as statistical means of ascertaining cause-effect relationship, whereas interdependence analysis are only concerned with ascertaining more general concurrence (as in correlation) relationships. This is a critical distinction not only from the methodological standpoint but also from the perspective of evidence creation, and thus will be more deeply explored next. It should be noted, however, that the ensuing examination of dependence- and interdependence-minded data analytic approaches focuses on topics that directly relate to decision-making evidence validation and substantiation – those interested in more exhaustive treatment of those topics are encouraged to reference one or more of numerous multivariate statistics focused sources.

Dependence Analysis

Just as the task of ascertaining causation is of fundamental importance to knowledge creation, dependence analysis can be seen as one of the key data analytic tools for objectively assessing the validity of suspected cause-effect relationships. Hence, developing a sound understanding of statistical assessment of 'dependence' as a source of decision-guiding evidence is contingent on developing sound foundational understanding of epistemology of causation.

Given its central role in knowledge creation, the notion of *causality* or *causation* has been a subject of centuries-long debate among scientists and philosophers alike. At the core of the debate has been the line of demarcation separating cause-and-effect from just simple concurrence-based relationships. Is factor A causing B, or do the two merely coincide? From the standpoint of philosophy of science, to be deemed causal an association has to exhibit temporal sequentiality (A has to precede B), associative variation (changes in A must be systematically associated with changes in B), the association between A and B has to be non-spurious (it should not disappear upon introduction of a third moderating factor), and lastly, it also has to have sound theoretical rationale (it has to 'make sense' or exhibit basic face validity). In spite of their somewhat foreboding names, temporal sequentiality and associative variation have a very simple meaning and application, as the conditions of occurring in sequence and doing so persistently are both intuitively obvious and relatively easy to demonstrate. For instance, one has to receive purchase incentive, such as a discount coupon, prior to making a purchase during which that coupon is redeemed (temporal sequentiality), and that sequence can easily be observed on recurring basis (associative variation).

The remaining two conditions – non-spuriousness and theoretical support – are somewhat more difficult to ascertain, as illustrated by the purchase incentive example. To provide an adequate proof of non-spuriousness, it is usually necessary to set up a controlled experiment, which is not always feasible, as it is indeed plausible that the observed concurrence of a product purchase and a purchase incentive (e.g., coupon redemption) is merely coincidental, rather than being causally related. In fact, one of the well-known problems with discount coupons is that those incentives do more to subsidize current (i.e., those who would likely repurchase the product without the incentive) than to attract new buyers. A bit of the same problem emerges when trying to establish theoretical support for a presumed cause-effect relationship. Continuing with the purchase incentive example, the same cause-effect relationship between purchase incentives and purchase behavior is likely to inspire one conceptual substantiation when the traditional economic theory is brought to bear, and a noticeably different one when behavioral economic reasoning is looked to for conceptual guidance.[23]

Within the confines of the 3E framework detailed in this book, the relative tangibility of temporal sequentiality and associative variation proofs warrants labeling those as 'hard' substantiations of causality, whereas the elusiveness of non-spuriousness and theoretical support suggests that those additional proofs be considered 'soft' substantiations. Given its practical reachability, the attainment of the hard causality substantiation should be considered convincing and sufficient indication of empirically validated cause-effect associations, whereas the attainment of the more practically elusive soft substantiation of causality should be considered further support of the already established causality.

Keeping the foundational cause-effect considerations in mind, there are numerous statistical means of estimating those relationships, with regression analysis, discriminant analysis, structural equation modeling, and analysis of variance being the most commonly used families of techniques. While all families of statistical techniques share the common foundation of expressly differentiating between 'cause' and 'effect' termed as 'dependent' and 'independent' variables, each set of methodologies approaches the very general task of causal assessment in a mathematically distinct manner. Moreover, each family of dependence techniques is comprised of multiple algorithms, with each algorithm offering an unambiguous process of solving a class of problems delimited by very specific combination of data characteristics and statistical assumptions (the discussion of which falls outside of the scope of this book). For example, the regression analysis family of statistical algorithms encompasses more than a dozen of distinct techniques including the relatively well-known linear and logistic regression techniques, as well as the typically lesser-known polynomial, quantile, ridge, lasso, ordinal, and other techniques. Moreover, each individual algorithm typically embodies a somewhat different set of data analytic process optimization and result validation considerations that have to be addressed to assure the validity and reliability of the resultant outcomes. In short, the conceptual goal of estimating cause-effect relationships using statistical methods of dependence analysis calls for a considerable amount of data due diligence and familiarity, and an equally considerable amount of statistical know-how. In general, the more methodologically and computationally complex the approach, the more involved the process of ascertaining the efficacy of the resultant knowledge claims.

Interdependence Analysis

Implied in the preceding discussion is that ascertaining the more general patterns of concurrence is methodologically and interpretationally less daunting. And indeed that is usually the case. From the evidentiary point of view, the task of proving that factors A and B co-occur presents a lower burden than the task of proving that A causes B because the latter does not attempt to control for the influence of other, not expressly accounted for, factors. Thus, within the conceptual realm of co-occurrence, A can cause B or there could be another, unaccounted for factor C that impacts both A and B – in either case, the general conclusion regarding the association between A and B remains the same.

In the context of statistical analyses of data, a widely used expression of co-occurrence is *correlation*, which is a quantity measuring a possible two-way linear association between variables. As discussed in more detail earlier in this chapter, correlation describes the behavior of pairs of variables in terms of two distinct dimensions of interdependence: the direction and the strength of the association. The former can be either positive, which is when an increase in one variable is associated with an increase in another, or negative, which is when an increase in one variable is associated with a decrease in the other; the latter can range from no association at all to perfect association, which is when the behavior of one variable is mirrored by the behavior of the other variable. It is important to note that perfect association can be either positive or negative – a positive perfect correlation is when the direction of change and the amount of change are the same for both variables, whereas a negative perfect correlation is when direction of change is different for each of the two variables (i.e., one goes up and the other goes down), but the magnitude of change is exactly the same. Commonly expressed on a standardized scale, perfect negative correlation is denoted by a coefficient of '−1', perfect positive correlation is denoted by a coefficient of '1' (with '+' being the implied qualifier) while no correlation is denoted by '0'. Given its standardized nature, correlation coefficients enable quick and easy strength of association comparisons.

There have been numerous types of correlation coefficients developed in the course of the past several decades, though most are based on, or derived from the two main types of correlation coefficients: Pearson's product moment and Spearman's rank correlation. Pearson's product moment correlation, typically denoted by 'r', assumes both variables to be continuous and normally distributed, and the (possible) relationship between them to be linear; it is affected by extreme values, which may exaggerate or dampen the strength of relationship. An alternative to Pearson's correlation, Spearman's rank correlation coefficient, denoted either by the Greek letter ρ (rho) or by r_s, is nonparametric (meaning, it does not assume variables to be normally distributed) and it is appropriate to use when one or both variables are at least ordinal or continuous but skewed; also, it is unaffected by extreme values.

Although the notion of correlation is commonly used to describe pairwise co-occurrence, the broader idea of variable interdependence is not limited to just bivariate associations. In fact, one of the important data curation considerations is *dimensionality reduction,* which is the process of decreasing the number of variables in a dataset by obtaining a set of principal components. Exemplified by the widely used methods of principal component analysis and factor analysis,[24] which are statistical algorithms designed to reduce the original set of variables into smaller sets of components or factors that account for most of the information found in the original variables, dimensionality reduction makes use of multivariate, or many variables, interdependence. In a more general sense, multivariate interdependence analysis is not limited to just the normally distributed, continuous variables – for instance, the method of principal component analysis has been extended to also include categorical variables (aptly named as categorical principal component analysis or CATPCA).

Notes

1 Meaning that patients are generally willing to follow the advice of their doctors, and multiple doctors treating a single patient typically work toward a shared goal of helping that patient.

2 To explain individual behavior, classical and neoclassical economic analyses make use of the rational choice model which posits that economic behavior is rational in the sense that it is governed by the principle of utility maximization; it could thus be argued that System 2 reveals itself in the manner described by the classical utility maximization.

3 For example, the 1995 passage of the Private Securities Litigation Reform Act by the US Congress, intended to limit frivolous securities lawsuits by means of changing pleading, discovery, liability, class representation, and awards standards, effectively rendered the pre-1995 data unreliable to post-1995 likelihood and severity of risk analyses.

4 For a comprehensive overview, see D. Kahneman's 2011 book *Thinking Fast and Slow*, Farrar, Straus and Giroux, New York, NY.

5 A physical phenomenon which occurs when pairs of particles interact in ways such that the quantum state of each particle cannot be described independently of the state of the other, even when the particles are separated by a large distance – in everyday language, it is akin to say that particles are simultaneously 'aware' of each other, regardless of the distance separating them.

6 A rather counterintuitive quantum mechanical principle according to which particles rather than existing in a single state or changing between a variety of states simultaneously exist in all possible states at the same time; it is a bit like saying that someone can be alive and dead at the same time.

7 For an easy to follow discussion, see B. Rosenblum and F. Kuttner's 2006 book *Quantum Enigma: Physics Encounters Consciousness* (Oxford University Press).

8 Since there is no operational limit to the number of tables comprising a relational database, it is not uncommon to encounter databases comprised of dozens of data tables.

9 It should be noted that the term 'buyer' is used here as a general descriptor of the unit of analysis (e.g., purchase vs. purchaser), rather than personally identifiable information, the use of which, as noted earlier, should be avoided.

10 Typically, this entails correcting for severely asymmetrical, or skewed, distribution (e.g., great many low-value records vs. comparatively very few high-value records, as might be the case with income or insurance claims cost).

11 For example, 'gender', which can be coded as 'female' and 'male' but could be easily re-coded into numeric indicators such as '1' for females and '2' for males.

12 For an easy to follow synopsis, see the F. Hartwig and B. Dearing's 1979 book, *Exploratory Data Analysis,* published by Sage; for a more methodologically thorough treatment, see J. Tukey's 1977 *Exploratory Data Analysis* book, published by Addison-Wesley.

13 In a very general sense, the notion of 'statistical significance', which is an integral part of the scientific method, is a widely used method of quantifying the likelihood that a relationship between two or more variables is caused by something other than random chance. However, when used with large volumes of data, the efficacy of significance testing can become questionable due to a combination of a large number of variables and the well-known sample size inflation, where the larger the sample size, the higher the likelihood of a particular relationship being seen as 'significant', or non-random (i.e., a relationship deemed not statistically significant will often become statistically significant when the underlying sample size is increased). Thus, exploratory analysis of 'big data' sources will likely produce overwhelming number of 'significant' relationships although the magnitude of at least some of those

relationships, as measured by methods such as correlation analysis, can be trivially small.

14 Attributed a 13th-century English Franciscan friar, William of Ockham, it posits that concepts should not be multiplied beyond necessity, or stated differently, everything else being equal, the simplest solution is preferred.

15 Perhaps the most common strategy is to use the following logic: If 'litigation date' = 'missing', then litigation = 0, else litigation = 1; in essence, the absence of a date implies that no litigation took place while the presence of any date implies the opposite.

16 Any numeric value can be measured using one of the four distinct measurement scales: nominal, ordinal, interval, and ratio – the first two are often grouped into 'categorical', and the latter two into 'continuous' categories.

17 Being bounded by two extremes does not contradict the idea of infinite number of values because the distance between those two extremes can be infinitely divided into ever smaller number of units.

18 A distribution is skewed if one of its tails is longer than the other; a positive skew means that the distribution has a long tail in the positive direction (i.e., higher values), whereas a negative skew means that the distribution has a long tail in the negative direction (i.e., negative values).

19 In situations in which there are an even number of data records (in which case there is no actual value that falls symmetrically in the center of the distribution), the median is computed by taking the average of the two values closest to the middle of the distribution.

20 The likelihood that a study will detect an effect when there is an effect there to be detected.

21 Although somewhat different outcome assessment methods and metrics are used with different statistical techniques, all are built around the general notion of the proportion of total variance explained by the model (i.e., the variable set used in the analysis).

22 Where statistical significance tests are used to differentiate between spurious and non-spurious effects and associations.

23 Traditional economics operates under the assumption that people are rational and make choices based on what is best for them and their situation, and those choices are a product of sound and rational cost-benefit calculations. Behavioral economics, on the other hand, suggests that people are quite irrational and their choices are often driven by impulses and habits that they cannot control, resulting in only a small percentage of choices being a product of careful cost-benefit analysis.

24 Two conceptually similar but methodologically distinct methods: In principal component analysis, the 'components' are actual orthogonal (independent) linear combinations that maximize the total variance, whereas in factor analysis, the 'factors' are linear combinations that maximize the shared portion of the variance.

9

SOURCING & ASSESSING

Research, Norms, and Judgment

A little more than a century ago when business schools first began to emerge as distinct academic units, their orientation was primarily occupational training oriented, which eventually began to attract criticisms from the more traditional parts of academic institutions. Wanting to shed the trade-school-like image, starting in the 1950s, schools of business began to aggressively pursue theoretical research agendas with the goal of becoming more university-like institutions, an effort which, by all accounts, was successful at shedding the practice-heavy image. In fact, it was so successful that by the 1980s business schools were commonly characterized as ivory towers producing graduates insufficiently prepared to assume managerial roles, or even to meaningfully participate in organizational functioning. Along the same lines, academe-produced intellectual research was just as often dismissed as esoteric and inapplicable, widely seen by management practitioners as overly theoretical, self-referential, and dismissive of practical considerations.

Perhaps management academics should be more application minded, and perhaps management practitioners should be more theoretically inquisitive. However, as noted earlier, management is not a formal profession framed by well-defined and universal body of knowledge manifesting itself in licensure measured competencies. Consequently, what constitutes 'meaningful body of knowledge' is open to interpretation, and by extension, what is considered practice-applicable research outcome is also a matter of individual perspective. Thus, in contrast to hard sciences or explicit rules based domains such as medicine or accounting, what managers are expected to know tends to be somewhat vague, from which it follows that the value of abstract academic research outcomes can be difficult to appreciate from the standpoint of management practice.

On the other hand, the value of objective operational data is usually quite clear, given its potential to spawn context-specific, decision-guiding knowledge. Not surprisingly, the explosive growth of all-things-data continues to inspire the collective imagination of organizational managers who see an ever-expanding informational possibilities. The ideas outlined in this book, however, are rooted in the fundamental belief that in all its many varieties, organizational data ultimately represent an addition to, not a replacement of other valuable decision-making contributors, which include scientific research, established industry norms, and well-considered expert judgment. That is because no source of knowledge is informationally complete, which means that to produce maximally valid and reliable insights, decision-makers need to leverage multiple sources of information. In that sense, while unique-to-none and known-to-all scientific generalizations or industry benchmarks might, individually, offer little help to decision-makers operating within specific sets of constraints, when thoughtfully synthesized with insights derived from other sources, including operational data, the results might be game-changing.

This chapter continues the overview of the mechanics of extracting decision-guiding evidence out of available information, now focusing on applicable academic and applied research, industry norms and best practices, and tacit professional knowledge. Together with the earlier (Chapter 8) discussed organizational data, the ensuring review offers a comprehensive summary of the means and methods of extracting decision-guiding knowledge out of available and diverse sources of information.

Thematic Analyses of Empirical Research

Interestingly, many of the challenges posed by operational data, as captured in the often-used 'volume, variety, and velocity' summarization, are the same challenges that are posed by synthesis of empirical research output. In fact, one avenue of decision-guiding insight extraction that might be more foreboding than the task of translating operational data into meaningful insights is the task of identifying, pooling, and synthesizing findings of empirical research studies. A conservative estimate pegs the number of academic journals at close to 29,000, and that does not include hundreds of trade journals, popular magazines, and an untold number of sporadic research dissemination sources, such as numerous research centers, consultancies, and other organizations that periodically contribute empirical research studies. And although only a subset of those sources are focused on pertinent to organizational decision-making domains, such as business management, the number of potential research outlets to be considered can still easily number in the hundreds. And that is just the number of outlets. According to research from the University of Ottawa, the combined output of just scientific research publishing-oriented sources totals approximately 2.5 million new scientific papers per year; if only 1% of those fall within a particular area of interest that is still about 25,000 potentially pertinent research contributions. Per year. Clearly, the 'big data' tagline seems as applicable to scientific research output as it is to commercial and social data.

Volume, of course, is only the initial challenge – the almost indescribable variability in the 'what', 'when', 'how', and 'why' of individual studies actually poses a far greater information processing challenge. The reason for that is the inherent subjectivity of research evaluation, coupled with the necessarily manual and thus incredibly tedious and time-consuming nature of that task. The search and pooling of potentially relevant research can benefit from the widespread content digitization which lends itself to process automation, effectively reducing the amount of time and effort required to compile the research outcomes of interest. However, when it comes to review and synthesis of the content of individual studies, technology offers very limited help. The obvious 'helpers' in the form of text mining and machine learning systems require extensive training on similar data, which renders those systems ineffective for processing highly heterogeneous bodies of research; hence, it is the task that ultimately requires careful and thorough review done by sufficiently knowledgeable individuals, which points to a yet another potential challenge: the inter-rater, inter-reviewer reliability, or concordance. When two different human reviewers examine the same research study, will both reach sufficiently similar conclusions? What should be done when reviewers reach different conclusions? An obvious solution might be to use multiple reviewers for each study and then employ some sort of a 'preponderance of conclusions' standard to select conclusions to be accepted. In theory that is a reasonable approach, but is it feasible in practice? How large a reviewer pool would be required to deploy such an approach to the 25,000 or so potentially worthwhile research outputs published annually in a domain of interest?

Synthesizing Empirical Research

In an organizational context, 'when' information is made available can be as important as 'what' information is available. In fact, there are numerous situations when rougher insights made available sooner can offer far greater value than more fine-tuned insights provided noticeably later. For instance, a key competitor decides to suddenly lower the price of its product – what is the best response? The nature of the underlying cross-product demand characteristics could be such that very immediate matching of that competitor's offer would be highly advisable, and being able to quickly secure such general insights would be far more beneficial than receiving more detailed information noticeably later. Although that is not always the case, it is nonetheless common for important organizational decisions to have relatively short time horizons.

The simple scenario briefly outlined above is but one of many illustrations of what is often referred to as the 'new normal' of modern, hypercompetitive business landscape in which rapid, and often unexpected change is the norm. On-point and timely information can reduce decision-making uncertainty and thus it is clearly a valuable asset, but that is provided that it is both on-point and timely. By and large, theory development focused academic research is primarily concerned with identifying and testing generalizable knowledge claims, which may or may not address idiosyncrasies of a particular situation. Moreover, the process of identifying and reviewing pertinent studies, synthesizing their findings, and extracting decision-related insights is tedious and time-consuming (in addition to also being chuck full of methodological challenges, such as the inter-reviewer concordance). Although the data processing and analysis-related technological advancements make rapid analyses of large volumes of diverse organizational data quite feasible, selecting, summarizing, and synthesizing research studies are 'manual', human judgment-rooted endeavors that do not yet lend themselves to meaningful automation (one could say that artificial-intelligence-based systems are still not sufficiently, well, intelligent). And yet, the currently prevailing conceptions of managerial evidence-based practice (as exemplified by the earlier discussed CEBMa's framework) emphasize grounding of organizational management related decision-making in systematic review and synthesis of applicable empirical research studies, without addressing the potentially large differences between decision and research synthesis time horizons. But once again, the 'when' of insights can be as important as the 'what'.

As more fully discussed in earlier chapters, research method-wise, empirical studies can fall into one of the three general categories: *observational*, which tend to utilize already existing data, such as point-of-sales transactions or insurance claims; *experimental*, which capture original data from specially designed tests, such as in-market promotional tests, and *research summaries*, which as the name suggests, review and synthesize individual observational and/or experimental studies focused on a particular theory or phenomenon. Given that, it seems likely (and can be easily shown in practice) that studies focused on a particular phenomenon will span all three, or at least two of the three general categories. Moreover, as even a casual review of several studies addressing the same phenomenon can reveal, virtually every study is likely to employ a different research design, sampling frame, and data analytical approach – moreover, it is also hard to look past a bias toward conducting 'new' research, rather than working to replicate the results of past research. When considered jointly in the context of research synthesis, it becomes clear that distinct within-type (e.g., all potentially relevant observational studies) research design and data analytical differences, as well as cross-type (e.g., all potentially relevant observational and experimental studies) research finding amalgamation obstacles need to be overcome. And so although 'distributed independence' (multiple researchers, spread across a wide array of academic and other research organizations, working independently on the same or similar research problems) notion widely touted by academic researchers is indeed a compelling idea, it poses a considerable practical problem. It is compelling because such diversity of effort should, in theory, lend credence to some ideas by virtue of multiple independent researchers reaching the same or similar conclusions, while effectively discrediting competing ideas that lack such corroboration. It poses a problem, however, because it spurs considerable variability in research design, methodological, analytical, and other results-shaping considerations, so much so that it renders side-by-side comparisons of overtly similar research findings difficult, at times even impossible.

In short, the sheer volume and methodological diversity of potentially applicable, to a decision problem at hand, empirical research studies, coupled with difficulties of reliable research findings synthesis, and the often short-time horizons of organizational decisions raise serious questions regarding the feasibility of instituting what could be characterized as 'grassroots-level' research summarization efforts in commercial (i.e., non-academic) organizational settings. Thus while conceptually compelling, Cochrane Collaboration-like empirical research summarization may not be feasible within the confines of management research. And yet looking past the potentially valuable insights that might be gleamed from research studies would be tantamount to willful degradation of the efficacy of decision-guiding knowledge. Not surprisingly, somewhere between 'all' and 'nothing' is the practically attainable solution, the outline of which is shown in Figure 9.1.

The Empirical & Experiential Evidence (3E) framework-aligned approach to empirical research synthesis is based upon the premise that research reviews undertaken by commercial organizations should build on the more fundamental work carried out by non-commercial organizations, such as universities and other research-oriented entities. After all, that is exactly the formula that is used in science and technology fields, where breakthrough ideas conceived and initially incubated in, typically, academic research centers are subsequently further developed by commercial entities. Why should business organizations try to duplicate the types of efforts for which very few of those organizations are well equipped in the first place?

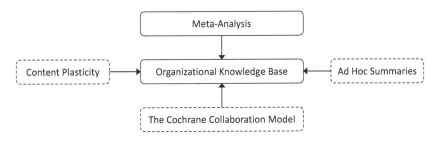

FIGURE 9.1 Organizational Synthesis of Theoretical Research.

The earlier described meta-analytic techniques can be seen as a key tool of such foundational research synthesis work. Commonly defined as a set of statistical procedures designed to assimilate results of topically related empirical studies with the goal of deriving generalizable conclusions, meta-analytic methods are particularly well suited to needs of organizational decision-makers because of those methods' reliance on quantitative effect size (e.g., magnitude of a relationship) estimates. For instance, pharmaceutical companies frequently use meta-analysis as a key component of new drug approval process – in fact, regulatory agencies, such as the US Food and Drug Administration, sometimes even require meta-analytic conclusions as broader (than a single study) substantiation of new drugs' efficacy. In a more general sense, practice-minded use of meta-analytic techniques is commonplace in fields such as medicine, education, and criminal justice, where applied researchers and clinicians both utilize those methodologies as bases for identifying the most effective diagnostic approaches and treatment strategies.

A key difference between meta-analysis and systematic reviews, which is the second of the two key empirical research summarization approaches (see Chapter 7), is that while the former emphasizes quantitative conclusions, the latter tends to produce noticeably more qualitative outcomes. That is because the stated goal of systematic reviews is to offer a more objective alternative to traditionally subjective (i.e., reflecting only the research authors' own assessment and interpretation) reviews of related research, which typically frame the context of scientific studies. Making use of replicable and transparent review processes, including formal audit trails of reviewers' choices and conclusions, all while maintaining the narrative review format results in reviewer bias reduction, which addresses one of the main shortcomings of academic research process. That said, how do systematic reviews benefit the organizational knowledge creation?

Implicit in that methodology's characterization is that systematic reviews do not usually expedite the process of research summarization – in fact, the added process due diligence tends to lengthen review timelines. That is primarily due to the fact that reviewer bias reduction is typically realized by means of a combination of engaging adequately large number of reviewers[1] and creation of explicit audit trails of individual reviewer's choices and conclusions, all of which requires extra time and effort. The resultant research review conclusions' validity and reliability gains offer a worthwhile payoff from the standpoint of theoretical knowledge development, but can rarely be justified by a practitioner operating within comparatively short decision timelines. Moreover, it is not clear to what degree the often highly abstract generalizations produced by systematic reviews offer 'plug and play' value to organizational decision-makers looking for context-specific insights. All considered, it is hard to avoid a conclusion that the mechanics of systematic reviews are simply not well suited to informational demands of business organizations. Hence, in contrast to the largely academic research focused evidence-based management philosophy discussed in Chapters 4 and 5 (which also happens to be shaped and advocated primarily by academic researchers), the 3E framework detailed in this book implicitly weighs the applicability of individual information summarization and processing approaches and techniques by their practical usability.

Summarizing Norms & Standards

The US Securities and Exchange Commission (SEC) is an independent agency of the federal government tasked with protecting investors, promoting fairness in the securities markets, and disseminating company information. Interestingly, the SEC has fewer employees, certainly fewer investigative employees, than there are companies publicly traded in the US,[2] which raises a question of how the agency is able to keep track of so much using so relatively few dedicated staff? A part of the answer is an extensive use of industry norms and key business ratios focused on matters such as solvency, efficiency, and profitability, which enable the agency to quickly assess the core aspects of multiple organizations in an unbiased yet adequately thorough manner. Certainly, the norms & standards based oversight has its limitations as illustrated by occasional accounting or corporate governance scandals (e.g., the Enron, Tyco, or Wells Fargo fiascos), but it is difficult to argue that since its inception in 1934, the SEC, and its benchmarking, contributed to fostering highly efficient and generally well-functioning financial markets.

Organizational evidence gathering can make use of similar reasoning. However, given the comparatively open-ended character of what constitutes, or what can be interpreted as 'norms' and 'standards', a more explicit framework is needed to assure the soundness of outcomes in terms of the earlier discussed utility, credibility, independence, and impartiality of results. With that in mind, the following norms and standards evaluation and summarization framework is recommended:

1   Evaluation guidelines

    a   Evidence gathering philosophy
    b   Evidence gathering plan
    c   Enumeration of competencies

2   Evaluation conduct

    a   Scope and objectives
    b   Timeliness and intentionality
    c   Methodology
    d   Communication and dissemination

3   Evaluation outcomes
    a   Quality assurance
    b   Quality control

Evaluation Guidelines

Before becoming immersed in the act of doing, it is important to carefully consider the 'why' and the 'how' of doing something. The SEC has a clear mandate, given to the Commission by the United States Congress in the form of the enabling legislative acts, and a clear purpose, which is that of safeguarding investors' interests, and by doing so assuring sound functioning of capital markets. In a similar vein, it is important for organizations to establish an explicit standards and norms evaluation guidelines, keeping in mind the specificities of the organization's informational needs, all while delineating a clear explanation of the purpose, scope, objectives, timelines, methodology, and subsequent usage of the resultant information. That is especially important when attempting to synthesize applicable norms and standards because that dimension of evidence is notoriously prone to subjective interpretations.

Thus, prior to delving into research and fact gathering, the organization should clearly spell out the purpose, means, and anticipated utility of evaluation outcomes. More specifically, the conduct of the ensuing assessment needs to be clearly described in terms of guiding objectives, the evaluative scope, expected timelines, proposed methodology, and anticipated outcomes, all of which fall under the broad umbrella of credibility and utility (two of the four defining qualities discussed earlier). In addition, specific provisions aimed at safeguarding independence and impartiality – the remaining two of the four evaluation defining qualities – should also be expressly delineated; those can take the form of comparative benchmarks to be used, or provisions for peer or external review.

A related but distinct aspect of developing explicit norms and standards evaluation mechanisms is planning. It is essential to draft an evaluation plan, which should be based on an explicit informational strategy, prepared with utility, practicality, and clear purpose in mind. To ensure maximum utility, plan preparations should include adequate consultations with organizational stakeholders, especially the intended users of anticipated informational outcomes. Moreover, the plan should also encompass a mechanism for informing the aforementioned stakeholders of the progress made in its implementation and should also include provisions for responding to ad hoc requests that were not included in the initial plan.

A yet another important foundational consideration is to enumerate competencies to be exhibited by those conducting the gathering and review work. Simply put, individuals engaged in designing, conducting, and managing standards and norms review and assessment activities should possess the core competencies required for their roles, in the form of skills, experience, educational background, and other attributes required to discharge their duties in a manner that will ensure the credibility and quality of outcomes. Those competencies typically encompass technical skills needed to access and make sense of specific domains of knowledge, communication skills needed to clearly convey findings and conclusions, and sufficient understanding of the basic tenets of evidence-based practice to guide the manner in which they synthesize informational outputs and frame their conclusions.

Evaluation Conduct

The operational aspects of norms and standards assessment are obviously of paramount importance and should be well thought out and clearly spelled out. In particular, there are four specific areas of interest: scope and objectives, timeliness and intentionality, methodology, and communication and dissemination of the resultant outcomes.

Evaluation scope and objectives should follow from the evaluation purpose, should be realistic and achievable, and should concretely explain the expected informational outcomes. They should be clear and agreed upon by key stakeholders. The scope should clearly delimit the boundaries of the evaluation while also acknowledging the limits of the evaluation, all while keeping the initiative's objectives in mind. Taken together, the scope and objectives should provide critical references for determining the optimal evaluation methodology.

In terms of timeliness and intentionality, assessments should be designed to ensure that they provide timely, valid, reliable, and relevant information while also clearly outlining the underlying intentionality. The rationale for 'why' specific evaluation is undertaken is as important as 'when' the outcomes are made available. Lastly, resource requirements (e.g., the number of man-hours and mix of skills) should also be expressly addressed to assure that the resultant outcomes are not only timely and relevant but also cost-effective.

To assure the highest possible degree of objectivity and result validity, evaluation methodologies must be sufficiently rigorous such that the evaluation reflects the earlier defined scope and objectives, can answer evaluation questions, ultimately producing complete, fair, and unbiased assessment. Specific methodological choices need to be made with a clear intent to provide credible answers to the evaluation questions. That can typically be accomplished by means of assuring validity and reliability of outcomes, in the sense of being sufficient to meet the evaluation objectives in a manner that is logically coherent and complete, meaning not speculative or opinion-based. That goal can be accomplished with the help of triangulation, or utilizing a combination of multiple data sources and multiple methods of analysis.

The last key aspect of evaluation conduct, communication and dissemination, should be guided by an effective communication strategy. Review and analysis produced knowledge needs to be actively shared with relevant stakeholders in a manner that encourages utilization. That goal can be furthered by adapting a simple, three-pronged strategy: First, evaluation outcomes need to contain elements of action, which is to say that the evaluation-derived knowledge needs to inform, explain, or suggest possible actions. Second, the manner in which those insights are communicated needs to address how the evaluation results may affect stakeholders as individual entities or as groups. Third, information should be presented in simple and easily understandable formats tailored to the specific needs of different audiences.

Evaluation Outcomes

The third and the final core element of the recommended norms and standards evaluation and summarization framework addresses the truthfulness and dependability of outcomes. The foundation of that aspect of the evaluation process is a sound quality assurance system, the design of which is typically one of the last steps in the overall evaluation process mapping. Perhaps the most essential feature of quality assurance is that it expressly addresses both the evaluation process and the outcomes of that process, which usually requires the use of either internal or external peer review, to assure the objectivity of the process.

In terms of the more operationally minded quality control considerations, those matters should be addressed during the initial design as well as during the final stage of the evaluation. At the design stage of evaluation, the quality should be controlled by examining whether the scope and methodology are appropriate to achieve the evaluation's objectives, whether it can ensure the collection of robust and triangulated data that can give rise to credible analysis and findings, and whether the evaluation team has an appropriate range of skills and expertise. During the final stage of evaluation, quality should be controlled by examining whether the evaluation was conducted according to quality-assured methodologies and processes and that any divergences were appropriately addressed, data were collected from sufficient and appropriate sources to ensure credibility of findings, and the resultant outcomes were based on valid analyses that were logically coherent and demonstrated requisite accuracy, validity, relevance, and usefulness.

Pooling Expert Judgment

A considerable amount of space was devoted in the earlier part of this book to the discussion of the many and varied cognitive biases and other impediments to sound subjective reasoning and choice-making. There is ample scientific and anecdotal evidence that explains and illustrates why and how those rationality-warping influences can negatively impact how individuals perceive and respond to reality, with some of the more salient points addressed in the first two chapters of this book. Still, it is hard to deny the important role intuitive conjectures played in the development of scientific thought; thus, it would be unwise to entirely dismiss subjective opinions of knowledgeable individuals. In his bestselling book *Blink*, Malcolm Gladwell showed how snap decisions can produce better outcomes than thoughtful analysis, and one of the leading researchers of behavioral intuition whose research contributed to Gladwell's ideas, Gerd Gigerenzer, argues in his book, *Gut Feelings: The Intelligence of the Unconscious*, that intuition is actually the result of unconscious mental processes that apply environment and prior experience-derived heuristics. He contends that the value of those 'unconscious considerations' lies precisely in being different from rational sensemaking as the former takes into account only the most useful, rather than all applicable information – in the sense then, knowing the right answer is often a product of instinctively understanding what information can be discarded as unimportant.

That line of thinking, and research, lends conceptual substantiation to applying the notion of *intuitive design* to human understanding, as a way of helping explain how gut feelings or hunches can precipitate scientific or commercial breakthroughs. In that context, intuitive design has been described as 'understanding without the use of instructions',[3] or in the words of Albert Einstein who once wrote that 'The intuitive mind is a sacred gift and the rational mind is a faithful servant. We have created a society that honors the servant and has forgotten the gift'. Coming from the man who gave us a new understanding of such fundamental physical phenomena as light and gravity, those words should not be taken lightly, but those words also come from the man who refused to accept quantum mechanics, which is the cornerstone of contemporary communications infrastructure. Clearly, intuition can be a source of brilliant insights, or a source of rather spectacular flops, and thus the perspective embodied by the 3E framework detailed in this book is that while some gut feelings should be dismissed as biased or unfounded impulses, other hunches might be nuggets of brilliant insights. The challenge of differentiating between the two is captured in the words of John Wanamaker, a late 19th- and early 20th-century department store magnate, who famously remarked that half the money he spent on advertising was wasted, the trouble was he did not know which half…

The organizational decision-making context suggests a rather obvious solution to the vexing problem of knowing which hunches should be trusted: seek and jointly consider intuitive conjectures from multiple individuals. Much like the earlier discussed transactional organizational data that combine dependable information and random error, views of experienced and otherwise knowledgeable professionals can be conceptualized as reflecting a combination of 'true' insights and 'biased' noise. Given the subjective and elusive nature of intuition, there is no plausible way to a priori validate the efficacy of a singular expert judgment, but the degree of concurrence of multiple experts' opinions can materially reduce the risk of embracing biased noise as true insights. Skeptics could argue that doing so might drown out the truly norm-breaking strike of genius – indeed, that possibility exists, but there is far stronger evidence pointing to the dangers of overreliance on unfounded beliefs, as illustrated by numerous once-thriving and now-gone business organizations including Circuit City, Radio Shack, Polaroid, Borders Books, or Wang Laboratories.

Delphi Approximations

Delphi[4] *method* is a systematic, interactive forecasting technique which relies on a panel of independent experts, originally developed at the beginning of the cold war to forecast the impact of technology on warfare. The method was conceived as a solution to the problem of developing credible estimates without the benefit of empirical evidence, in response to which Douglas Aircraft Company started Project RAND (*Research ANd* Development, now an independent nonprofit think tank) to study 'the broad subject of inter-continental warfare other than surface'. Finalized as a methodology by the late 1950s, Delphi method is based on the principle that forecasts from a structured group of experts are more accurate than those from unstructured groups or individuals; since its inception, the method has been adapted to a variety of business applications, including new product design and marketing.

It works as follows: The carefully selected experts answer questionnaires in two or more rounds. After each round, a facilitator provides an anonymous summary of the experts' forecasts from the previous round as well as the reasons they provided for their judgments, and participants are encouraged to revise their earlier answers in light of the replies of other members of the group. During that process, which is iterative, the range of answers tends to decrease, and the group begins to converge toward a singular answer. Finally, the process is stopped after a predefined stop criterion, such as the number of rounds or the achievement of consensus or the stability of results, and the mean or median scores of the final round determine the outcomes.

In terms of its philosophical underpinnings, Delphi method is based on the notion of *successive approximations*, which is a method of estimating the value of unknown quantity via repeated reshaping of the original estimates. The process of successive approximations is used extensively in computational mathematics, behavioral psychology, educational research, health treatment, and other areas where repeated interactions with the outside (to a respondent) environment are deemed beneficial to shaping of the final outcome. It has proven itself to be an effective method of arriving at the most reasonable estimates in

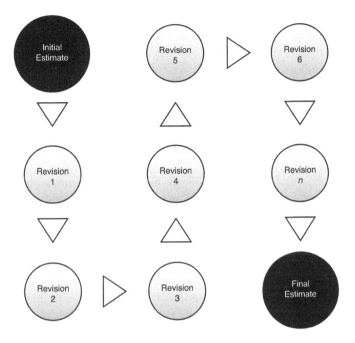

FIGURE 9.2 Delphi Approximations.

situations where potentially large disparities in judgment exist. The outcome of the Delphi method inspired evaluative process can be seen as a stress-tested results of subjectively initiated but objectively validated approximations estimates, termed *Delphi approximations* within the confines of the 3E framework, and graphically summarized in Figure 9.2.

An important aspect of Delphi approximations is the inter-expert reliability assessment, the aim of which is to capture the degree of similarity across individually derived estimates. Higher inter-rater reliability (IER), values are indicative of higher initial forecast homogeneity which, under most circumstances, is preferred, as it is indicative of higher initial consensus. IER can be operationalized by correlating individual item responses across responders using simple correlation discussed earlier in the context of exploratory analysis, and detailed in Appendix B. A general rule of thumb (also detailed in Appendix B) can be used to determine whether the initial spread of estimates is compact enough to warrant engaging in iterative approximations.

Problem Scoping

The quality of answers often hinges on the clarity of questions. Within the confines of expert judgment, where multiple individuals might be asked to provide their forecasts or other expertise-derived inputs, it is critical to assure interpretational uniformity of stated questions. Here, the time- and application-tested psychometric survey design principles can offer worthwhile guidance. Those include the following:

- *Plan to pretest.* Prior to using to collecting expert inputs, questions to be posed to experts should be tested for uniformity of interpretation. Doing that does not necessitate using respondents possessing deep knowledge of the subject matter since the goal of this step to assess interpretational uniformity only.
- *Avoid vague or imprecise terms.* While the use of technical terms is often discouraged in general, for example, consumer, surveys, the use of carefully chosen technical terms is appropriate in expert surveys, precisely because of the deep technical knowledge of respondents. In those situations, the use of typically narrowly and clearly defined technical terms will likely result in greater interpretational uniformity than the use of vague, interpretation-prone terms.
- *Avoid complex sentences.* Sentences with too many clauses or unusual constructions often confuse respondents because they tend to draw attention to different cue or stimuli. Using the basic question structure of 'verb + subject + noun', such as 'what is the probability of recession in 2019?', where 'what' is the verb, 'probability' is the subject, and 'recession' is the noun will greatly enhance interpretational uniformity of questions.
- *Avoid double-barreled questions.* Questions that touch upon more than a single issue yet seek only a single answer tend to compel different respondents to zero-in on only one of the issues, resulting in an invariant frame of reference. For instance, asking experts to assess the risk of an earthquake by considering the likelihood and the potential impact of such an event will likely cause some experts to focus on the probability of occurrence while compelling others to focus on the potential damage (i.e., the impact), for essentially random reasons.
- *Provide appropriate frames of reference.* Additional clarifications, such as those addressing time and/or location, are often necessary to ensure interpretational uniformity. For example, the aforementioned earthquake risk estimation should be further contextualized to a specific location, for example, San Francisco, and a timeframe, for example, the next 10 years.
- *Avoid questions using leading, emotional, or evocative language.* Rationality is an essential aspect of evidence construction; thus, expert judgment should be focused on generating well-reasoned, logical conclusions. In some instances, the underlying emotional linkages can be quite subtle – for instance, asking about immigration reforms proposed by President Trump may evoke divergent responses because of how different respondents may feel about President Trump, rather than how they feel about reforming immigration policies.

Expert Selection

A common definition of an expert is a person who has a comprehensive and authoritative knowledge of, or skill in, a particular domain of knowledge. Recalling the earlier (Chapter 1) discussion of knowledge and knowing, a person's expertise can stem from explicit or tacit sources, where the former is a factual and objective outcome of formal education, typically manifesting itself in one of more formal degrees, and the latter is interpretive and subjective product of experience. Given their implicitly symbiotic relationship, explicit and tacit learning modes produce three somewhat distinct dimensions, or manifestations of knowledge: semantic, which encompasses knowledge of (largely) abstract ideas or concepts, procedural, which entails skills and behaviors necessary to execute specific activities, and lastly episodic, which is the ability to recall and cite illustrative examples.

Given that very general outline of what it takes to be considered an expert in a particular field, several distinct expertise prerequisites can be delineated, which are as follows:

- *Technical credentials*. Education is the cornerstone of the technical dimension of a person's expertise, with advanced degree in closely related fields being the most readily recognized foundation. In professional practice areas, such as medicine, law, or accounting, that offer or even require licensing by recognized accrediting bodies, appropriate license further strengthens the technical dimension of one's expertise. Lastly, membership in professional societies may add a yet another, albeit softer accentuation of technical expertise.
- *Relevant experience*. Although generally viewed as complementary to education, there are some aspects of knowledge that can only be acquired by means of 'doing'. For example, a management scholar and an experienced business manager might exhibit noticeably different understanding and interpretation of certain aspects of organizational behavior.
- *Independent contributions*. A subset of virtually all education- and experience-based groups are those that made unique, even trend-setting contributions to their field. In any domain of knowledge and professional practice there are a handful of individuals – just think of names like Einstein, Shakespeare, or Buffett – whose achievements or contributions make them stand out in their respective peer groups.
- *Forecasting ability*. Although education and experience offer a foundation upon which one can draw to form professional judgment about related but new situations, those foundations alone are not sufficient to form credible professional opinions. What is also required is the ability to generalize, or draw inferences from one's accumulated knowledge and experience in a manner that retains those aspects that are generalizable (i.e., can be applied

to multiple similar situations) while setting aside those that are unique to individual instances.

*   *Willingness to engage.* Many expert judgment situations may require more than just scratching of one's 'expert head' – some situations may demand even the most knowledgeable and experienced experts to devote time and effort to learning specifics of situations of interest, and even engaging in additional topical research. To be a valid expression of one's expertise, opinions of experts need to be expressions of thoughtful and careful considerations.

Putting It All Together

Political, business, military, religious leaders, ancient philosophers, media pundits and commentators, and even standout athletes and coaches have been invoked in different situations as authoritative sources of secrets to success. The stage first created by the early mass media of television and radio, subsequently expanded by the rise of the Internet, and more recently the social media platforms, make it possible for the ever larger armies of self-anointed 'experts' to espouse their views on topics ranging from the most important to the most inconsequential. And though the marvels of modern communication technology ushered in the age of truly global interconnectedness by all but eliminating the obstacle of physical distance, finding true expertise can be as difficult today as it was in the decades past. In the age of relentless self-promotion, fake news, and unsubstantiated claims, the truly knowledgeable and authoritative voices are often drowned out by what is, in an informational sense, nothing more than background noise.

Moreover, even factually substantiated knowledge and experience base does not guarantee the applicability of individual experts' bases of knowledge. For example, numerous individuals may be described as risk management experts, but their individual domains of knowledge may range from insurance underwriting to insurance claim management to risk estimation to risk transfer, to name just a few of numerous distinct subdomains of the broad area of risk management. And depending on the informational need at hand, some of those risk management experts might be either supremely, marginally, or not even at all qualified to provide dependable insights because of substantially dissimilar knowledge and experience bases.

And yet, a carefully assembled panel of knowledgeable professionals can make worthwhile evidentiary contributions to a decision at hand. For that to happen, however, deliberate due diligence process is necessary, not unlike what is used to assess the quality of organizational data or research outcomes. More specifically, the overall endeavor of sourcing expert opinions needs to be approached in a rational and systematic manner that expressly addresses the three distinct aspects of expert search, expert evaluation, and expert utilization.

I   Expert search:

    1   *Delineate and describe sought informational inputs.* Taking inventory of what information is sought is, in a sense, the most elementary and the first step to be taken when initiating expert search. Singling out clearly described informational inputs to be provided by experts, preferably in the form of unambiguously framed and phrased research questions or topical areas, should be undertaken prior to considering expert qualities.

    2   *Settle on, describe, and disclose expert identification criteria.* Although the idea of seeking expert advice sounds simple, clearly defining and characterizing what constitutes 'expertise' is often considerably less straightforward, and even more often not carefully framed. Hence, clear domain of knowledge and/or practice definition needs to be thoughtfully sketched out, along with educational and experiential characteristics deemed essential to substantiating expert designations.

    3   *Identify sufficiently knowledgeable degree of expertise evaluators.* Echoing the (not always flattering) expression that it 'takes one to know one', those evaluating prospective experts' backgrounds, skills, and competencies have to themselves have adequate understanding of the domain of interest to conduct sound evaluations. Arguably, evaluators do not have to have expert-level qualifications, but nonetheless have to have strong enough understanding of that particular domain to recognize and appreciate the true depth of expertise.

II   Expert evaluation:

    1   *Educational background.* One of the core elements of professional expertise, formal educational attainment is usually the foundation upon which additional, typically experiential knowledge is built. It is important to note that it not only matters what degrees, e.g., PhD, MD, JD, a presumed expert earned but also the closeness of the field of study to the domain of expertise of interest.

    2   *Applied, research, and other applicable experience.* The second core element of expertise, practical experience, can take form of either applied industry experience or more theoretically oriented research experience. Deceptively easy to decode, it actually often requires closer scrutiny because of its often nuanced nature, which necessitates paying closer attention to demonstrated functional skills, competencies, and work outcomes, rather than more broadly defined areas of expertise. For instance, the earlier mentioned risk assessment area encompasses qualitative, judgment-based threat identification and description, as well as highly quantitative, statistics and machine learning driven numeric risk modeling – depending on the type of expert judgment sought,

either one aspect of experience could be more applicable, but the two can rarely be found in the same person (at least at a level warranting expert designation).

3   *Interest, willingness, and availability.* For reasons ranging from time constraints to preferences, an otherwise well-qualified expert may not be willing or able to provide the sought informational inputs. It is a comparatively pragmatic consideration, but underscoring it is the implicit 'engagement of time and mind' requirement which should not be overlooked, as rushed or half-hearted inputs can do more harm than good.

4   *Potential conflicts of interest.* Being free of any possible evaluation-impacting influences is of paramount importance. This includes not only economic but also intellectual impediments to provide unbiased inputs. For instance, industry consultants may have client or other financial relationships that may prejudice their views on certain topics, whereas researchers may have what could be characterized as 'vested intellectual interest' stemming from expressed preferences for certain philosophies, conceptualizations, or interpretations of facts, which can also bias their assessments.

III   Expert utilization:

1   *Level-set.* Ad hoc pooled groups of experts rarely make natural teams – in fact, groups of highly accomplished individuals may prove themselves to be difficult to manage. Clearly defined informational goals, rules of engagement, and expectations often help smooth out any potentially undesirable group dynamics.

2   *Use well conceptualized, structured, and pretested questions.* The 'what' and 'how' of framing research questions to be address by the expert panel is of paramount importance to assuring interpretational uniformity. Even the seemingly syntactically simple and semantically obvious questions ought to be pretested as doing so offers the only credible assurance of clarity.

3   *Provide meaningful frames of reference.* It is usually safe to assume that each expert's experience is somewhat different from other experts' experiences – in a sense, a panel of properly vetted, well-qualified professionals can be thought of as a set of somewhat skewed samples. With that in mind, the more contextualized the question at hand the more the individually skewed experiences can be 'bent' to the specifics of the situation of interest, by implicitly compelling experts to draw inferences from their individualized experiences and applying those learnings to the described situation.

As outlined above, finding, engaging, and trusting experts can – really, should – require more time and effort than might be initially expected. Given the subjectivity of individual expert's opinions, and the iterative mechanics of the Delphi approximations process outlined earlier, each member of the overall expert pool should be chosen carefully. In the broader decision-guiding evidence generation sense encapsulated by the 3E framework, cumulative wisdom of highly knowledgeable professionals offers an important dimension of the total of external-to-self (i.e., the decision-maker) knowledge, but capturing that wisdom requires a rational, disciplined, and thorough process.

Notes

1 As suggested by the Law of Large Numbers, as the number of reviewers increases, their (i.e., sample) mean estimate becomes a progressively more accurate approximation of the true (i.e., population) mean.
2 According to the most recent, publicly available headcount, the SEC had about 4,300 employees. The count of publicly traded companies fluctuates constantly, but in 2018 there were about 4,000 companies traded on the New York (NYSE) and NASDAQ exchanges, and another 15,000 stocks traded over-the-counter, or decentralized exchanges although it should be noted that many of the latter do not files financial reports with the SEC.
3 In Theo Humphries' 2012 paper 'Considering Intuition in the Context of Design, and of Psychology'.
4 The name 'Delphi' is derived from the Delphic oracle, the most important oracle of the classical Greek world; the creators of this method were not happy with that particular name, feeling it implied 'something smacking a little of the occult', but the name stuck nonetheless.

PART IV

Evidence-Based Decision-Making in Organizations

10

INTERNAL DESIGN & DYNAMICS

How many of the estimated 35,000 or so decisions made by an average person on daily basis are truly individual, given the profound role played by organizations in modern society? While it may not be feasible to arrive at a sound numeric estimate, it is safe to assume that a significant proportion of small and big choices is made in a group setting. Taking up a large proportion, even the majority of an average person's functioning time, engagement with school, work, social, or professional organizations should be expected to account for a proportional share of daily decisions. Thus, many of the 35,000 daily decisions are likely made in a group setting, and many of those that are not directly or indirectly impacted by group dynamics, understanding of which is an important part of fully leveraging the decision-making value of the Empirical & Experiential Evidence (3E) framework.

Organizational culture is one of the perhaps most celebrated and at the same time most elusive manifestations of group dynamics, often described in terms of a combination of physical features and behavioral norms. Pixar, a well-known movie animation studio, offers its animators and engineers a host of enviable physical amenities at its 22-acre Emeryville, California campus including gourmet cafeteria with a cereal bar, a soccer field, a swimming pool, billiards and foosball tables, whereas organizations such as Kayak, a travel company, place more emphasis on somewhat less visible perks such as flexible hours, travel bonuses, team excursions and games. Some organizations' design features only implicitly address decision-making, as is the case with Kayak, where employees are hired on the basis of being smart and then encouraged to think 'outside of the box' and put their ideas to work, while in case of others, best illustrated by Zappos, an online retailer, altogether eschew traditional management structure in favor of organizational designs such as holacracy, where employees define their own job titles, everyone has a voice, and rather than reporting to individual managers, employees work in groups and are accountable to groups.

In a more general sense, organization-unique combinations of structure, culture, and founders' or managers' philosophy create contexts within which organizational choices are made. Not only what information and how much of it is utilized in the choice-making process but also the very manner in which organizations, as collections of individuals, learn are all heavily influenced by a combination of structural, cultural, and philosophical organizational attributes. This is the first of two chapters addressing the moderating impact of those factors on the efficacy of evidence-based practice in general, and the 3E framework in particular. More specifically, this chapter addresses the key 'micro', or internal (to the organization) factors falling under broad umbrellas organizational culture, or shared assumptions, values, and beliefs governing how people behave in organizations, and organizational dynamics, conceptualized here as an organization's approach to managing and promoting organizational learning.

Organizations as Human Collectives

At their core, organizations are groups of people joined together in pursuit of shared goals. As it is intuitively obvious from that broad definition, the reason humans tend to join together is because doing so helps with the attainment of goals, which, in turn, can be seen as manifestations of a wide range of human needs. Those needs range from the most fundamental, namely self-preservation, to those that could be considered refined or evolved, most notably self-actualization. It thus follows that organizations are formed to pursue a wide array of goals – in fact, throughout human history, organizations have been steadily expanding into more spheres of life while also growing in size and complexity. And so as aptly summarized by a noted organizational scholar Amitai Etzioni, '...our society is organizational society'. Most individuals are born in hospitals, educated in schools, employed by business, governmental or other organizations; those individuals then elect to join social, religious, or professional organizations. From birth through death, at work or at play, life in modern societies is increasingly conducted in organizational settings, so much so that in view of many sociologists, organizations are now the dominant institutions of modern societies.

When looked at from the most general of perspectives, organizations can be either formal or informal. The former are characterized by clearly defined structure, which usually entails division of labor, specialization, and expressly defined authority and responsibilities; moreover, formal organizations tend to be deliberately impersonal, in the sense of being driven by reasoned goals rather than emotions, and typically seek to grow and expand. The latter are somewhat more difficult to concisely portray, primarily because those organizations tend to lack easily discernible structure. That said, informal organizations tend to coalesce around often unwritten beliefs and norms, and belonging to those organizations is usually contingent on adherence to common rules or beliefs.

While offering a reasonable point of departure in a review of organizational types, the formal-informal distinction offers little operational clarity, given that, for instance, it is hard to think of an informal business organization.[1] In fact, the earlier mentioned assertion of modern society being an organizational society alludes to formal organizations, as schooling, employment, even spiritual or professional pursuits usually take place within the confines of formal organizations. Recognizing the typological and practical inefficacy of the formal vs. informal organization distinction, organizational scholars tend to set aside informal organizations and instead focus their attention on developing more granular typologies of formal organizations. The resultant classificatory schemas can themselves be clustered based on the type of grouping considerations employed, which fall into one of three general descriptors: (1) function, (2) beneficiaries, and (3) power. Numerous typologies have been proposed within each of those differently minded formal organization type grouping bases, and while no two are exactly alike, a clear pattern of higher-order similarities is evident.

Organization grouping typologies built around 'function' tend to differentiate between production/economic, political/managerial, integrative, adaptive, and maintenance organizations. Production/economic organizations are focused on wealth creation through the manufacture of goods or provision of services to be consumed by society; for-profit business companies are examples of such organizations. Political/managerial organizations are primarily concerned with the attainment of political goals, adjudication, coordination and control of resources, people, and subsystems; legislative and executive government branches best exemplify such organizations. Integrative organizations are concerned with settlement of conflicts, integration, and coordination of various segments of society to work together and provide stability in the society; judicial courts, police, and social agencies offer the best examples of such organizations. Adaptive organizations are focused on knowledge creation and dissemination, with universities and non-university research institutions offering the best examples. Lastly, maintenance organizations are focused on societal continuity as expressed in the form of enduring values or culture, with cultural and religious institutions offering the best examples.

Typologies built around 'beneficiaries' base their classificatory logic on who is the direct recipient of organizational output, resulting in four types of organizations. Mutual benefit associations, which represent the first of the four types, primarily benefit their members, and are exemplified by political parties, trade unions, and professional associations; those organizations are primarily concerned with the attainment of their shared goals. Business organizations represent the second main type of who-benefits defined organizations – here, it is the organizational owners who are the primary beneficiaries, and their objective is typically wealth or value maximization. Service organizations represent the third beneficiary defined organizational type, and in this type of organization it is the clients who are the primary beneficiaries. In contrast to the first two organizational types, the beneficiaries of service organizations, such as educational institutions or social service agencies, do not have control over those organizations. The fourth and the final type are commonwealth organizations, which provide administrative or protective functions for the public at large, which is those organizations' primary beneficiary; police and fire departments, as well as the military and the post office are all examples of commonwealth organizations.

Typologies built around 'power' see the manner in which organizations subordinate some members under the authority of others as a key source of cross-organization differences. In view of the broad notional scope of the idea of power, organizational scholars tend to draw a distinction between two somewhat separate dimensions of power: authority and compliance. The former can take the form of charismatic, traditional, and legal, whereas the latter can be coercive, utilitarian, or normative. Thus, within the confines of that view of organizations, leaders can derive their power from uniquely compelling personal characteristics (charismatic authority), a sanctioned position (traditional authority), or from a system of rules and procedures stemming from recognized rules and policies (legal authority). Moreover, leaders can coerce the desired subordinate behavior through a threat (or an actual application) of sanctions, they can compel those behaviors using physical rewards such as compensation (utilitarian power) or can compel those behaviors using symbolic rewards such as achievement awards (normative power). As it is clear from the preceding overview, power-based organizational characterizations are of more narratively descriptive than classificatory nature, especially when contrasted with those built around organizational function or beneficiaries – that said, those portrayals nonetheless add an informationally worthwhile dimension to the study of organizational types.

Organizational Structure

A more tangible aspect of organizations is represented by a manner in which organizations approach decision-making. Commonly referred to as organizational structure, the typically hierarchical arrangement of authority, communications, rights and duties of distinct organizational stakeholders, it determines how the roles, power, and responsibilities are assigned, controlled, and coordinated, and how information flows between the different organizational decision-making units.

Typology-wise, the study of organizational structures can be thought of as being comprised of two somewhat distinct subsets: The first is made up of 'mature' types of organizational structures, which are those that have been widely used for decades (or longer), and thus are well understood and richly described. Those include *functional*, also called bureaucratic, organizational structure which divides the company based on specialty, such as production, marketing, finance; *divisional*, which uses product/service or brand distinctiveness as the basic structural units; or *matrix*, which is a blend of the functional and division structures, and which tries to retain the specialization of the former while also attempting to infuse more decision-making flexibility of the latter (which can be a source of ambiguity or even confusion).

The second of the two subsets organizational structure types is comprised of newer, or emergent types of structures. Those include *flatarchies*, which eschew the 'tall' hierarchical structures, typically associated with the above outlined mature organizational controls, in favor of greater collaboration believed to result from spreading decision-making power across multiple positions by means of removing or flattening (hence the name) the traditional managerial hierarchies. Another emerging type of organizational structure is *holacracy*, which tries to go beyond flatarchy by further distributing decision-making while giving all employees the freedom to work on what they do best. Any remaining structure, as considered from a traditional command-and-control perspective, is based on 'circles' roughly resembling departments, rather than distinct individuals as centers of authority. It should be noted that, at least at the time of writing of this book, flatarchies and holacracies are still relatively rare, and are typically found in smaller and start-up companies.

However, the combined effect of globalization, hyper-competition, rapid technological change, and environmental and market turbulence are changing the nature of work, and effectively forcing organizations to become more adaptive, not only in terms of 'what' and 'how' they do but also in terms of how they function. The resultant adaptiveness imperative directly impacts not only business process design, organizational core competencies and behaviors but also compels greater structural fluidity. That means de-emphasizing formal hierarchies in favor of informal networks, or moving away from specialized departments to improvised processes or temporary project teams. And while it might be premature to proclaim the doom of the traditional, fixed, and rigid organizational structures geared toward control, similarity and ideal competencies, it is safe to suggest that the emergent organizational mindset favors diversity of competencies, adaptability, and improvisation capability. Stated differently, to be successful tomorrow, business, as well as other types of organizations, should seek fluidity of structure and capabilities as the mean of responding to environmental, market, and technological turbulence.

Organizational Culture

Perhaps no organizational characteristic is as elusive as organizational culture, which are those often hard to put into words ways of 'organizational living' that tend to be shared and maintained, and that tend to distinguish one organization from others. Recalling the earlier discussion of organizational types and structures, organizational culture can be seen as a product of coercive and normative processes, and it tends to be experienced as routine behaviors, norms, rules of conduct, or dominant philosophies, all of which can be communicated tacitly and explicitly, and are often intended to reduce ambiguity.

The key to discerning organizational culture is understanding the source of it. In most business organizations, culture emanates from their founders or leaders, from demonstrated success, and from new members. Founders and leaders usually sow the seeds of organizational culture through the process of implementing their personal beliefs, values, and assumptions regarding strategies, competition, and the environment; those beliefs, values, and assumptions precipitate patterns of thinking and behavior learned and adopted by organizational members. If and when the resultant business strategies and philosophies lead to success, they are then embraced as cherished organizational values. Over time, it is common for business organizations to enshrine the key elements of their culture as core organizational values, prominently displayed and eagerly passed onto new organizational members.

The explicitly communicated aspects of organizational culture are primarily cognitive and tend to encompass everyday organizational rules, such as the dress code, which are typically unambiguous. The tacitly communicated aspects, on the other hand, are predominantly symbolic and thus highly interpretive. Cherished (or at least subscribed to) organizational beliefs and values usually constitute the core of symbolic elements of culture – under most circumstances, organizational stakeholders need to make sense of those noticeably more ambiguous elements of organizational culture on their own. Not surprisingly, misinterpretation of the tacitly communicated, symbolic elements of organizational culture is a common occurrence, especially in environments in which organizational culture can be characterized as highly participative, adaptive, and organic. Offering explicit cultural references or points of reference is a proven ambiguity reducing strategy, but it requires the degree of organizational introspective that is often missing, especially among younger, less mature organizations.

When considered from an inescapably reductive outsider's perspective,[2] organizational culture is often characterized in terms of a handful of key attributes reflecting the manner in which the organization copes with external adaptation and with internal integration. Externally, organizations interact directly with their customers, suppliers, creditors, and – if applicable – regulators; business organizations also interact indirectly with their competitors, and, for public companies, with their shareholders. Internally, organizations need to address the needs of their employees and processes, both of which are influenced by broad societal, legal, and environmental forces. Hence, from the point of view of an external onlooker, organizational culture can be reduced to the degree of, and the manner in which it responds to internal and external forces. In a very broad sweep, organizational cultures can be characterized as participative, adaptive, and organic, or as detached, inflexible, and synthetic. Though those descriptive labels themselves sound value-laden, that is actually not the case. As a matter of just simple practicality, embracing participative culture is considerably more viable for a small start-up than a large, geographically and operationally dispersed organization; moreover, participative culture might also be more desirable for a small firm focused on growth, than a large, established organization more concerned with preservation and control. Some of the same reasoning applies to the organic vs. synthetic distinction. Young, entrepreneurial business organizations tend to have naturally organic cultures, largely because they may not yet have found their truly defining values and beliefs, while established, successful organizations' cultures are typically synthetic precisely because they are large and successful (i.e., their cultural values served them well). In a similar vein, organizations proudly displaying their 'core beliefs' are, by extension, culturally inflexible, in a manner notionally similar to religious organizations; many of those still looking for their 'cultural DNA' are usually characterized as adaptive.

The above considerations notwithstanding, technological and environmental turbulence, globalization and hyper-competition are not only changing how work is done but are also reshaping the often long-standing cultural norms. Ranging from fundamental organizational reconfiguration ushered by the emergence of more egalitarian organizational structure models such as flatarchies and holacracies, to the steady rise of alternative working models as exemplified by telecommuting, the long-standing cultural norms are not just being challenged – they are being slowly dismantled. And so whereas in a traditional 'command-and-control' organizational setting the bulk of organizational decision-making was directed toward internal persuasion, which typically took the form of promoting ideas down the organizational command chain, in a hierarchically flatter organizational setting, in which more decision-making authority is horizontally distributed rather than being vertically concentrated, a significantly higher proportion of organizational decision-making is outwardly directed. Doing so not only reduces bottlenecks but even more importantly it relegates domain-specific choice-making to those with greater, if not the greatest, domain expertise. In doing so, business organizations can not only respond more rapidly but they can also respond more knowledgeably.

Choice-making by business organizations is also subject to additional considerations reflecting the unique manner in which those entities interact with their various and different stakeholders. The next section offers a high-level summary of those matters.

Business Organizations

While developing a sound understanding of organizational structure and culture is essential to making sense of choice-making mechanics in a very broadly conceived organizational setting, decision-making in for-profit business firms is also subject to a number of unique influences. As economic entities, business firms have customers, owners, quite commonly non-owner managers, and employees – in addition, being participants in the economic value creation process, business firms tend to participate in capital markets and are subject to at least some regulatory oversight. Consequently, the traditional view of business firms depicts those organizations as distinct economic entities aiming to fulfil the needs of their customers but operated for the benefit of their owners, subject to constituent interests of other stakeholders.

However, that once-dominant view of business organization is giving way to the enterprise perspective, which sees business firms as social institutions operated for the benefit of multiple stakeholders, including shareholders, employees, customers, creditors, regulators, and the public at large. Thus, whereas within the context of the traditional view of business firms organizational choice-making was seen as being shaped by a combination of customers' needs and owners' objectives, the emerging enterprise perspective paints a considerably more complex picture, with numerous stakeholder groups exerting some degree of direct or indirect influence on organizational choices. Moreover, implicit in the distinctiveness of individual stakeholder groups are differences in organizational interaction modes and motivations: For instance, in spite of being its legal owners shareholders tend to have infrequent, if any, direct contact with the business organization in which they hold stock, and their expectations rarely extend beyond opportunistic arbitrage. On the other hand, employees usually have constant direct interactions with the organization and their expectations tend to emphasize continuity and conditions of employment; still other stakeholder groups, such as customers or creditors have periodic interactions with the company and their expectations tend to reflect the fulfillment of implicit or explicit commitments.

In a more general sense, enterprise theory suggests that business organizations can be viewed as networks of distinct constituents. The theory further implies that firms strive to promote an efficient and effective functioning of their stakeholder ecosystems through instituting formal systems of rules, practices, and processes, to serve as bases of organizational decision-making. Broadly known as corporate governance, those rules aim to ensure accountability and fairness in organizations' relationships with individual stakeholder groups. Naturally, the degree to which firms meet those goals can be questioned by different stakeholder groups leading to corrective or remediative actions,[3] which can target firms as distinct legal entities, or firms' directors and officers as organizational decision-makers, or both. In general, those actions are reactive, as they reflect stakeholder evaluations of a priori management actions in the context of obligations imposed by formal and informal rules comprising corporate governance. Thus, to be fully understood, business-related decision-making needs to be examined within the context of organizational stakeholder ecosystems.

Businesses as Stakeholder Ecosystems

There is a long tradition of likening different aspects of business to natural phenomena – notions of 'evolution', 'natural selection', 'lifecycle', or 'ecosystem' all offer interesting contexts for capturing different aspects of socioeconomic interactions that form the foundations of modern commerce. The earlier mentioned enterprise theory-promoted view of business interactions draws particularly close parallels to the concept of *ecosystem*. Defined, in its original scientific context, as the totality of living organisms and nonliving elements inhibiting a particular area and interacting with one another, individual ecosystems are generally assumed to exhibit a certain degree of distinctiveness, and their overriding purpose is typically framed in the dual context of survival and self-perpetuation, or using business vernacular, to remain a going concern.

Given the highly reductive but nonetheless widely used conception of business organization as a group of individuals joined together in pursuit of commercial goals, a question of how those individuals are 'joined together' needs to be addressed. While a broader overview of different legal organizational forms falls outside of the scope of this overview, let it suffice to say that corporation is the most common type of business organization, at least in the US. One of the distinguishing characteristics of that particular organizational form is that a corporate entity is considered a stand-alone legal body that is both distinct and independent from the individuals who make it up, which means that the very individuals who comprise a business corporation can be thought of as organizational constituents, rather than the organization itself. Furthermore, as hinted by the notion of stakeholder ecosystems, any external to the organization entity that interacts with the firm and contributes to the creation or to the consumption of its economic output can also be considered its constituent. All considered, a publicly owned (i.e., one whose shares are traded on a public stock exchange, such as the New York Stock Exchange or NASDAQ) corporation can have up to seven distinct sets of constituents: shareholders, employees, regulators, customers, creditors, suppliers, and competitors, all of whom have constituent interest in the corporation's decisions.

Shareholders, defined as any person, company, or other entity that owns at least a single share in a company, are the first of the seven common stakeholder groups. Although it is rare for shareholders to have direct interactions with organizations in which they own stock, as owners they nonetheless have numerous rights, many of which translate into binding obligations – or liability – on the part of the management. (It should be noted that, in the US, the exact makeup of those rights depends on the state in which a company was incorporated, as laws governing corporations are derived from state rather than federal laws; that said, nearly half of all US public companies, and more than 60% of Fortune 500 corporations, are incorporated in the state of Delaware, in spite of the fact that most are domiciled elsewhere.)

The second key stakeholder group is employees, defined as persons who work for a business enterprise in return for financial or other compensation. Within the confines of stakeholder ecosystems, there are two distinct employment classes: executive and non-executive. The former shape and enforce organizational policies that the latter are expected to follow, which points to noticeably different interactions with the organization: From the standpoint of corporate governance, executive employees are effectively legal proxies of the organization they manage hence can be viewed as endogenous to the firm, whereas non-executive employees are exogenous to the firm, thus can be considered a distinct external stakeholder group.

Regulators are the next key stakeholder group. Although there are numerous federal (more than 500 in the US, according to official sources), not all have rulemaking powers and of those that do, not all have oversight over business conduct of organizations. Overall, regulatory agencies with rulemaking powers and business conduct oversight can be grouped into two broad categories: (1) business-general and (2) industry-specific. The former, exemplified by the Securities and Exchange Commission, the Federal Trade Commission or the Equal Employment Opportunity Commission regulate those aspects of business that apply to all companies, whereas the latter, exemplified by the Food and Drug Administration or the Nuclear Regulatory Commission, focus on matters that are specific to only certain industries. Hence, it follows that while all organizations that are involved in commercial activities within the US are subject to at least one US regulatory agency's oversight, the number of applicable regulatory overseers will vary across industries and, to a lesser degree, across companies. Also, it should be noted that individual states (in the US) regulate some limited aspects of business, such as insurance, which may translate into additional regulatory demands, directly or indirectly impacting organizational decision-making.

Considering that no business organization can remain a going concern without earning income from the sale of its products and/or services, customers should be viewed as yet another distinct group with a constituent interest in business organizations. In many regards, interacting with customers can be seen as most information intensive, primarily because the customer-company linkage is highly tenuous. It is hard to think of a product or a service that is not competitive, in the sense of differently branded but functionally substitutable offerings, which translates into ongoing, information-intensive customer acquisition and retention efforts.

The next two stakeholder groups – creditors and suppliers – are similar, yet distinct. They are similar insofar as both supply product or service creation and delivery required inputs, which means both sets of relationships tend to be governed by contractual agreements centered on the truthfulness of all requisite disclosures as well as adherence to the agreed upon terms. They are distinct because interacting with each entails different decisions and calls for different types of information.

The last and probably the most unlikely organizational stakeholder groups are the firm's competitors. It is important to note that when taken at its face value, the nature of competitor constituency is fundamentally different from those discussed above: While virtually all of the other organizational stakeholders have symbiotic relationships with business organizations in which they hold constituent interest, that is generally not the case with competitors. However, when looked at from a more macroeconomic point of view, firms that compete in a particular product or service category have a vested interest in making sure that others (i.e., competitors) adhere to the agreed upon rules of engagement, broadly known as trade practices. Thus following that line of reasoning, firms have constituent interest in governance-related decisions of their competitors, which places additional demands on firms' decision-making related information creation and dissemination.

Stakeholder Ecosystems and Organizational Decision-Making

A handful of exceptions notwithstanding, corporate decision-making is controlled by corporate managers who have legal rights to make decisions on behalf of business firms (assuming those are organized as corporations and are thus considered person-like entities in the eyes of the law), the opportunity given to them by virtue of exercising control over business assets, and the obligation to act, emanating from what is known as the 'duty of care'.[4] When coupled with the already complex picture painted by organizational ecosystems and resultant constituent interests of distinct stakeholder groups, the result is a highly contextualized decision-making setting. However, the picture gets even muddier once the earlier discussed organization-specific structural and cultural characteristics are added in, as both can be seen as moderators of the individual organization-stakeholder group interactions. And so while some of the stakeholder-specific rights might transcend organizational structure and culture, decentralized organizations that encourage a wide range of participative decision-making can nonetheless be expected to assimilate more of stakeholder inputs than centralized, command-and-control firms. The reason for that assertion is that the former tend to go beyond legal rights to also take into account rising social consciousness, whereas the latter tend to limit those inputs to just those that emanate from recognized legal rights and obligations. All considered, the manner in which distinct organizational stakeholder groups directly or indirectly affect organizational decision-making cannot be understood outside of the organization-specific structural design features and cultural norms.

Organizations and Decision-Making

One of the common characteristics shared by all formal organizations is the need for ongoing decision-making. Earlier defined as commitment to a course of action intended to serve a particular end goal, many – perhaps even most – organizational decisions can be seen as outcomes of boundedly rational processes, so characterized because of being commonly constrained by limited/incomplete information as well as cognitive and time limitations. The mental heuristics and proximal mechanisms that produce judgments and choices are still poorly understood, which in a way is not surprising given the paradoxical complexity of human cognition – how does one make sense of one's sensemaking? Moreover, as implied by the preceding overview of cultural and structural forces affecting institutional functioning, organizational decisions are shaped not only by cognitive but also by psychological, emotional, and social factors.

Still, making decisions is an inescapable aspect of human functioning – as noted earlier, it has been estimated that a person makes about 35,000 decisions a day. If that estimate seems exceedingly large that is probably because many choices are so routine and, in a sense, unordinary that they don't seem like 'real' decisions, as illustrated by a simple process of walking which entails making numerous, almost automatic choices. One of the many implications of that assertion is that decisions can vary significantly in terms of frequency, importance, and difficulty, and the combination of those three decision-shaping factors can produce materially different decision scenarios. For instance, many routine everyday choices are frequent, important, and comparatively easy, from the decision-making standpoint, as illustrated by the task of crossing a busy roadway. From the decision-making standpoint, the choices entailed in crossing a busy street are, under most circumstances, characterized by nearly perfect information and adequate decision time, and require relatively straightforward cognitive processing of the available information; other decisions, such as choosing a college, can be characterized as non-routine, important, and complex from the standpoint of information seeking and processing.

When decisions are made within an organizational setting, the additional consideration of group dynamics needs to be taken into account. Defined as attitudinal and behavioral determinants of collective functioning, group dynamics effectively adds another evaluative dimension to the decision-making process. More specifically, it necessitates explicit differentiation between single- and multiple-actors choice-making mechanics and considerations, especially the interplay between personal and interpersonal factors that shape the final organizational choice-making outcomes. While the most salient single-actor-decision-influencing factors – most notably learning and knowledge, sensemaking, and the impact of cognitive bias – have been discussed in Chapter 1, the added context of group dynamics further expands the scope of outcome shaping considerations.

A good starting point in considering the combined effect of personal and interpersonal choice-influencing factors is offered by McKinsey & Company, a consultancy, which developed a 2 × 2 decision categorization schema which, at least implicitly, touches upon some of the key single- and multiple-actors considerations. Framed by 'scope and impact', which can be narrow or broad, and 'level of familiarity', which can be either unfamiliar and infrequent or familiar and frequent, McKinsey's schema yields four distinct types of decisions: (1) big-bet decisions, which are broad in scope, infrequent, and deal with unfamiliar choices, (2) cross-cutting decisions, which are also broad but are comparatively frequent and tackle familiar choices, (3) delegated decisions, which are frequently made and deal with familiar and narrow matters, and (4) ad hoc decisions, which also deal with narrow, but unfamiliar and infrequent choices. The first two decision types – big-bet and cross-cutting – necessitate collaborative, that is, multi-actor choice evaluation, whereas the latter two decision types – delegated and ad hoc – can be tackled either by individuals or by teams.

The relative gravity of the decision at hand notwithstanding, all decisions call for either a simple, typically binary (i.e., yes vs. no), or a complex set of determinations. From the standpoint of rational choice-making, the former can be seen as being shaped, primarily, by the preponderance of 'for' vs. 'against' evidence, whereas the latter entail far more nuanced sets of considerations. Stated differently, complex organizational decisions in particular tend to require more evidence and more involved evidence evaluation, which, in turn, highlights the importance of a singular evidentiary sensemaking framework. That is not to say that human decision-makers should become robot-like, but it does mean that the influence of common interpersonal differences, emanating from factors such as culture or motivation, need to be taken into account. Moreover, the potential impact of individual actors' *implicit social cognition* also needs to be reckoned with. Broadly defined as mental processes that occur outside of conscious awareness or control in relation to socio-psychological phenomena, those instinct-like sensemaking mechanisms are believed to be responsible for many of an individual decision-maker's attitude-based responses, including the use of stereotypes. All considered, implicit social cognition can bring about noticeably different interpretation of the same sets of facts, some of which can be in the form of informative insights, and some can be a manifestation of perception-warping bias. A strategy that has proven itself successful at stimulating the former and suppressing the latter is to provide explicit points or frames of reference, but being aware of those factors is the key to successfully managing choice-making within the confines of group dynamics.

The Role of Evidence

To be 'evident' is to be obvious to the eye or mind, thus *evidence* encompasses facts or other organized information presented to support or justify beliefs or inferences. The notion of evidence is of central importance to such transcendental and diverse tasks as the pursuit of social justice and the search for scientific truths. Arguments that are rooted in sound, objective evidence are inherently more compelling and persuasive, and the search for evidence can be considered to be the single most important aspect of analyses of data. Not surprisingly, evidence plays a critical role in organizational decision-making, especially in situations in which outcome uncertainty or ambiguity is high, or in situations in which multiple and divergent points of view collide. And so either by means of science rooted notion of 'weight of evidence', or more legally framed notion of 'preponderance of evidence', facts and other organized information ought to be seen as means of optimizing organizational choice-making.

Implied in the above reasoning is the importance of external-to-self aspect of evidence. In many situations, especially in group decision-making where differences of perspectives are common, the most persuasive arguments tend to be those that can be substantiated by objective, that is, external, information, as captured by the 'empirical' dimension of the 3E framework detailed in this book. This is not a novel idea: Scientific theories are validated using independent observations, medical diagnosis rely on tests, and legal disputes are resolved by independent facts. In general, by virtue of stemming from larger and more representative fact base, data analyses and empirical research derived evidence can be considered to be more valid and reliable than perception-colored and possibly atypical experiential evidence.

Still, although empirical evidence tends to be more persuasive in a group setting, experiential evidence can play a disproportionately influential role in shaping the point of view of an individual. A professional's experience tends to weigh heavily on his or her judgment precisely because it is personal, in the sense that any resultant beliefs feel intuitively correct. In fact, experience-rooted beliefs can overshadow more objective evidence because experiential knowledge is closely linked to one's self-esteem. Not surprisingly, however, when put in the context of organizational decision-making, strong preference for *self-referential knowledge*, or persistent partiality for internal-to-self explanations and interpretations, can adversely impact group dynamics, when differences in self-referential knowledge emerge. Those and related considerations play an important role in the 3E framework's evidence scoping and agglomeration logic, which attempts to balance the relative efficacy of different sources of evidence (through an explicit hierarchy of evidence) with group dynamics (through combining empirical and experiential sources of evidence).

Group Dynamics

Conventional wisdom suggests that groups make better decisions than individuals because of greater capacity to accumulate and deal with more information, encourage divergent and innovative thinking, point out group members' errors, and reduce the impact of cognitive bias. However, research in areas of social cognition and social psychology paints a somewhat different picture, one which suggests that cognitive, social, and situational influences determine the quality of decision-making, and that groups don't always outperform individuals. While interactions taking place within groups indeed increase decision confidence, that does not necessarily translate into higher decision quality because of two main reasons: First of those is the phenomenon often referred to as 'groupthink', a dysfunctional pattern of thought and interaction during group decision-making characterized by closed-mindedness, uniformity expectations, and group bias. The second is biased information search, characterized by strong preference for information that supports the group's view. Thus, thinking of organizations as communities specializing in knowledge creation and transfer, it is essential to recognize that while groups have the potential to enhance the capacity, objectivity, and creativity of organizational thinking, the realization of that promise is contingent on containing cognitive diversity-suppressing aspects of group dynamics.

An aspect of cognitive diversity that is of particular importance is *critical thinking*, a summary construct capturing an individual's ability to evaluate and analyze an issue of interest in a rigorous manner. More specifically, a critical thinker examines the underlying assumptions, is able to discern hidden values, has the capacity (in the sense of cognitive abilities and reasoning/analytic tools) to evaluate evidence, and assess the efficacy of conclusions. While framed using common attributes, critical thinking is inescapably individual because it calls upon both explicit and tacit knowledge to produce a unique perspective, ultimately giving rise to cognitive diversity at a group level. In that sense, individual-level critical thinking is a core determinant of the efficacy of group-level decision-making – the aforementioned phenomena of groupthink and biased information search suppress the degree of cognitive diversity of a group by curtailing the individual group members' critical thinking.

A yet another important, organizational decision-making-related aspect of group dynamics is group conflict. As suggested by social exchange theory, which views the stability of group interactions through a theoretical lens of negotiated exchange between parties, individual group members are ultimately driven by the desire to maximize their benefits, thus conflict tends to arise when group dynamics take on more competitive than collaborative character. Keeping in mind that the realization of group decision-making potential requires full contributory participation on the part of individual group members, within-group competition reduces the willingness of individuals to contribute their best to the group effort. The reason for that, according to research from social psychology, is trust, believed to be one of the strongest determinants of an individual's willingness to share his or her knowledge with a group. Thus, in many common business situations, the more competitive the nature of group dynamics the greater the inclination of individuals to perceive group sharing as detrimental to their self-interest, which translates into limited group thinking involvement and superficial participation.

As could be expected, the quality of group outputs will be proportional to the quality of group inputs, as predicted by the earlier mentioned research findings. Unfortunately, while the solution to this problem may seem simple, there are endemic obstacles that stand in its way, most notably the inherently competitive character of organizational reward and recognition systems. Although terms like 'collaboration' and 'teamwork' are used to compel full group commitment and participation, the commonly pyramid-like organizational reward structures tend to produce more within-group competition than collaboration. The desire to change that is one of the reasons behind the emergence of more community-minded organizational structures such as flatarchies and holacracies discussed earlier.

An important aspect of competition vs. cooperation themed group dynamic is the extent of information sharing. Research focused on group decision-making-related information pooling points toward a consistent tendency to pool and repeat more of shared than unshared information, a phenomenon now known as *information-sampling bias*. Considering that in-group competition activates individuals' fears of being exploited (while also heightening the desire to exploit others) and makes individuals more focused on standing out in comparison of competencies with others, group information processing is also characterized by the tendency to evaluate one's own information more favorably than information of others', a tendency known as *ownership bias*, and the inclination to evaluate more positively any information that is consistent with one's initial preferences, a psychological phenomenon known as *preference effect*. It is important to note, however, that those generally undesirable information processing instincts are at least somewhat involuntary, ultimately stemming from causes that could be considered physiological in the sense that preference-consistent information is usually more salient and thus more accessible from memory. Reasons notwithstanding, the combination of ownership bias, preference effect, and poor unshared information pooling can materially degrade the efficacy of group decision-making, ultimately negating that which is often held out as the reason for trusting group-derived conclusions.

Still, there is more. As posited by the Motivated Information Processing in Groups model, information processing in groups is driven by two orthogonal motivational factors of epistemic and social motivations. Individual-framed epistemic motivation captures individuals' willingness to expend effort to achieve thorough and accurate understanding of the problem at hand, whereas group-described social motivations capture individuals' preferences for sharing in outcome distributions. Thus, developing of sound understanding of the impact of group dynamics on what and how much information is processed and assimilated also calls for discerning those two key motivational dimensions that exert meaningful impact on the extent and the degree of involvement in truly participating in group-based choice-making.

Organizational Learning

Chapter 1 introduced the general idea of learning, discussed in the context of the relatively general inductive and deductive learning modes, and the more refined observational, theoretical, computational, and simulational learning paradigms. Broadly characterized, inductive learning generalizes from specific instances, whereas deductive learning applies generalized principles to arrive at specific conclusions. Products of the ferment of the Renaissance and Reformation movements that swept through Europe in 16th and 17th centuries and saw science becoming an autonomous (from philosophy) discipline focused on the pursuit of knowledge through observation and experimentation, inductive and deductive learning captured the essence of learning at that time. The more recent learning paradigms -observational, theoretical, computational, and simulational -can be seen as products of perhaps not as grand a revolution,[5] but a revolution nonetheless, commonly referred to as the Information Age. The rise and rapid proliferation of the ever-increasing varieties of transactional and communication data are now opening up new avenues of learning, ones that reach far beyond just observation and experimentation to also include data-enabled constructed, or virtual reality based learning. And while the inductive-deductive duality is still meaningful, it is more instructive to examine organizational learning through the lens of the more complete typology of observational, theoretical, computational, and simulational learning, which better reflects the 'who' and the 'how' of current-day learning.

Observational learning is a product of sensory experiences, a curious mind driven to understand the world through careful observation and subsequent generalization, which closely resembles the traditional inductive learning paradigm. Along the similar lines, the *theoretical* learning paradigm closely resembles deductive learning, which produces specific knowledge claims by means of applying general theories or conjectures to specific situations. *Computational* learning can be seen as a direct consequence of the emergence and rapid growth of electronic transaction processing and communication infrastructure along with rapid maturing of computer science; the combined effect of the two manifests itself in the ability to discover new insights (exploratory analyses) as well as validate the truthfulness of prior beliefs (confirmatory analyses). And lastly, simulational learning represents an evolution of computational learning, a direct result of coming together of vast and varied volumes of data and the ever-advancing data processing capabilities, which together enable knowledge creation by means of computer-rendered virtual reality. Moreover, learning is no longer an exclusively human endeavor -machines are now also capable of learning (see chapters 1 and 3 for more details), and as evidenced by recent advances in the field of artificial intelligence, machine learning capabilities are improving at a staggering pace.

Let us pause here. If the traditional conception of learning implies acquisition of knowledge by individuals, what then constitutes organizational learning? In a sense, it is easier to say what it is not, and it is not a simple sum of knowledge acquired by members of an organization although that is certainly a part of it. It has been noted earlier that organizations are essentially groups of individuals joined together in pursuit of common goals, and so as those groups mature, in the sense of moving from a simple collection of individuals toward a complex, integrated system, they begin to preserve certain behaviors, norms, and values, which, together with the sum of individually held explicit and tacit knowledge, can be broadly characterized as organizational learning. As such, the slowly accumulating institutional knowledge enables organizations to build organizational understanding and interpretation of their environment, and as such it is of key importance to organizations' ability to assess their strategies, and ultimately, to the attainment and maintenance of competitive advantage.

Content-wise, organizational learning encompasses the two independent dimensions of *behavior*, or the act of doing, and *cognition*, or the process of knowing. The former commonly takes the form of what is known as lower level learning, which is the process of forming rudimentary behavior-outcome associations, whereas the latter usually takes the form of higher level learning, which is the process of discerning overall rules and norms (rather than just specific activities and behaviors). Both the lower and higher learning are shaped by four broad, contextual factors: (1) culture, or shared beliefs, ideologies, and patterns of behavior, (2) strategy, or organizational goals and objectives that provide boundaries and context for decision-making and thus focal points for learning, (3) structure, or the organizational arrangement of authority, which can either reinforce past behaviors (as is the case with centralized, mechanistic structures) or facilitate shifts in beliefs and actions (typically the case with de-centralized, organic structures), and (4) environment, or the relative complexity and stability of the context within which organizations function. Individually and collectively, those four broad contextual factors shape what and how much an organization learns, though it should be noted that environmental complexity and stability exert particularly strong influence on organizational learning – in general, the less complex and more stable the organization's environment, the more effective the organizational learning.

The socio-cognitive view of organizational learning summarized above suggests that organizational learning takes place in a complex web of individual interactions and cultural structures that define organizations, which draws attention to the importance of the idea of *social cognition*, first raised in the context of organizational culture. Placing the ideas learning and knowing, or cognition, in the context of interpersonal interactions yields more realistic collective cognitive representations of organizational learning. More specifically, by bringing to light conscious and subconscious human information processing, the theoretical lens of social cognition unmasks the otherwise hidden learning influencers that directly or indirectly shape organizational learning in complex social and structural interactions. For instance, the perspective offered by social cognition helps to better understand the interplay between learning and emotions – do managers feel threatened when challenged by more knowledgeable subordinates, and what effect does that have on a broader landscape of organization-wide learning?

The term 'learning organizations' is often used to characterize actual or aspirational capability to adapt to opportunities and threats by means of identifying and assimilating appropriate knowledge and implementing necessary changes. Popularized by consultants dispensing sage advice and surefire solutions promising to deliver a lot and fast, the concept of learning organizations became a yet another[6] 'quick fix' managerial remedy. Setting aside a nagging question prompted by the idea of learning organizations – are there organizations that do not learn? – the applied conception of learning organizations seemed to have accomplished one thing, which was to turn an important set of socio-cognitive ideas aimed at understanding how organizations learn into a faddish buzzword.

Accepting that some manner and degree of learning can be considered an inescapable aspect of organizational (or personal, for that matter) existence, or stated differently, that learning is endemic to organizational functioning, cross-organization performance variability suggests that not all organizations learn equally well (as discussed in Chapter 7 in the context of contrasting fortunes of the now defunct Circuit City and still thriving Best Buy). As noted earlier, structural and cultural differences, in addition to strategic and environmental factors shed some fairly general explanatory light on cross-organization learning effectives. For instance, centralized, mechanistic organizational structures tend to reinforce past behaviors and impede new ideas, whereas de-centralized and more organic structures, as exemplified by flatarchies and holacracies, are more conducive to shifts in beliefs and behaviors. Looking beyond those relatively coarse explanations, deeper understanding of cross-organization learning efficacy can be realized by differentiating among different types of organizational learning, which can be grouped into the following three modalities:

1 *adaptive learning*, which encompasses mostly automatic changes needed to accommodate changing environmental demands or requirements,
2 *generative learning*, which describes purposeful acquisition and dissemination (within the organization) of new knowledge or skills as a mean of attaining organizational goals, and
3 *transformative learning*, which encapsulates strategic shifts in organizational structure, tasks, or goals, typically in response to outside opportunities or threats.

Starting with the premise that, as noted earlier, all organizations can be assumed to learn, a more in-depth assessment of the degree of adaptive, generative, and transformative learning can shed light on the variability in cross-organizational learning efficacy. It seems likely that most organizations exhibit comparable degrees of adaptive learning, and that there are more notable cross-organization differences in generative learning, and even more pronounced differences in transformative learning; lastly, those learning dissimilarities ultimately help to explain cross-company performance differences. All considered, the 'what' and 'how' of organizational learning represent important albeit complex aspects of organizational behavior. Deeper understanding of the efficacy of organizational learning requires careful and thoughtful study of the socio-cognitive fabric of individual organizations, with particular emphasis on organizational structure, culture, and the intricate web of interpersonal interactions. In a more forward-looking, prescriptive sense, building and sustaining maximally effective organizational learning habits also calls for an equally deliberate study of the sources and types of knowledge, as captured in the 3E framework.

The 3E Framework & Organizational Dynamics

The 3E framework is not expressly individual or group focused in its orientation primarily because there is no clear line of demarcation between individual and organizational learning. In any formal organizational or informal group setting, some learning will be shared across members as explicit knowledge, and some will be intimately personal, resulting in what is commonly known as tacit knowledge (see Chapter 1 for a more in-depth discussion of explicit and tacit knowledge). At the same time, all learning taking place in an organizational context is influenced by a combination of organizational, interpersonal, and contextual factors. From the perspective of choice-making, the key organizational factors that shape, or at least influence learning include group characteristics in the form of culture and structure, individual factors, most notably cognition, behaviors and emotions, and contextual considerations in the form of expected learning outcomes, framed in the context of three types of learning: adaptive, generative, and transformative. Hence while the 3E framework does not expressly contemplate individual or group level decision-making, the latter clearly brings to bear additional considerations that need to be taken into consideration.

Figure 10.1 re-introduces the 3E framework, discussed in detail in Chapter 7.

As graphically depicted in Figure 10.1 and in a manner conceptually similar to other evidence-based practice conceptualizations, the 3E framework is built around an implied progression of systematically identifying, evaluating, and making use of decision-related evidence. Moreover, though it may not be immediately clear from the framework's graphical summarization, the earlier detailed operational mechanics of the framework emphasize the importance

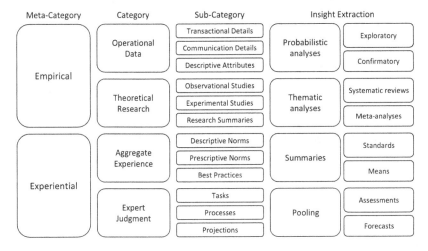

FIGURE 10.1 The Empirical & Experiential Evidence Framework.

of operational data to organizational decision-making. In fact, the genesis of the 3E framework is the failure of other evidence-based practice-related conceptualizations to recognize that in the information/big data age, it is the broadly defined organizational data that is the primary source of decision-guiding knowledge, which is particularly so in the context of business decision-making.

Still, even the most impressive, as seen from the perspective of a casual observer, or overwhelming, as seen from the perspective of a potential user, collections of organizational data are rarely informationally sufficient on their own for two basic reasons: First, the available data are incomplete and noisy. More specifically, the key focal points of organizational data including behavioral outcomes, as exemplified by product or service purchases, or attitudinal states, as exemplified by product or service reviews, are not fully described by the available (in this case transactional and communication) data, and the available data include some, typically unknown, amount of error. Second, data analytic methods are probabilistic, which means their outcomes are only approximately true.

Looking beyond organizational data, all other sources of decision-shaping information – most notably, empirical research studies, industry norms, standards and benchmarks, as well as individual-level experience – are also singularly imperfect. Thus, when confronting routine or atypical choices, *informational triangulation,* or cross-source insight verification, enhances the efficacy of decisions by strengthening the degree of dependability of available evidence. This is precisely why the rationale behind the 3E framework is built around the idea of expressly taking into account all available and decision-pertinent knowledge. With that in mind, when considering the task of identifying, amalgamating, and synthesizing decision-related information in the confines of organizational learning, the earlier outlined organizational decision-making influencing factors of organizational culture and structure, individual learning-shaping factors of cognition, behaviors and emotions, and contextual, or learning type (adaptive, generative, and transformative) considerations also need to be taken into account.

The Impact of Organizational Culture and Structure

The elusive, intangible nature of organizational culture is conducive to overlooking that important aspect of an organizational fabric. It is usually not so with organizational structure, which, as a system of roles and responsibilities is one of the most visible, and even one of the most defining organizational features. And so while organizational culture embodies a fundamental 'feel' of an organization, organizational structure embodies the more tangibly ascertainable intentions, aspirations, and purposes, which are particularly well demonstrated by flatarchies and holacracies, the newly emergent, norm-breaking organizational structures. In that sense, organizational structure can be as much as an instrument for efficient operation as a manifestation or even legitimation of organizational power holders' values and beliefs.

Organizational culture and structure are mutually interdependent and both rely on the reflexivity and dynamics of organizational members to develop the necessary organizational functions, and ultimately to achieve the stated organizational objectives. Broadly held beliefs, often summarized under the umbrella of institutional theory, suggest that organizations have to adapt to societal and sectoral values that spell out appropriate organizational forms, but the very emergence of the aforementioned norm-breaking organizational forms cast doubt on the validity of those beliefs. Though still only anecdotal in nature (given the small, non-representative sample size), recent evidence nonetheless suggests that values of dominant organizational power holders, particularly the founders, have norm-setting impact on defining organizational fabric. In fact, rather than having to adapt to prevailing norms, highly influential power holders can effectively re-write those norms.

Culture and structure are also closely related to organizational learning. While (mostly academic) research suggests that organizational learning shapes organizational structure, a view supported by rather frequent organizational restructurings, a more pragmatic perspective suggests that organizations typically have to choose a particular system of roles and responsibilities at the very onset of their existence, before any appreciable amount of organizational learning has accrued. It thus seems reasonable to see organizational culture and structure both as determinants and outcomes of organizational learning, which has important implications for the 3E framework.

As graphically illustrated in Figure 10.1, the general process of systematic identification, assessment, and synthesis of multi-sourced, decision-related information is at the core of the 3E framework. When that process is considered from the perspective of organizational structure, centralized organizations, which are those in which all key decisions are made at the top level, produce materially different learning outcomes than de-centralized organizations, which distribute at least some of the decision-making power throughout their hierarchies. By virtue of concentrating decision-making powers in the hands of relatively few individuals (typically the top executives), centralized organizational structure reduces the aggregate amount of experiential evidentiary knowledge produced throughout the organization. De-centralized organizations, on the other hand, tend to generate comparatively greater, and likely also informationally richer, aggregate volumes of experiential learning as a result of delegation of decision-making authority.

When the general process of systematic identification, assessment, and synthesis of multi-sourced, decision-related information is considered from the perspective of organizational culture, it is clear that the empirical dimension of decision-guiding evidence generation is most directly affected. By monopolizing the core elements of organizational decision-making, centralized organizations effectively discourage the pursuit deeper exploration of the available data and applicable academic research. Recalling the three distinct dimensions of organizational learning discussed earlier – adaptive, generative, and transformative – centrally controlled organizations implicitly encourage adaptive learning, which encompasses reactive changes primarily brought about by internal pressures, while at the same time implicitly discouraging generative (acquisition of new skills and knowledge) and transformative (strategic shifts in skills and knowledge) learning. In a more general sense, the non-participatory, often rigid decision-making structure of centralized organizations tends to reduce broader organizational learning to mechanistic responses to environmental demands while suppressing higher-order, critical thinking, and social cognition rooted learning. Conversely, non-centralized organizations tend to run the risk of insufficiently inducing lower-level, that is, adaptive, learning while implicitly promoting, even nurturing as in the case of flatarchies or holacracies, more organic and systemic higher-order learning.

Lastly, recalling that learning takes the two somewhat distinct forms of 'doing' or behaviors, and 'thinking' or cognition, under most circumstances organizational structure most directly impacts the behavioral aspect of organizational learning, whereas organizational culture primarily affects the cognitive aspect of learning. Reasons for that are as follows: In the context of organizational learning, behaviors and cognitions are interrelated to the degree to which at least some of the aggregate organizational learning can be seen as an outcome of de facto experimentation. Reasonable choices, supported by a combination of reasonable assumptions and sound empirical knowledge, take the form of organizational actions, the vast majority of which are ultimately speculative, given the presence of numerous environmental uncertainties. In that sense, individual organizational decisions can be – in fact, should be – evaluated as applied experiments, outcomes of which should be assessed against predetermined evaluative benchmarks. In that context, learning is a function of 'thinking' surrounding the logic of organizational actions, and 'doing', which takes the form of executing of ideas. Given all that, one of the inescapable characteristics of centrally controlled organizations is that by concentrating choice-making powers in the hands of few, such organizations offer limited behavioral learning opportunities to many. And by extension, they also offer limited incentives to engage broad employee base in more systemic social cognition efforts, as centralized organizational structures are most commonly associated with non-participative, predominantly mechanistic and often inflexible cultures, which ultimately provide limited incentives to engage in broad base, systemic cognitive learning.

It is difficult to escape the conclusion that to truly flourish, organizational learning requires a combination of supportive structure and culture. The slogan-laden, superficial 'employee engagement' campaigns of mechanistic (effectively), non-participatory command-and-control organizations are unlikely to yield meaningful and systemic organizational learning outcomes because the very essence of such organizational designs creates natural learning disincentives, even barriers. In the end, though organizational learning is more than a simple sum of individual members' knowledge, no organization can amass competitively advantageous knowledge base without individual-level learning involvement and commitment.

Cognitive, Behavioral, and Emotive Factors

When massive open online courses (MOOCs), self-paced, prerecorded learning modules aimed at unlimited participation and open access via the web were first introduced around the year 2006 and began to quickly garner widespread interest, many in higher education circles became worried about the future of traditional, face-to-face educational institutions. A bit more than a decade later, although MOOCs are still alive and well they are no longer seen by traditional universities, many of which developed their own, albeit typically limited MOOC offerings, as an equally big existential threat – why? While numerous potential explanations can be cited here, the one that is of particular interest from the standpoint of organizational learning is that, as suggested by research from social psychology, people simply prefer learning from other people, whom they deem knowledgeable and trustworthy, than from documents or digital sources.

To go a step further toward understanding the underlying dynamics, a person learning from another person can be conceptualized as a process incorporating social interaction and dyadic trust (e.g., a student's faith in teacher) as critical antecedents of effective knowledge transfer. This realization is particularly important to deciphering the mechanisms that facilitate organizational dissemination of experiential knowledge, which is one of the two meta-categories of the 3E framework. Stepping a bit deeper into abstract considerations, group learning situations characterized by high trust and emotionally positive context tend to produce better organizational experiential learning outcomes, as the initially individual cognitions ('I think that...') are slowly transformed into shared cognitions ('We think that...') which ultimately give rise to shared institutionalized reality ('It is true that...'). When that happens, the experiential knowledge of organizational thought and practice leaders can be disseminated throughout the organization, effectively enhancing the aggregate knowledge base. Thus, the realization of decision-making efficacy gains made possible by more thorough and systematic identification, assessment, agglomeration, and assimilation of available and applicable experiential evidence hinges on creating of socially and emotionally conducive learning environments. In addition, as posited by social identity theory, closeness of organizational identification of individual member with the organization also has strong impact on learning outcomes. If being a part of the organization contributes to building a positive self-esteem, that is, is a source of positive social identity, readiness and willingness to learn will be greater.

Although empirical evidence, which is the second of the two meta-categories that define the evidentiary scope of the 3F framework, is arguably considerably less 'personal', the means and the manner in which that knowledge is produced and disseminated are also directly influenced by the cognitive, behavioral, and emotive aspects of group dynamics. Although cognitive diversity is generally beneficial to organizations, it can also pose challenges. Cognitive bias is ubiquitous and takes on numerous forms (see Appendix A for a partial list) – it follows that greater organizational cognitive diversity will also manifest itself in a wider range of cognitive bias manifestations. Greater cognitive diversity also tends to produce pluralistic data analytical and (academic) research findings evaluation perspectives. For instance, probability estimation, which is one of the core elements of statistical inference, can be approached from two fundamentally different methodological perspectives. The first one is Bayesian, which treats probability as a manifestation of the state of knowledge known and available to the decision-maker at decision time; as such, it combines subjective prior beliefs (of the decision-maker and/or decision-influencers) with analyses of past outcomes (i.e., objective data). The second one is the frequentist approach, which limits probability estimation inputs to just objective data collected by means of experiments or recorded historical occurrences, explicitly barring any subjective (e.g., prior beliefs) inputs. Under most circumstances, the two approaches will yield numerically different estimates which can give rise not only to informational ambiguity but can also be source of group conflict, which as noted earlier tends to adversely impact creativity and flexibility of group thinking.

And there is more. While evidence gathering related group interactions may increase the confidence of the ultimate conclusion, socio-psychological research suggests that does not necessarily translate into greater decision efficacy because of two commonly observed phenomena. The first is popularly labeled as 'groupthink,' and it is characterized by pressure toward group uniformity stemming from overestimation of the value of the group and the corresponding scorn of the individual. The second of the two phenomena, biased information search, can be seen as a consequence of groupthink as it manifests itself as favoring information that supports the group's view. In a more general sense, when confronted with diverse and divergent data analytical or research evidence, the desire for uniformity may impede critical thinking, or more specifically, may bias the examination of assumptions and hidden values associated with differently sets of outcomes and findings, ultimately leading to distorted evaluations and conclusions.

Overcoming the potential cognitive, behavioral, and emotive challenges that may arise in a group setting is tantamount to enabling organizational readiness to learn. As groups mature, which is to say they evolve from a simple collection of individuals into more complex, integrated systems, and develop a stronger sense of identity, they also begin to solidify their behaviors, norms, and values. Nurturing the desirable aspects of groups, most notably the diversity of perspectives, all while dissuading forced uniformity is not simple but it is necessary for organizations to learn in a manner that builds organizational understanding and interpretation of their environment.

Learning Outcome Differences

It could be argued that learning is an inescapable part of existence. While often thought of as episodic and purposeful acquisition of specific know-how, learning is in fact considerably more elementary and ongoing. It encompasses an almost impossibly broad array of memories ranging from basic behavioral adaptations, as exemplified by discovering, early on, the painful consequences of touching a hot object, to developing an abstract understanding of concepts such as the force of gravity, to acquiring a deeper sense of morality, or learning to make sense of highly emotional experiences. Perhaps we say that 'it is human to err' because learning is such an inseparable part of our existence.

Within the somewhat more amorphous context of group dynamics and organizational decision-making, learning can be looked at from three different perspectives: the level of learning, the manner of learning, and the modality of learning. The first two of those three characterizations – the level and the manner of learning – are both built around dichotomous and conceptually similar categorizations and so can be combined into a single, more richly detailed perspective. Here, organizational learning is seen as being comprised of lower and higher levels, where the former focuses on outcomes that form rudimentary associations of behaviors and consequences, whereas the latter emphasizes abstract cognitive understanding of rules and norms. When considered from that perspective, organizations, as groups of individuals, learn behaviors from repetition and routine, and then somewhat separately develop cognitive understanding of the underlying rules and norms through new insights and through acquisition of new skills. Within that conceptual context, the reasoning embedded in the 3E framework is beneficial to lower level learning, but it is essential to higher level learning. Lower level learning can benefit from thorough and objective identification, assessment, and synthesis of situation-applicable behaviors, with particular emphasis on experientially sourced learnings. The 3E framework is essential to higher level learning because of the framework's emphasis on broad (organizational data, scientific research, industry benchmarks, and expert judgment) and assimilative information sourcing and assessment, and the importance of the resultant unbiased insights to advance organizational knowledge and understanding.

Conceptually and typologically distinct perspective on learning modality portrays organizational learning through three distinct outcome focused modalities: adaptive, generative, and transformative. Adaptive learning encompasses mostly automatic responses to changing environmental demands; thus, it tends to be highly reactive. However, while behavioral adaptations themselves can be seen as automatic, the task of identifying and interpreting of environmental stimuli cannot be assumed to be automatically sound. In fact, the frequency, volume, and variability of environmental stimuli make adaptive learning increasingly more difficult, especially for larger organizations, suggesting that more systematic and anticipatory mechanisms are called for to aid in timely identification of appropriate environment-precipitated adjustments. That conclusion is even more fitting for generative learning, which embodies purposeful acquisition of new skills as a mean of attaining organizational goals. In contrast to externally compelled adaptive learning, generative learning is motivated and regulated by the organization itself, which underscores the importance of broad and assimilative informational inputs to guide organizational learning choices. And lastly, the same can be said about transformative learning, the third learning modality encapsulating strategic shifts in organizational structure, tasks, or goals in response to outside opportunities or threats. Deliberate and deliberative gathering, assessment, and evaluation of expected future needs are of the most fundamental importance to that mode of organizational learning, and while future is a mystery to all, those with better knowledge of the emerging trends are usually better equipped to anticipate it.

All considered, the type of organizational learning outcome notwithstanding, the purposeful, evaluative, and agglomerative logic of the 3E framework can yield considerable organizational learning benefits by providing systematic and well-structured information gathering and assimilation framework. Although some organizational learning can be expected to happen organically, almost naturally, the type of learning that produces and sustains competitive advantage requires an underlying knowledge creation and dissemination infrastructure. In the manner that is somewhat reminiscent of formal educational systems, the 3E framework can form a foundation of organizational knowledge creation mechanisms, one that will not only suggest appropriate behavioral adaptations but will also give rise to competitively advantageous organizational cognition.

Notes

1 An informal organization business would lack the basic decision mechanisms which are necessary to make choices regarding such basic business considerations as resource allocation or opportunity prioritization, not to mention other essential choices such as those regarding reward and recognition.
2 When assessing the unknown, it is natural to want to reduce ambiguity by summarizing or reducing the description of the phenomenon of interest to a manageable number of easy to categorize descriptive characteristics.
3 In the US, which is one of the few countries that allow class action lawsuits, in which a group of individuals with the same or similar injuries or other grievances (such as financial losses) caused by the product or action sue the defendant as a group.
4 The legal concept of organizational managers' *duty of care* compels those with the power to make decisions on behalf of corporate entities to be actively involved in the affairs of organizational decision-making. It amounts to say that it is unacceptable to be a figurehead passively watching the company-impacting events unfold, or not to pay attention at all; indeed, it is incumbent upon the organization's leadership to actively engage in activities aimed at helping to positively affect the well-being of the organization. Stated differently, the decision-making power placed in the hands of corporate leadership does not come with an option to act – it comes with an obligation to act.
5 After all, the Scientific Revolution of the 16th and 17th centuries brought an end to roughly 2,000 years of Greek philosophy dominated approach to study of natural phenomena.
6 Knowledge management, agile management, talent management, employee engagement, lean, business process re-engineering, and emotional intelligence are all examples of other still in use or already faded quick fix management frameworks.

11

EXTERNAL FORCES & INFLUENCES

Looking beyond internal structural and cultural factors discussed in the pre-vious chapter, organizational decision-making is also affected by numerous external, typically uncontrollable influences, such as market, legal, technolog-ical, or competitive forces. The uncontrollable character of those broad envi-ronmental influences represents perhaps the largest source of organizational choice-making uncertainty, which, in turn, tends to compel organizational decision-makers to look to 'tried and true' decision guides for help. Learn-ing organizations, employee engagement, agile management, and emotional intelligence all exemplify such ostensibly proven answers to nagging manage-ment questions. In-tune with the zeitgeist and offering novel, though rarely radical solutions to even intractable management problems, those quick fix management recipes come chock-full of fun anecdotes, buzzwords, and stories of excellent companies, offering to deliver a lot and fast, and helping adaptors feel effective and cutting-edge. And though in fact bits of ideas imbedded in those frameworks might indeed work in some contexts some of the time, what is often positioned as 'evidence' of their efficacy is as illusory as con-clusions drawn from statistically nonrepresentative samples. When evaluated from the perspective of time and experience, those miracle cures to manage-ment ailments are more aptly described as management fashions, or transitory collective beliefs that certain management techniques are at the forefront of management progress.

Decision uncertainty infused by uncontrollable environmental factors also fosters the embrace of another form of self-deception known as *management lore*, which encompasses flawed axioms, anecdotes, or beliefs that are so pervasive that they erroneously achieve the status of immutable facts. Perhaps best exem-plified by Walt Disney's famous axiom 'if you can dream it, you can do it', or the popular 'sky is the limit' expression, some such beliefs are nearly axiomatic to Western society and culture. And yet, empirical evidence from social psychology shows that, for instance, dreaming big can actually be detrimental to individuals' performance, even to their career success because adopting unrealistic fantasies of success can lead to becoming accustomed to the fantasy as if it was already a reality, which, in turn, can lead to overconfidence and failure to commit the effort required to actually achieve the big goals. The same is true of another widely subscribed to management lore, according to which group creativity always benefits from diversity. And while diversity might indeed be desirable for a wide range of societal reasons, there is no empirical evidence supporting the creativity-diversity link. In fact, group dynamics related research suggests that even if diverse individuals privately generate substantially different ideas, teams do not often discuss all ideas thought of by individual members, and thus distally related concepts do not necessarily produce coherent wholes. Along the same lines, the widely subscribed to belief that the idea of emotional intelligence is one of the best predictors of organizational employees' performance lacks sound theoretical basis or meaningful practical measurement approaches, thus cannot be backed either by scientific research or by verifiable practical outcomes.

There are no universal, off-the-shelf shortcuts to reducing organizational decision-making uncertainties brought about by uncontrollable environmental factors – the only viable solution to those problems lies in thoughtful, systematic, and holistic use of available and applicable choice-making evidence. Uncertainty is not the same as unknowability – there are numerous and well-documented examples of organizations that consistently outperform their competitors by taking better advantage of the available information. In fact, the relatively recent explosion of interest in business analytics and data science can be, at least in part, attributed to the growing realization of the value of situation- and organization-specific decision-guiding knowledge, which can only be produced by thorough and sound synthesis of available evidence. This is the second of two chapters addressing the value of, and obstacles to organization-wide adoption of evidence-based management in general, and the Empirical & Experiential Evidence (3E) framework in particular, this time focusing on the key external choice-making influences.

External Forces

The task of identifying distinct external influences of organizational decisions is not an easy one, as the efficacy of any classificatory typology can be called into question. Further complicating the task at hand is a lack of clarity regarding the level of abstraction, given the trade-off between generalizability, which favors higher level of classificatory schema abstraction, and operational utility, which is typically better served by less abstract schemas.

Starting from the premise that the modern networked economy casts a long shadow over organizational choice-making, in an abstract sense, both direct and indirect external influences of organizational decisions can be characterized as forces acting upon organizations. As suggested by organizational research, those can be summarized into five general categories of market demand, political and legal, social and ethical, technological, and competitive. Being aware of the manner in which those abstractly framed forces influence organizational decision-making represents one of the core manifestations of *organizational consciousness*, broadly defined as organization's awareness of itself in terms of identity, reason for existing, and relations with others. To be deemed conscious, an organization needs to exhibit choice-making and sensemaking unity across operational divisions (assuming it is indeed comprised of multiple units, which tends to be the case with business firms). In more operationally clear terms, organizational consciousness manifest itself in three distinctive behavioral characterizations: reflexive, which explains how an organization makes sense of its position based on its unique attributes; social, which summarizes an organization's conception of its place and contribution to a larger whole; and collective, which captures the degree to which an organization functions as a horizontally and vertically integrated unit guided by a shared purpose.

When considered from the standpoint of the five broad external forces, organizational consciousness gives rise to organizational memories, by means of which knowledge resulting from past experiences and events influences present organizational choices. Those memories can be divided into two general types: declarative and procedural, where the former encompasses any facts or events that can be consciously recalled (or 'declared', hence the name), whereas the latter encapsulates largely unconscious memory of how to perform specific tasks. An important consideration from the standpoint of decision-making is that human memory, and thus by extension organizational memories, is emotion laden – in other words, memories of past experiences and events are bounded by accompanying emotions. As suggested by neuropsychological research, situational emotional activation may trigger special encoding and consolidation mechanisms that facilitate memory formation, which explains why recollection of certain events tends to also trigger specific emotional responses. In an organizational setting, emotion-laden experiences tend to be disseminated by stories and dialogs, over time leading to aspects of institutionalized reasoning becoming devoid of clear justification (which may have been lost or only exists in the subconscious), which offers some insight into why organizations may respond irrationally to environmental changes. The adverse impact of emotion-laden recall is further compounded by an effect known as *bounded rationality*. Irrespective of mental capacities, organizational decision-makers are beset by three inescapable constraints: (1) limited in amount and imperfect in terms of validity and reliability information, (2) limited cognitive capacity to evaluate and process the information that is available, and (3) limited amount of time to make a decision. Thus, when confronted with a complex problem, as exemplified by the need to assess broad and somewhat vaguely framed external environment, even the most committed rational choice-making efforts are, well, bound to make suboptimal choices.

While thinking about the impact of external-to-organization influences in terms of abstract notions of 'organizational consciousness' and 'environmental forces' is beneficial to the development of robust understanding of deeply seeded root causes, it offers comparatively little decision-making guidance. Here, the more operationally clear notion of *organizational ecosystems* might be more operationally meaningful. Defined from the standpoint of a single organization, ecosystem can be characterized as self-sustaining community of interdependent economic, political, or social entities with constituent interest in that organization. All business, social, and other organizations have their respective ecosystems, and while similar organizations would likely have similar ecosystems, ecosystems are ultimately highly organization specific.

Organizational ecosystems, however, should not be assumed to be inherently cooperation-minded – just because the individual economic, political, or social entities comprising a particular ecosystem are interdependent does not mean they work together toward a common goal.[1] In fact, one of the core aspects of ecosystem dynamics is the conflict vs. cooperation duality, which reflects the nature of dyadic relationships between the organization and each individual member of its ecosystem. Within the confines of business organizations, customers, who in aggregate represent the market demand dimension of environmental influences, tend to have generally cooperation-minded interest in organizations whose products or services they purchase and use, whereas competitors' constituent interest can be generally characterized as adversarial-minded. In a more general sense, all external entities' constituent interest in a business organization generally emanates from either economic or regulatory basis, as individual organization-constituent group interactions are motivated either by some form of economic exchange or by the desire to enforce binding rules or regulations. It thus follows that at least a partial understanding of the implied or explicit influence of environmental forces on organizational decision-making can be derived from a closer examination of the individual organization-stakeholder group interactions.

The 3E Framework and Environmental Forces

The single largest factor confounding organizational decision-making is uncertainty, especially regarding external to the organization environment. Market and competitive, as well as societal, political, and technological forces exert at times direct, and at times indirect influence on organizational choices.

And while some degree of ambiguity can be considered endemic to external environmental forces, the degree of uncertainty of their potential impact can be materially and systematically reduced through judicious use of the available information. Given the potentially overwhelming breadth and depth of each of the very broad environmental influences, the organizational ecosystem encapsulated view of those forces offers a way of narrowing the scope to just the aspects that are most meaningful to individual organizations. It also makes it possible to relate the resultant informational needs to the types of information that need to be produced by the 3E framework-framed informational synthesis.

Figure 11.1 depicts the high-level view of how the two meta-categories – empirical and experiential – as well as the more narrowly framed four constituent categories – operational data, empirical research, norms & standards, and expert judgment – align with informational needs that emanate from the distinct environmental forces. The intent behind the reductive summary shown in Figure 11.1 is to bring forth the primary sources of insight that can be used to reduce environmental force specific decision-making ambiguity. For instance, although all sources of information encompassed in the 3E framework can contribute some competition- and market-related information, the operational data dimension of empirical evidence should be considered the principal source of competition- and market-related information because that source offers the best combination of recency and rich dimensionality (i.e., many details produced by numerous types and sources of data), ultimately yielding unparalleled decision-guiding insights. Thus while supplementary insights can be sourced from the remaining sources of empirical (empirical research) or experiential (norms & standards and expert judgment) evidence, operational data should be looked to for core competition- and market-related decision-guiding inputs. In a similar manner and as graphically summarized in Figure 11.1, empirical research should be considered the chief source of the societal dimension of decision-relevant environmental forces, broadly defined norms & standards should be deemed the core source of political and legal information, and

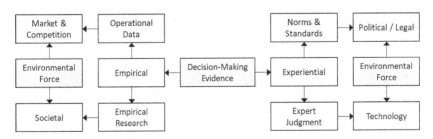

FIGURE 11.1   The 3E Framework and Environmental Forces.

lastly, expert judgment should be deemed to be the most important source of technology-related insights.

Assessing Market & Competitive Forces

Discussed in detail in Chapters 7 and 8 and looked at as a diverse but at least somewhat delimited set, operational data encompass recordings of routine functioning and activities of organizations, such as for-profit businesses, non-profit service or social organizations, or governing entities. In more operationally clear terms, the 'routine functioning and activities' of organizations manifest themselves as stakeholder interactions taking place within individual organizational ecosystems, and so operational data represent recordings of those interactions. Given the rapid digitization of human interactions, both the volume and the variety of operational data are continuously expanding. Starting with the rise and rapid proliferation of electronic transaction processing (e.g., the now ubiquitous bar code scanners) in the 1970s to the more recent explosive growth of electronic social networking, organizations now can tap into enormous quantities of highly detailed ongoing streams of behavioral and attitudinal data. The resultant arrays of available, and potentially applicable data can be staggering, as illustrated by just one limited 'slice' in the form of customer data, which include transactional and descriptive details sourced from multiple electronic interchange systems and, typically, distributed across numerous capture, storage, and management systems, further divided (within each system) into numerous tables and/or files.

As noted earlier, organizational data can be seen as mix of informative 'signal', which can yield decision-guiding insights, and informationless 'noise'. That characterization, however, needs to be considered in the context of another important data portrayal dichotomy, the distinction between 'smooth' and 'rough'. Jointly considering those two data characterizations suggests that the distinction between informative and informationless contents of data are iteratively determined, and thus in effect are multi-layered. Restated in more everyday terms, that (part of data) which may be deemed noise in one context may turn out to be informationally useful in a different context. For example, in the context of insurance claim analyses, the 'accident date' field might be deemed noise when analyzing claim cost variability, while it would likely be quite informative to likelihood of accident estimation.

Estimation of market-level demand can be seen as a natural extension of consumer choice analyses, subject to generalizability and projectability considerations discussed in Chapter 8. While forecasting the future demand – or any other future outcome – is inescapably imperfect, careful analyses of ongoing streams of purchase data can nonetheless offer the most dependable means of estimating future market demand. There are certainly contexts, such as developing markets with limited data or new product categories, in which that assertion may be questioned, but under most common scenarios, large pools of objective, fact-based and recent operational data contain more signal relative to noise than other sources of evidence discussed in this book. Moreover, given their longitudinally compounding flows, operational data give rise to point-in-time as well as time-over-time insights, with the former bringing to light the recency aspect of market information, whereas the latter capturing macro trends, yielding insights into persistence of potential future-suggesting trends.

Similar reasoning applies to competitive insights. While organizations, especially business firms, tend to carefully guard their own operational data, quite a bit of competitive data is nonetheless available. For instance, companies traded on public US stock exchanges are required by law to publicly disclose details about their financial condition, operating results, management compensation, and other areas of their business,[2] all of which is readily available to other companies.

Assessing Societal Forces

The human brain sees change differently depending on how it encounters it. This neurologic glitch is called *change blindness* and it's one of the many cognitive biases that affect all decision-makers (all humans for that matter). The essence of that well-documented phenomenon is that gradual, regularly experienced change tends to go unnoticed, and perhaps the most surprising part is that it happens not because of willful of even careless disregard, but because of the manner in which the human brain processes information. One could say that mankind is wired to disregard slow everyday change and that has a direct impact on how organizational decision-makers take into account – or not – societal changes.

The idea of social change is often looked at in the context of defining and clearly visible events, as exemplified by a wave of social unrests that swept through the Middle East and North Africa and have come to be jointly known as the 'Arab Spring' (because those events generally began in the spring of 2011). However, careful analysis of broader patterns of societal transformations suggests that while historical flashpoints can indeed be a source of significant societal changes, as was the case with French or Soviet revolutions, a far more commonly encountered pathway is that of an ongoing series of small alterations to the initial status quo. The gay rights movement in the US, and elsewhere, took decades of individually small but collectively significant changes of societal norms, views, and legal standards, so much so that the 'before' and 'after' only become visible upon very close examination. That has direct and significant implications for the manner in which the assessment of the nature and trajectory of societal forces that might be applicable to a decision at hand is undertaken.

Heraclitus, a Greek philosopher, observed that change is the only constant in life. And since ubiquitous change is also unnoticeable, discerning patterns of change requires a systematic and purposeful study. Here, methodologically sound empirical scientific research offers the best means of assessing of decision-applicable societal forces because it offers the means of circumventing cognitive bias, most notably the earlier discussed change blindness, by expressly drawing attention to patterns that might otherwise go unnoticed.

Assessing Legal Forces

Within the confines of organizational ecosystems, a combination of legally binding obligations and behavioral norms gives rise to stakeholder group specific expectations, perhaps best illustrated by organization-shareholder dyads. The US federal securities laws guarantee shareholders of business firms traded on public US exchanges the legal right to expect managers of those companies to timely, completely, and accurately disclosure details of those companies' financial performance.[3] Those clearly stated and binding obligations are examples of 'black letter law', a broad category encompassing the basic standard elements or principles of law which are generally known and free from doubt or dispute (in American legal system, well-established case law also falls within the domain of black letter law).

Shareholder rights, however, are not limited to provisions emanating from black letter law. A distinct, though conceptually related expectation-shaping influence takes the form of judicial decisions, especially those made within the context of torts, or civil wrongs (as opposed to criminal transgressions, which fall outside the scope of this overview). As a common law country, the US derives many of its legal standards from judicial decisions which tend to fill the legal void in matters not expressly addressed by existing legislative acts or other black letter law standards. It is worth mentioning that in everyday business vernacular, legislative and judicial forces are often lumped together under a single 'legal requirements' umbrella – though in some situations such a generalization may be warranted, it is important to note that the two are separate and distinct. The legislative aspect of shareholder rights is largely driven by the ever-changing political sentiments producing new legislative acts, which can be seen as manifestations of changing societal priorities, whereas the judicial aspect is shaped by evolving interpretations of already existing legislative acts and legal standards.

Of particular interest to company-shareholders dyadic interactions are the concepts of *business judgment rule* and the *duty of care*. The former is a corporate law notion which states that directors of a corporation are clothed with the presumption, which the law accords to them, of being motivated in their conduct by a bona fide regard for the interests of the corporation whose affairs the shareholders have committed to their charge. Stated differently, business judgment rule extends a certain degree of immunity to corporate managers, so long as they manage the organization to the best of their abilities. The duty of care, on the other hand, captures the legal responsibility placed upon corporate directors and officers, which demands adherence to a standard of reasonable care while engaging in behaviors that could foreseeably harm the constituents of companies they govern. There are numerous manifestations of the duty of care that relate to executive actions, with one of the most visible ones being that of public disclosures: As custodians of organizations, corporate managers are responsible for the accuracy of oral and written statements (as in general communications and casual comments, as well as the formal financial reporting discussed earlier) that reflect their companies' performance, prospects, and the overall well-being. Furthermore, it is instructive to note that in the wake of high-profile corporate governance scandals (e.g., Enron, Tyco International, Bank of America Merrill Lynch), the scope of directors' and officers' duty of care has been expanding, especially in the area of expected prudence and competence. Lastly, it is also important to note that the disclosure accuracy is an absolute requirement, which means that it makes no distinction between intentional and unintended errors or misstatements (in legal terms, it does not require a discernible intent to deceive).

Although dyadic interaction between a business organization and its outside shareholders is only one of numerous potential organizational ecosystem interdependencies, it is nonetheless illustrative of the importance of focusing on applicable norms and standards when assessing the potential impact of broadly defined legal and political forces on the decision at hand.

Assessing Technological Forces

A 2017 survey conducted by CEMS (formerly the Community of European Management Schools and International Companies) concluded that technological change was seen as the biggest threat to business organizations, having been selected as the #1 threat by 68% of respondents, compared with 60% who cited shifts in economic and political power, and 59% who named climate change as the biggest threat. Encompassing invention, innovation, and diffusion of technologies or processes, technological change is difficult to anticipate not only because of the often spontaneous, at times even unexpected character of scientific breakthroughs, but also because of uncertainties surrounding user adoption of those breakthroughs. Typically, new technologies are not immediately successful primarily because overcoming of the 'known-to-me' factor can be a challenge, especially if the new technology requires significant behavioral re-learning on the part of its users, or if its user benefits are not immediately compelling. In fact, that is one of the key reasons the new and the old technologies tend to coexist during technological transition, which affords time for organizations to adapt to resultant changes.

There are numerous examples illustrating the potential length of technological transformation, as well as the importance of early recognition of the discontinuous impact of the new technology. The August 22, 1787 successful trial of a 45-foot steamship on the Delaware River in Philadelphia (in the presence of the members of the US Constitutional Convention) is commonly considered to be the beginning of the era of steam-powered ships, but it took decades before the new technology displaced sailboats as the primary means of water transport. Similarly, the world's first single chip microprocessor was introduced by Intel in 1971, though at the time few could foresee the enormous transformational impact of that breakthrough on business and the society at large, and the transition from 'paper and pencil' to electronic information storage and dissemination was a gradual process although not nearly as lengthy as was the transition from wind to steam powered shipping. And as the speed of innovation accelerates, so does the speed of adoption of new technologies. The now ubiquitous personal computers first arrived about 40 years ago but it took a couple of decades or so for those devices to become a staple in business and personal life; yet, smartphones were introduced about a decade ago and today it seems nearly everyone is gazing at those glowing, handheld computers, and 'wearable devices', such as Fitbit or Apple watch, are an even newer innovation but are already as commonplace as smartphones or personal computers. In aggregate, the technology-driven societal transformation has been nothing short of revolutionary affecting virtually all aspects of how we live and work, an avalanche that started with that one tiny single-chip microprocessor developed by Intel in 1971. Since then, computer chips have become increasingly more powerful (and less expensive), as over the last five decades the number of transistors, which are the tiny electrical components that perform basic operations, on a single chip have been doubling about every 18 months, as predicted by Moore's Law, and the resultant innovations continued to spawn more innovations.[4]

A lesson imbedded in the above observations is that technological change makes for retrospectively fascinating stories, but its future impact can be devilishly difficult to surmise, even by those deeply immersed in a particular area. Kodak and Polaroid were both technological innovators not only in their traditional businesses of film-based photography but also in the area of digital photography – in fact, both companies developed industry leading digital cameras that were ahead of their competitors. Yet, in spite of their early technological advantage, the management of both organizations refused to truly embrace their own new digital technologies because they feared it would destroy their highly profitable film-based business. As famously captured by a senior Polaroid manager's comment – 'Why should we accept a 38% margin [of digital photography]? I can get 70% in film' – the organizational leadership of Polaroid (and Kodak alike) saw digital photography as an alternative to film-based photography, rather than what it truly was – an existential threat to their addictively profitable film business.

Lastly, technological or process change is not a one-size-fits-all phenomenon. Over the years, academic researchers and business consultants proposed numerous typologies of technological change, but the one that fits the greatest array of situations is a simple dichotomy that distinguishes between incremental and dis-ruptive (also referred to as discontinuous) innovation. The former usually takes the form of improvements in an existing technology or process, whereas the latter entails introduction of a brand new technology or process. Telephone, television, and the Internet are all examples of disruptive innovations offering new, radically different (from the standard of the time) means of communication, whereas cellular telephone, color television, and the World Wide Web all can be seen as incre-mental improvements that added new features and user functionality to telephone, television, and the Internet, respectively. As it is intuitively obvious, incremental innovation is both easier to anticipate and easier to manage than discontinuous technological innovation, which tends to break with established norms and disrupt historical trends. In both cases, however, as suggested by analyses of a cross-section of technological product and process innovations, the past is rarely a good indicator of the future, primarily because factors that drive product and process innovations tend to change over time, often in an unpredictable manner. Naturally, that casts doubt on technological change predicting efficacy of any evidence stemming from historical patterns or events. Thus, operational data, empirical research, as well as established norms and standards are all poor indicators of new technologies, or even of incremental improvements in existing technologies or processes.

The last of the four broad categories of evidence, expert judgment, offers the best potential window – though still quite imperfect – into potentially disruptive technological change. The reason that outlook of highly qualified and practiced in-dividuals tends to be the best potential predictor of technological change is rooted in the very essence of expertise: Encompassing often unique combinations of tacit and explicit knowledge, subject matter expertise manifests itself in deeper understand-ing of strengths, weaknesses, and evolutionary patterns of 'what-is', which, in turn, is likely to precipitate a clearer vision of 'what-could-be'. Also, in a more pragmatic sense, technological innovation is ultimately a product of human ingenuity, or more tangibly, an outcome of product and process improvement and/or development efforts of those with expert knowledge in a particular domain of knowledge, and thus those individuals are usually best equipped to anticipate technological change.

It is important to note that as discussed within the confines of the 3E frame-work, expert judgment can take the form of expertise in distinct *tasks* or gen-eral *processes*, as exemplified by highly experienced insurance claim adjustors, or making future *projections*, as demonstrated by weather or economic forecasters. In other words, the label of 'expert' can be applied to experienced task handlers, or to highly knowledgeable researchers, but it is the latter who are in a unique posi-tion to anticipate technological change. A practicing engineer, for instance, could be expected to have strong knowledge of current technologies, but not necessar-ily an equally robust 'feel' for what might be coming next, whereas a researcher studying technological trends or developing new technologies or processes would typically be in a far better position to anticipate upcoming technological change. Stated differently, just being proficient with 'what-is' is not likely to be sufficient to produce credible forecasts regarding 'what is likely to be'.

Non-Systematic Influences

Market, competitive, societal, and technological forces can be thought of as systematic influences on organizational decision-making because of their nearly mechanical cogency. As such, those forces represent perhaps the most profound and, in a sense, most obvious external influences; those factors aside, organizational choices are also impacted by numerous non-systematic although potentially just as impactful situational factors. Those factors can be grouped into two general categories: estimable risks, which encompass recurring adverse events, and non-estimable threats, which encompass any highly irregular or feasible but not-yet-materialized dangers to organizational continuity.

Estimable Risks

Identification, assessment, and responding to numerous manifestations of adverse events are one of the most critical dimensions of organizational management – in fact, the efforts to manage risk in commercial setting have a long and distinguished history, dating as far back as 2000 BC. However, it was not until the 17th century that the contemporary notions of speculative risk transfer and risk pooling began to emerge, ultimately giving rise to insurance marketplace and alternative risk financing mechanisms. The modern practice of risk management began to take shape around the same time; originally focused on sea shipping, the management of risk expanded to property following the Great London Fire of 1666, and then onto other aspects of commerce. Today, the theory and practice of risk management extend into natural disasters, man-made crises and liability, as well as other manifestations of operational risk, such as health care, banking and finance, security and crisis management, outdoor recreation, project management, information infrastructure maintenance, communication, and numerous others. It is also not surprising that, from the standpoint of organizational risk management, the management of multiplicity of risks can be approached holistically, a practice that has come to be known as enterprise risk management (ERM).

As the 'gold standard' in contemporary organizational risk management, ERM is built around a stepwise process of identification, estimation, mapping, and response to individual risks, all of which are treated as a part of a larger organizational risk profile, which offers maximum risk management efficiencies. Considered from a very high-level perspective, ERM assumes that managing a portfolio of risks is more efficient than managing each risk individually. The scope of organizational ERM efforts typically incorporates traditionally known (i.e., recurring with a certain degree of regularity) risks, such as accidents or product liability claims, and unknown (i.e., possible but not yet materialized) threats, such as extreme weather events, and its scope encompasses downside (loss only) as well as upside (loss or gain) threats. ISO 3100 and COSO[5] are the two dominant ERM frameworks offering normative enterprise-wide risk management processes; while both have been praised for the thoroughness of their risk identification, mapping, and response logic, they have also been frequently criticized for offering inadequate 'how-to' operational guidance, especially in the area of risk estimation. This is one of the reasons that the 3E framework can play nothing short of a transformative role as an enabler of more systematic and rational means of operationalizing the promise of those, and other risk management frameworks.

An objective and thorough assessment of what is already known, and what else might be knowable is the most fundamental benefit of using the 3E framework as the source of risk management related knowledge. While the discussion of different types, sources, and manifestations of operational risk falls outside the scope of this book, let it suffice to say that there are numerous non-systematic or random events that can materially impact organizational well-being, and the ability of organizations to identify those events and to estimate their potential impact is contingent on what could be characterized as *analytic creativity*, or the willingness and ability to use different informational sources to attain valid and reliable likelihood of occurrence and severity of impact estimates. Some manifestations of operational risk, as exemplified by casualty accidents such as worker injuries, recur with a fairly consistent regularity and thus their future impact can be fairly reliably estimated using readily available accident or insurance claim data; other facets of operational risk, such as wildfires, are far more irregular and as such are not easy to estimate using historical occurrence data, which necessitates the use of other informational sources, such as expert opinions. With that in mind, the comprehensive informational scope of the 3E framework will enable organizations to develop more robust estimates of distinct manifestations of organizational risk by aligning risk-type-specific informational needs with the appropriate informational dimension of the 3E framework, and then making use of the informational dimension-specific analytic logic.

Non-Estimable Threats

Not everything that is worth knowing is knowable. The vigorous, at times heated, and at times even dogmatic-sounding debate surrounding the topic of climate change – one of the existential threats confronting humanity – illustrates the difficulty of persuasively asserting even the most fundamental truths. The roughly 100 or so years of detailed weather measurements is generally considered sufficient to produce widely accepted near-term weather forecasts, but when the same general body of information is used as bases for discerning long term, more fundamental trends, many experts feel that much more than that is needed to produce equally believable estimates of climate change-like fundamental macro phenomena. Also, the common practice of normalizing data by means such as smoothing out of data patterns considered to be aberrant is sometimes called into question and used as a yet another reason to question the veracity of climate change forecasts. In the end, while the scientific community is in general agreement that rapid and unimpeded climate change would have catastrophic societal consequences, there is enough skepticism regarding empirical estimates of climate change to effectively derail such consensus regarding the immediacy of climate change. As a result, enormous threats, such as the likely release of mass volumes of methane, a powerful greenhouse gas, from seas and soils in the now-melting permafrost regions of the Arctic are not spurring the badly needed decisive global risk mitigation steps.

While climate change may be one of the most extreme examples of difficult to assess threats, within the far more confined context of organizational management there are numerous other events that could potentially threaten organizational survival. Some of those threats may manifest themselves as extremely low frequency, high impact events seen in the past, whereas others might be recognized as possible future developments that may not yet have been observed. Both the empirically-manifest-but-infrequent and the not-yet-empirically-evident events encompass natural disasters, as exemplified by tsunami-caused Fukushima nuclear disaster in Japan, or man-made catastrophes, as exemplified by the accounting scandal that precipitated the demise of Enron, a Houston-based energy company. Sometimes labeled as 'black swans', in recognition of their rarity (although that particular species of swan is actually quite common in their native regions of southwestern and southeastern Australia), those events are extremely difficult to forecast, which necessitates different means of mitigating their potential impact. That very realization was the impetus that spurred the emergence of a distinct, from the earlier discussed risk management, field of practice and research known as 'organizational resilience'. Rooted in ecology, where it is defined as the capacity of an ecosystem to respond to a disturbance by resisting damage and by recovering quickly, organizational resilience is about developing threat absorptive capacities. Hence, in contrast to risk management, which focuses on shielding organizations from known (i.e., estimable) events, organizational resilience is concerned with developing capacity to absorb the impact of, and subsequently bounce back from largely unforeseeable, and potentially very harmful events.

Both as a research and applied area, organizational resilience is comparatively new. In fact, the discipline can be seen as an evolutionary amalgamation of two previously distinct disciplines: disaster risk reduction and business continuity management (both of which are themselves fairly recent, having came of age in the course of the past four decades). The rise of systematic disaster risk reduction efforts can be seen as a product of the rising awareness of the importance of planned and purposeful mitigation of the impact of disasters and catastrophes, whereas the growing dependence of businesses and governments on electronic communication and data infrastructure was the motivation behind systematic business continuity management efforts. That said, while the idea organizational resilience is widely embraced, organizational actions that may be required to truly adopt its spirit tend to be disputed, in a manner quite similar to implications of climate change.

Worrisome climate change forecasts and unnerving organizational resilience scenarios are often disputed on the grounds of unidimensionality, scarcity, and subjectivity of evidence, which is precisely why the all available information focused 3E framework can be quite helpful. Amalgamating and objectively synthesizing all topically related information has the potential to yield maximally convincing conclusions, and ultimately compel the most appropriate – in view of the totality of available evidence – organizational actions. This assertion is supported by the fairly intuitive conclusion that development of organizational capabilities that can be deemed sufficient to allow organizations to withstand the impact of often unforeseen adverse events demands careful consideration of events that might have had some historical precursors, as well as those for which no clear historical precedent exists. The former is well illustrated by superstorm Sandy that ravaged large swaths of New York and New Jersey in 2012 causing nearly $70 billion in damage; that particularly severe weather event materialized because of an extremely rare (estimated as 1-in-500 years) trifecta of a powerful hurricane, an unusually shaped dip in the jet stream, and lunar high tides (that raised the sea level by several feet along the East Coast of the US). Given the very remote chances of those three independent developments happening at exactly the same time, anticipating such an event in the sense of taking resource-committing preparatory steps relying only on a singular source of information is unrealistic, primarily because the dependability of such information can be, and usually will be, called into question. However, when a similar recommendation stems from thorough and thoughtful assessment of all available information, disbelief is less likely to arise. The same reasoning applies even more to plausible but not-yet-materialized (in terms of past occurrences) threats, assessment of which demands an approach that identifies, amalgamates, and synthesizes all available sources of information. That is precisely what the 3E framework enables and empowers organizations to achieve.

Notes

1 For a more in-depth overview of organizational constituent groups and forces shaping their dyadic interactions with business organizations see Banasiewicz, A. D. (2015), 'The Ecosystem of Executive Threats: A Conceptual Overview', *Risk Management*, 17(2), pp. 109–143.
2 Publicly owned companies prepare two annual reports, one for the US Securities and Exchange Commission (SEC) and one for their shareholders. Form 10-K is the annual report made to the SEC, and its content and form are strictly governed by federal statutes (most notably, the Securities Act of 1933, the Securities Exchange

Act of 1934, and the Sarbanes-Oxley Act of 2002); it contains detailed financial and operating information, as well as a management response to specific questions about the company's operations.

3 See endnote 2.

4 Named after Gordon Moore, a cofounder of Intel, who in 1965 observed that the number of transistors on a chip doubled every year (while the cost halved); a decade later, he revised his initial estimate to doubling every 2 years, later adjusted to 18 months to account for the combined effect of number and speed of transistors.

5 International Organization for Standardization (ISO) is an international standard-setting body comprised of representatives from various national standards organizations; Committee of the Sponsoring Organizations (COSO) is a joint initiative of five private sector finance and accounting associations.

APPENDIX A

COGNITIVE BIASES

The following is a running repository of cognitive biases reported by researchers throughout the past several decades. Biases listed below affect belief formation, business and economic decisions, and human behavior in general; as a rule, they tend to arise as a replicable result of a specific condition. It should be noted that although a considerable amount of effort was invested in identifying distinct and recurring manifestations of generalizable cognitive distortions, the list shown below may not include all reported effects, and some of the reported effects might represent a somewhat different way of describing the same underlying phenomenon.

Ambiguity effect: The tendency to avoid options for which missing information makes the probability seems unknown.

Anchoring: The tendency to rely too heavily on one trait or piece of information when making decisions (usually the first piece of information acquired on that subject).

Attentional bias: The tendency of our perception to be affected by our recurring thoughts.

Automation bias: The tendency to depend excessively on automated systems which can lead to erroneous automated information overriding correct decisions.

Availability heuristic: The tendency to overestimate the likelihood of events with greater 'availability' in memory, which can be influenced by how recent the memories are or how unusual or emotionally charged they may be.

Availability cascade: A self-reinforcing process in which a collective belief gains more and more plausibility through its increasing repetition in public discourse (as the expression goes, 'repeat something long enough and it will become true').

Backfire effect: The reaction to disconfirming evidence by strengthening one's previous beliefs.

Bandwagon effect: The tendency to do (or believe) things because many other people do (or believe) the same; related to groupthink and herd behavior.

Base rate fallacy or base rate neglect: The tendency to ignore base rate information (generic, general information) and focus on specific information (information only pertaining to a certain case).

Belief bias: An effect where someone's evaluation of the logical strength of an argument is biased by the believability of the conclusion.

Ben Franklin effect: A person who has performed a favor for someone is more likely to do another favor for that person than they would be if they had received a favor from that person.

Berkson's paradox: The tendency to misinterpret statistical experiments involving conditional probabilities.

Bias blind spot: The tendency to see oneself as less biased than other people, or to be able to identify more cognitive biases in others than in oneself.

Change blindness: A perceptual phenomenon that occurs when a change in a visual stimulus is introduced and the observer does not notice it.

Cheerleader effect: The tendency for people to appear more attractive in a group than in isolation.

Choice-supportive bias: The tendency to remember one's choices as better than they actually were.

Clustering illusion: The tendency to overestimate the importance of small runs, streaks, or clusters in large samples of random data (i.e., seeing phantom patterns).

Confirmation bias: The tendency to search for, interpret, focus on, and remember information in a way that confirms one's preconceptions.

Congruence bias: The tendency to test hypotheses exclusively through direct testing, instead of testing possible alternative hypotheses.

Conjunction fallacy: The tendency to assume that specific conditions are more probable than general ones.

Conservatism in belief revision: The tendency to revise one's belief insufficiently when presented with new evidence.

Continued influence effect: The tendency to believe previously learned misinformation even after it has been corrected.

Contrast effect: The enhancement or reduction of a certain perception's stimuli when compared with a recently observed, contrasting object.

Courtesy bias: The tendency to give an opinion that is more socially correct than one's true opinion, so as to avoid offending anyone.

Curse of knowledge: When better-informed people find it extremely difficult to think about problems from the perspective of lesser-informed people.

Declinism: The belief that a society or institution is tending toward decline, leading to the predisposition to view the past favorably (rosy retrospection) and future negatively.

Decoy effect: Preferences for either option A or B change in favor of option B when option C is presented, which is similar to option B but in no way better.

Denomination effect: The tendency to spend more money when it is denominated in small amounts (e.g., coins) rather than large amounts (e.g., bills).

Disposition effect: The tendency to sell an asset that has accumulated in value and resist selling an asset that has declined in value.

Distinction bias: The tendency to view two options as more dissimilar when evaluating them simultaneously than when evaluating them separately.

Dunning-Kruger effect: The tendency for unskilled individuals to overestimate their own ability and the tendency for experts to underestimate their own ability.

Duration neglect: The neglect of the duration of an episode in determining its value.

Empathy gap: The tendency to underestimate the influence or strength of feelings, in either oneself or others.

Endowment effect: The tendency for people to demand much more to give up an object than they would be willing to pay to acquire it.

Exaggerated expectation: Based on the estimates, real-world evidence turns out to be less extreme than our expectations (conditionally inverse of the conservatism bias).

Experimenter's or expectation bias: The tendency for experimenters to believe, certify, and publish data that agree with their expectations for the outcome of an experiment, and to disbelieve, discard, or downgrade the corresponding weightings for data that appear to conflict with those expectations.

Focusing effect: The tendency to place too much importance on one aspect of an event.

Forer effect or Barnum effect: The observation that individuals will give high accuracy ratings to descriptions of their personality that supposedly are tailored specifically for them, but are in fact vague and general enough to apply to a wide range of people.

Framing effect: Drawing different conclusions from the same information, depending on how that information is presented.

Frequency illusion: The illusion in which a word, a name, or other thing that has recently come to one's attention suddenly seems to appear with improbable frequency shortly afterwards (not to be confused with the recency illusion or selection bias).

Functional fixedness: Limits a person to using an object only in the way it is traditionally used.

Gambler's fallacy: The tendency to think that future probabilities are altered by past events, when in reality they are unchanged; it usually arises from an erroneous conceptualization of the law of large numbers.

Hard-easy effect: Based on a specific level of task difficulty, the confidence in judgments is too conservative and not extreme enough.

Hindsight bias: Sometimes called the 'I-knew-it-all-along' effect, the tendency to see past events as being predictable at the time those events happened.

Hot-hand fallacy: The 'hot-hand fallacy' is the fallacious belief that a person who has experienced success with a random event has a greater chance of further success in additional attempts.

Hyperbolic discounting: Discounting is the tendency to have a stronger preference for more immediate payoffs relative to later payoffs; it leads to choices that are inconsistent over time, such as making choices today that would not be made in the future, despite using the same reasoning.

Identifiable victim effect: The tendency to respond more strongly to a single identified person at risk than to a large group of people at risk.

IKEA effect: The tendency for people to place a disproportionately high value on objects that they partially assembled themselves, such as furniture from IKEA, regardless of the quality of the end result.

Illusion of control: The tendency to overestimate one's degree of influence over other external events.

Illusion of validity: Belief that furtherly acquired information generates additional relevant data for predictions, even when it evidently does not.

Illusory correlation: Inaccurately perceiving a relationship between two unrelated events.

Illusory truth effect: A tendency to believe that a statement is true if it is easier to process, or if it has been stated multiple times, regardless of its actual veracity.

Impact bias: The tendency to overestimate the length or the intensity of the impact of future feeling states.

Information bias: The tendency to seek information even when it cannot affect action.

Information-sampling bias: The tendency to pool and repeat more shared than unshared information in group decision-making settings.

Insensitivity to sample size: The tendency to under-expect variation in small samples.

Irrational escalation: The phenomenon where people justify increased investment in a decision, based on the cumulative prior investment, despite new evidence suggesting that the decision was probably wrong, also known as the *sunk cost fallacy*.

Law of the instrument: 'If all you have is a hammer, everything looks like a nail'.

Less-is-better effect: The tendency to prefer a smaller set to a larger set judged separately, but not jointly.

Look-elsewhere effect: An apparently statistically significant observation may have actually arisen by chance because of the size of the parameter space to be searched.

Loss aversion: The disutility of giving up an object is greater than the utility associated with acquiring it.

Mere exposure effect: The tendency to express undue liking for things merely because of familiarity with them.

Money illusion: The tendency to concentrate on the nominal value (face value) of money rather than its value in terms of purchasing power.

Moral credential effect: The tendency of a track record of non-prejudice to increase subsequent prejudice.

Negativity bias: Psychological phenomenon by which humans have a greater recall of unpleasant memories compared with positive memories.

Neglect of probability: The tendency to completely disregard probability when making a decision under uncertainty.

Normalcy bias: The refusal to plan for, or react to, a disaster which has never happened before.

Not invented here: Aversion to contact with or use of products, research, standards, or knowledge developed outside a group.

Observer-expectancy effect: When a researcher expects a given result and therefore unconsciously manipulates an experiment or misinterprets data to find it.

Omission bias: The tendency to judge harmful actions as worse, or less moral, than equally harmful omissions (inactions).

Optimism bias: The tendency to be over-optimistic, overestimating favorable and pleasing outcomes (see also wishful thinking, valence effect, positive outcome bias).

Ostrich effect: Ignoring an obvious (negative) situation.

Outcome bias: The tendency to judge a decision by its eventual outcome instead of based on the quality of the decision at the time it was made.

Overconfidence effect: Excessive confidence in one's own answers to questions. For example, for certain types of questions, answers that people rate as '99% certain' turn out to be wrong 40% of the time.

Ownership bias: The tendency to view and evaluate one's own information more positively than information of others'.

Pareidolia: A vague and random stimulus (often an image or sound) is perceived as significant, for example, seeing images of animals or faces in clouds, the man in the moon, and hearing non-existent hidden messages on records played in reverse.

Pessimism bias: The tendency for some people, especially those suffering from depression, to overestimate the likelihood of negative things happening to them.

Planning fallacy: The tendency to underestimate task-completion times.

Post-purchase rationalization: The tendency to persuade oneself through rational argument that a purchase was good value.

Preference effect: A tendency to evaluate more positively information that is consistent with one's initial preferences.

Pro-innovation bias: The tendency to have an excessive optimism toward an invention or innovation's usefulness throughout society while often failing to identify its limitations and weaknesses.

Projection bias: The tendency to overestimate how much our future selves share one's current preferences, thoughts, and values, thus leading to suboptimal choices.

Pseudo-certainty effect: The tendency to make risk-averse choices if the expected outcome is positive, but make risk-seeking choices to avoid negative outcomes.

Reactance: The urge to do the opposite of what someone wants you to do out of a need to resist a perceived attempt to constrain your freedom of choice.

Reactive devaluation: Devaluing proposals only because they purportedly originated with an adversary.

Recency illusion: The illusion that a word or language usage is a recent innovation when it is in fact long-established.

Regressive bias: A certain state of mind wherein high values and high likelihoods are overestimated, whereas low values and low likelihoods are underestimated.

Restraint bias: The tendency to overestimate one's ability to show restraint in the face of temptation.

Rhyme as reason effect: Rhyming statements are perceived as more truthful ('If the gloves don't fit, then you must acquit').

Risk compensation/Peltzman effect: The tendency to take greater risks when perceived safety increases.

Selective perception: The tendency for expectations to affect perception.

Semmelweis reflex: The tendency to reject new evidence that contradicts a paradigm.

Sexual over-perception bias/sexual under-perception bias: The tendency to over-/underestimate sexual interest of the opposite sex in oneself.

Social comparison bias: The tendency, when making hiring decisions, to favor potential candidates who don't compete with one's own particular strengths.

Social desirability bias: The tendency to over-report socially desirable characteristics or behaviors in oneself and underreport socially undesirable characteristics or behaviors.

Status quo bias: The tendency to like things to stay relatively the same (see also loss aversion, endowment effect, and system justification).

Stereotyping: Expecting a member of a group to have certain characteristics without having actual information about that individual.

Subadditivity effect: The tendency to judge probability of the whole to be less than the probabilities of the parts.

Subjective validation: Perception that something is true if a subject's belief demands it to be true.

Survivorship bias: Concentrating on the people or things that 'survived' some process and inadvertently overlooking those that didn't because of their lack of visibility.

Time-saving bias: Underestimations of the time that could be saved (or lost) when increasing (or decreasing) from a relatively low speed and overestimations of the time that could be saved (or lost) when increasing (or decreasing) from a relatively high speed.

Third-person effect: Belief that mass communicated media messages have a greater effect on others than on themselves.

Triviality/Parkinson's Law: The tendency to give disproportionate weight to trivial issues.

Unit bias: The tendency to want to finish a given unit of a task or an item.

Weber-Fechner law: Difficulty in comparing small differences in large quantities.

Well-traveled road effect: Underestimation of the duration taken to traverse oft-traveled routes and overestimation of the duration taken to traverse less familiar routes.

Zero-risk bias: Preference for reducing a small risk to zero over a greater reduction in a larger risk.

Zero-sum bias: A bias whereby a situation is perceived to be like a zero-sum game (i.e., one person gains at the expense of another).

APPENDIX B
INTER-EXPERT RELIABILITY

The inter-expert reliability, or IER, coefficient can be computed using the following formula:

$$IER = \sqrt{\frac{\sum_{i=1}^{n}\left(X_i - \overline{X}\right)^2}{n-1}}$$

where,
IER is inter-expert reliability
X_i is response of expert 1

As a general rule, the strength of inter-rater reliability can be estimated using the following decision rule:

$$|IER| \geq \frac{2}{\sqrt{n}}$$

where,
n is the number of individual experts/opinions

For example, if IER = 0.80 and there are 15 individual experts, then the measurement can be deemed reliable if IER is 0.52 or higher.

AUTHOR BIOGRAPHY

Dr. Andrew D. Banasiewicz is the director of data science and analytics programs at Merrimack College, a professor of business analytics at Cambridge College, and the founder of Erudite Analytics, a data analytical consultancy focused on risk measurement. Prior to embarking on full-time academic and consulting career, Andrew spent nearly two decades in the private industry as a senior-level quantitative business analyst. His primary area of expertise encompasses research design and sampling, predictive analytics, text mining, and impact measurement; he has extensive, hands-on data analytical experience in a wide range of industries including energy, utilities, automotive, financial services, pharmaceuticals, consumer packaged goods, gaming, and hospitality. He is the author of four other analytics-focused books, in addition to multiple methodological journal articles and industry white papers. A frequent speaker at professional meetings and conferences in North America, Europe, Australia, Asia, and Africa, Andrew is also a fellow of the Center for Evidence-Based Management, and the Australian Academy of Business Leadership, and a member of the Board and the Chair of Professional Practices for the Society of Risk Management Consultants.

Andrew holds a Ph.D. in business from Louisiana State University, and lives in Bristol, Rhode Island, with his wife, Carol, and their three children: Alana, Katrina, and Adam.

INDEX

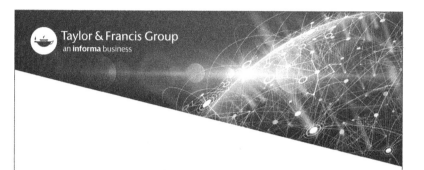